RECKLESS FAITH

RECKLESS
FAITH

When the Church Loses
Its Will to Discern

John F. MacArthur

CROSSWAY BOOKS • WHEATON, ILLINOIS

A DIVISION OF GOOD NEWS PUBLISHERS

Reckless Faith:
When the Church Loses Its Will to Discern

Copyright © 1994 by John F. MacArthur, Jr.

Published by Crossway Books
      a division of Good News Publishers
      1300 Crescent Street
      Wheaton, Illinois 60187

Cover design: The Puckett Group

Book design: Mark Schramm

Manuscript editing: Leonard G. Goss

First printing, 1994

Printed in the United States of America

ISBN 0-89107-793-6

All Scripture quotations in this book, except those noted otherwise, are from the *New American Standard Bible*, © 1960, 1962, 1963, 1968, 1971, 1972, 1973, 1975, and 1977 by The Lockman Foundation, and are used by permission.

Quotations marked KJV are from the *King James Version*.

02	01	00	99	98	97	96	95					
15	14	13	12	11	10	9	8	7	6	5	4	3	2

*To Marcel Cotnoir, missionary,
pastor, friend, who for many years
has fought the battle for truth
against the Roman system and is
seeing the Gospel triumph*

CONTENTS

ACKNOWLEDGMENTS

T HIS BOOK is the fruit of many people's labors. I'm grateful to God for the dedication of numerous dear friends and colleagues whose long hours of behind-the-scenes labor makes my busy writing ministry possible. Phil Johnson applied his exceptional skills to his usual task of editing my sermons, and in this book also developed some of the material on the Apostles' Creed and the evangelical-Catholic accord.

Special thanks to Allacin Morimizu for her diligence and extraordinary skill in making the indexes, and proofreading the final manuscript under a nearly impossible deadline. Thanks also to Jean-Paul Chenette and Tim Wydo, who proofread and critiqued the earliest manuscripts. Others who helped meet rigorous proofreading deadlines include Garry Knussman, Jay Flowers, Mike Taylor, and Ralph White. My deepest gratitude goes to my entire staff, especially Lance Quinn, Dick Mayhue, and Tom Pennington, for their advice and encouragement all along the way.

I'm also very thankful for the staff at Crossway—especially Lane Dennis and Leonard Goss, whose enthusiasm never flagged, even when this project fell behind schedule. Our partnership is something I am very grateful for.

Some of the seminal thoughts for chapter 6 came from a book

review by Gary Johnson. He was kind enough to send me a preview copy of the review which will be published in early 1995 in *Reformation and Revival Journal.*

I also want to thank Iain Murray for his superb biography of Jonathan Edwards. In addition to being one of the finest biographies I have ever read, it was a great encouragement to me as a pastor— and it helped shape my thinking on some of the crucial issues addressed in this book.

INTRODUCTION

MANY PEOPLE mistakenly think of faith as inherently noble. A popular song extols the virtue of believing: "I believe for every drop of rain that falls, a flower grows." No one *really* believes that, of course, but that is not the point. The song is a paean to faith—without regard to the *content* of that faith. The *object* of faith was of no concern to the songwriter. The sentiment that song expresses is by no means biblical. It is an echo of one of the worst lies of our age—the notion that it isn't important what you believe, as long as you believe passionately enough.

Did you know that faith can actually be seriously harmful? Some varieties of faith actually lead away from the true God—substituting superstition, falsehood, or faith itself in place of truth. Such faith inevitably leads to spiritual disaster. It is *reckless faith*.

Reckless faith goes to two extremes. At one end of the spectrum it looks within—relying on feelings, inner voices, fantasy, or subjective sensations. At the other extreme it fixes its hope on some external human authority—the teachings of a supreme leader, religious tradition, magisterial dogma, or some other arbitrary canon.

An obvious non-Christian example of the first extreme is New-Age mysticism. An obvious non-Christian example of the second is Islam. But even among groups that profess Christianity, both varieties of reckless faith are clearly in evidence. The charismatic movement, for example, tends toward the first extreme; Roman Catholicism epitomizes the second. Among religious beliefs that are labeled "Christian" are countless ideas that involve reckless faith of one variety or the other—and often a mixture of tendencies from both extremes.

Note that at both poles reckless faith seeks spiritual truth apart from Scripture—and that is the very point at which it becomes reckless. Both kinds of reckless faith also have this in common: they are irrational and anti-intellectual. "Anti-intellectual" doesn't mean they oppose intellectual snobbery. It means they spurn the intellect and encourage blind, uncritical trust. Anti-intellectuals often set faith *against* reason, as if the two were opposites. That kind of "faith" is gullibility. It is foolishness, and not biblical faith. Biblical faith is never irrational.

At the outset three very careful distinctions must be made. First, in defending rationality, I am not suggesting that human reason even at its best can lead a person to saving truth. Sin has corrupted and darkened the mind and heart of every person so that none of us could ever reason our way to salvation. That is why God has given us supernatural revelation in His inspired Word, the Bible. Scripture is *God's* revelation to us. It is true because God is true (Rom. 3:4). We don't reason our way to this truth. Rather, we begin by taking God at His Word, and we make Scripture the foundation on which all reason builds.

Second, to say that people can't reason their way to the truth of Scripture is not to imply that Scripture itself is irrational. The Bible is perfectly reasonable, consistent with itself, true in all its parts, reliable as a foundation for our logic, dependable as a basis for good judgment, and trustworthy as the definitive test of sound doctrine. Because it is pure truth, it is perfectly rational.

Third, to argue against irrationality is not to argue in favor of *rationalism*. *Rationalism* is a philosophy that denies divine revelation. Rationalism is anti-supernatural, anti-biblical, and often cynical toward all religion. Rationalists make human reason both the source and the final test of all truth. In short, they set human reason in place of Scripture. Christians have always rightly rejected rationalism as inimical to the Christian faith.

This is the point: although we must reject *rationalism*, we dare not repudiate *rationality*—the right use of sanctified reason, sound logic, clear thought, and common sense. Those who reject rationality render all truth nonsense. They discard all the mental faculties essential to understanding. They portray faith as a blind leap in the dark, something that bypasses the intellect. Such "faith" is either feeling-based, or it is made to be a sheer act of the will. Either way, it is reckless faith.

Authentic faith can never bypass the mind. It cannot be irrational. Faith, after all, deals with truth. Truth is objective data to be known, studied, contemplated, and understood. All those are activities that engage the intellect.

That means genuine Christianity *cannot* be anti-intellectual. The body of truth on which our faith is based has depths that are mysterious—unfathomable to the merely human mind, or inscrutable—but truth is *never* irrational. The difference is all-important. God cannot lie (Titus 1:2). Therefore what God says is true—and the antithesis must be false. Truth cannot be self-contradictory. Truth makes sense; nonsense cannot be true.

Moreover, the doctrine on which we base our faith must be *sound*—which is to say it must be biblical (1 Tim. 4:6; 2 Tim. 4:2-3; Titus 1:9; 2:1). "If anyone advocates a different doctrine, and does not agree with sound words, those of our Lord Jesus Christ, and with the doctrine conforming to godliness, he is conceited and *understands nothing*" (1 Tim. 6:3-4, emphasis added). Sound, biblical doctrine therefore underlies all true wisdom and authentic faith. The attitude that scorns doctrine while elevating feelings or blind trust cannot legitimately be called faith, even if it masquerades as Christianity. It is actually an irrational form of unbelief.

God holds us accountable for *what we believe* as well as *how we think* about the truth He has revealed. All Scripture testifies to the fact that God wants us to *know* and *understand* the truth. He wants us to be wise. His will is that we use our minds. We are supposed to think, to meditate—to be discerning. Consider, for example, these well-known verses. Note the repeated use of words like *truth*, *knowledge*, *discernment*, *wisdom*, and *understanding*:

- "Thou dost desire truth in the innermost being, and in the hidden part Thou wilt make me know wisdom" (Ps. 51:6).

- "The fear of the Lord is the beginning of wisdom; a good understanding have all those who do His commandments" (Ps. 111:10).

- "Teach me good discernment and knowledge, for I believe in Thy commandments" (Ps. 119:66).

- "Make your ear attentive to wisdom, incline your heart to understanding; for if you cry for discernment, lift your voice for understanding; if you seek her as silver, and search for her as for hidden treasures; then you will discern the fear of the Lord, and discover the knowledge of God. For the Lord gives wisdom; from His mouth come knowledge and understanding" (Prov. 2:2-6).

- "The beginning of wisdom is: acquire wisdom; and with all your acquiring, get understanding" (Prov. 4:7).

- "We have not ceased to pray for you and to ask that you may be filled with the knowledge of His will in all spiritual wisdom and understanding" (Col. 1:9).

- "In [Christ] are hidden all the treasures of wisdom and knowledge" (Col. 2:3).

- "All Scripture is inspired by God and profitable for teaching, for reproof, for correction, for training in righteousness" (2 Tim. 3:16).

As Christians, we need not fear using our rational faculties. We need not distrust sound logic. We need not—we dare not—abandon reason.

When Martin Luther was summoned to the Diet of Worms in 1521 and asked to recant his teaching, he replied, "Unless I am convinced by Scripture and plain reason, my conscience is captive to the Word of God. I cannot and I will not recant anything, for to go against conscience would be neither right nor safe. God help me. Here I stand, I can do no other."[1]

Luther's well-known formulation, "Scripture and plain reason," is the only basis on which we can properly ground true spiritual discernment. *Discernment* is the ability to understand, interpret, and apply truth skillfully. Discernment is a cognitive act. Therefore no one who spurns right doctrine or sound reason can be truly discerning.

Authentic spiritual discernment must begin with Scripture—revealed truth. Without a firm grounding in divine revelation, human reason always degenerates into skepticism (a denial that anything can be known for certain), rationalism (the theory that reason is a *source* of truth), secularism (an approach to life that purposely excludes God), or any number of other anti-Christian philosophies. When Scripture condemns human wisdom (1 Cor. 3:19), it is denouncing not reason per se, but humanistic ideology divorced from the divinely-revealed truth of God's Word. In other words, reason *apart from* the Word of God leads inevitably to unsound ideas, but reason subjected to the Word of God is at the heart of wise spiritual discernment.

The Westminster Confession of Faith clearly recognizes the formula of *Scripture and sound reason* as the basis of discernment. The Confession states: "The whole counsel of God . . . is either expressly set down in Scripture, or by good and necessary consequence may be deduced from Scripture" (chapter 1, section 6). In other words, sound and careful logic must be applied to Scripture to yield a full and mature understanding of the spiritual truth God has revealed. This is no denial of the sufficiency of Scripture. The formula is not Scripture plus philosophy, but Scripture interpreted by careful, sensible, thoughtful, Spirit-directed reasoning. That is the essence of discernment.

In short, anti-intellectualism is incompatible with genuine spiritual wisdom. Those who think of faith as the abandonment of reason cannot be truly discerning. Irrationality and discernment are polar opposites. When Paul prayed that the Philippians' love would "abound still more and more in real *knowledge* and all *discernment*" (Phil. 1:9, emphasis added), he was affirming the rationality of true faith.

He also meant to suggest that knowledge and discernment necessarily go hand in hand with genuine spiritual growth.

Biblical faith, therefore, is rational. It is reasonable. It is intelligent. It makes good sense. And spiritual truth is meant to be rationally contemplated, examined logically, studied, analyzed, and employed as the only reliable basis for making wise judgments. That process is precisely what Scripture calls *discernment*.

This book is a plea for discernment. It is a reminder that God's truth is a precious commodity that must be handled carefully—not diluted with whimsical beliefs or bound up in human traditions. When a church loses its will to discern between sound doctrine and error, between good and evil, between truth and lies, that church is doomed.

The apostle John drew a very sharp distinction between Christianity and the spirit of antichrist—and he zealously held the line: "Anyone who goes too far and does not abide in the teaching of Christ, does not have God; the one who abides in the teaching, he has both the Father and the Son. If anyone comes to you and does not bring this teaching, do not receive him into your house, and do not give him a greeting; for the one who gives him a greeting participates in his evil deeds" (2 John 9-11). Thus John commanded those under his spiritual oversight to be watchful and discerning—and to have nothing to do with Christ-denying error or the purveyors of it.

Contrast today's Christians who soothe themselves with the opinion that few things are really black and white. Doctrinal issues, moral questions, and Christian principles are all cast in hues of gray. No one is supposed to draw any definitive lines or declare any absolutes. Every person is encouraged to do what is right in his own eyes—exactly what God forbade (cf. Deut. 12:8; Judg. 17:6; 21:25).

The church will never manifest its power in society until we regain a passionate love for truth and a corollary hatred for error. True Christians cannot condone or disregard anti-Christian influences in their midst and expect to enjoy God's blessing. "Now it is high time to awake out of sleep: for now is our salvation nearer than when we believed. The night is far spent, the day is at hand: let us therefore cast off the works of darkness, and let us put on the armour of light" (Rom. 13:11-12, KJV).

> My son, if you will receive my sayings, and treasure my commandments within you, make your ear attentive to wisdom, incline your heart to understanding; for if you cry for discernment, lift your voice for understanding; if you seek her as silver, and search for her as for hidden treasures; then you will discern the fear of the Lord, and discover the knowledge of God. For the Lord gives wisdom; from His mouth come knowledge and understanding (Prov. 2:1-6).

1

The War Against Reason

TRUE DISCERNMENT has suffered a horrible setback in the past few decades because reason itself has been under attack within the church. As Francis Schaeffer warned nearly thirty years ago in *The God Who Is There*, the church is following the irrationality of secular philosophy. Consequently, reckless faith has overrun the evangelical community. Many are discarding doctrine in favor of personal experience. Others say they are willing to disregard crucial biblical distinctives in order to achieve external unity among all professing Christians. True Christianity marked by intelligent, biblical faith seems to be declining even among the most conservative evangelicals.

THE ABANDONMENT OF OBJECTIVE TRUTH

The visible church in our generation has become astonishingly tolerant of aberrant teaching and outlandish ideas—and frighteningly *in*tolerant of sound teaching. The popular evangelical conception of "truth" has become almost completely subjective. Truth is viewed as fluid, always relative, never absolute. To suggest that any objective criterion might be used to distinguish truth from error is to be egregiously out of step with the spirit of the age. In some circles, Scripture itself has been ruled out as a reliable test of truth. After all, the Bible can be interpreted in so many different ways—who can say which interpretation is right? And many believe there is truth beyond the Bible.

All this relativity has had disastrous effects on the typical Christian's ability to discern truth from error, right from wrong, good from evil. The plainest teachings of the Bible are being questioned among people who declare themselves believers in the Bible. For example, some Christians are no longer certain whether homosexuality should be classed as a sin. Others argue that the feminist agenda is compatible with biblical Christianity. "Christian" television, radio, books, and magazines serve up a preposterous smorgasbord of ideas from the merely capricious to the downright dangerous—and the average Christian is woefully ill-equipped to sort out the lies from the truth.

Even to suggest that a sorting between lies and truth is necessary is viewed by many as perilously intolerant. There is a notion abroad that any dispute over doctrine is inherently evil. Concern for orthodoxy is regarded as incompatible with Christian unity. Doctrine itself is labeled divisive and those who make doctrine an issue are branded uncharitable. No one is permitted to criticize anyone else's beliefs, no matter how unbiblical those beliefs seem to be.

A recent article in *Christianity Today* exemplifies the trend. The article, titled "Hunting for Heresy," profiled two well-known Christian leaders who had "come under withering attack for controversial writings."[1]

One is a popular speaker on the college lecture circuit and a best-selling author. He wrote a book in which he encouraged homosexuals to establish permanent live-together relationships (albeit celibate ones). He suggests the evangelical community suffers from "homophobia." He is convinced that permanent living arrangements between homosexuals are the only alternative to loneliness for people he believes are "born with a homosexual orientation." This man's wife has published an article in a homosexual magazine in which she "enthusiastically affirms" monogamous sexual relationships between homosexuals. The speaker-author says he has a "very, very strong" disagreement with his wife's approval of homosexual sex, but his own view seems to allow homosexuals to engage in other kinds of physical intimacy short of actual intercourse.

The other Christian leader profiled in the *Christianity Today* article is a woman who, with her husband, is a featured speaker for a popular, nationally-syndicated radio and television ministry. Their ministry is not a weird offshoot from some fringe cult, but an established, well-respected mainstay from the evangelical heartland. She also serves as chairperson of one of the largest evangelical student organizations in the world. This woman has written a book in which she chronicles some rather peculiar spiritual experiences. She dedicates the book to her male alter ego, an imaginary person named "Eddie Bishop" who romances her in her dreams. This woman says she also has visions of "the Christ child that is within" her. He appears to her as a drooling, emaciated, barefoot "idiot child" in a torn undershirt—"its head totally bald and lolled to one side." The woman has engaged the services of a Catholic nun who serves as her "spiritual director," helping to interpret her dreams and fantasies. The book mingles mysticism, Jungian psychology, out-of-body experiences, feminist ideas, subjective religious experience, and this woman's romantic fantasies into an extraordinary amalgam. The book is frankly so bizarre that it is disturbing to read.

The remarkable thing about the *Christianity Today* article is that the story was not written to expose the aberrant ideas being taught by these two leading evangelicals. Instead, what the magazine's editors deemed newsworthy was *the fact that these people were under attack for their views*.

In the world of modern evangelicalism, it is allowable to advocate the most unconventional, unbiblical doctrines—as long as you afford everyone else the same privilege. About the only thing that is taboo nowadays is the intolerance of those who dare to point out others' errors. Anyone today who is bold enough to suggest that someone else's ideas or doctrines are unsound or unbiblical is dismissed at once as contentious, divisive, unloving, or unchristian. It is all right to *espouse* any view you wish, but it is not all right to *criticize* another person's views—no matter how patently unbiblical those views may be.

When tolerance is valued over truth, the cause of truth always suffers. Church history shows this to be so. Only when the people of God have mounted a hardy defense of truth and sound doctrine has the church flourished and grown strong. The Reformation, the Puritan era, and the Great Awakenings are all examples of this. The times of decline in the history of the church have always been marked by an undue emphasis on tolerance—which leads inevitably to carelessness, worldliness, doctrinal compromise, and great confusion in the church.

ADRIFT ON A SEA OF SUBJECTIVITY

That the church would lose her moorings in this particular age, however, poses greater dangers than ever. For in the past hundred years or so, the world has changed in a dramatic and very frightening way. People no longer look at truth the way they used to. In fact, we live under a prevailing philosophy that has become hostile to the very idea of absolute truth.

From the beginning of recorded history until late last century, virtually all human philosophy assumed the necessity of absolute truth. Truth was universally understood as that which is true, not false; factual, not erroneous; correct, not incorrect; moral, not immoral; just, not unjust; right, not wrong. Practically all philosophers since the time of Plato assumed the objectivity of truth. Philosophy itself was a quest for the highest understanding of truth. Such a pursuit was presumed to be possible, even necessary, because truth was understood to be the same for every person. This did not mean that everyone agreed what truth was, of course. But virtually all agreed that *whatever* was true was true for everyone.

That all changed in the nineteenth century with the birth of *existentialism*. Existentialism defies precise definition, but it includes the concept that the highest truth is *subjective* (having its source in the individual's mind) rather than *objective* (something that actually exists outside the individual). Existentialism elevates individual experience and personal choice, minimizing or ruling out absolute standards of truth, goodness, morality, and such things. We might accurately characterize existentialism as the abandonment of objectivity. Existentialism is inherently anti-intellectual, against reason, irrational.

Danish philosopher Søren Kierkegaard first used the term "existential." Kierkegaard's life and philosophy revolved around his experiences with Christianity. Christian ideas and biblical terminology reverberate in many of his writings. He wrote much about faith and certainly regarded himself as a Christian. Many of his ideas began as a legitimate reaction against the stale formalism of the Danish Lutheran state church. He was rightly offended at the barren ritualism of the church, properly outraged that people who had no love for God called themselves Christians just because they happened to be born in a "Christian" nation.

But in his reaction against the lifeless state church, Kierkegaard set up a false antithesis. He decided that objectivity and truth were incompatible. To counter the passionless ritualism and lifeless doctrinal formulas he saw in Danish Lutheranism, Kierkegaard devised an approach to religion that was *pure* passion, altogether subjective. Faith, he suggested, means the rejection of reason and the exaltation of feeling and personal experience. It was Kierkegaard who coined the expression "leap of faith." Faith to him was an irrational experience, above all a personal choice. He recorded these words in his journal on August 1, 1835: "The thing is to find a truth which is true *for me*, to find *the idea for which I can live and die*."[2]

Clearly, Kierkegaard had already rejected as inherently worthless the belief that truth is objective. His journal continues with these words:

> What would be the use of discovering so-called objective truth.... What good would it do me if truth stood before me, cold and naked, not caring whether I recognized her or not, and producing in me a shudder of fear rather than a trusting devotion?... I am left standing like a man who has rented a house and gathered all the furniture and household things together, but has not

yet found the beloved with whom to share the joys and sorrows of his life. . . . It is this divine side of man, his inward action, which means everything—not a mass of [objective] information.[3]

Having repudiated the objectivity of truth, Kierkegaard was left longing for an existential experience, which he believed would bring him a sense of personal fulfillment. He stood on the precipice, preparing to make his leap of faith. Ultimately, the idea he chose to live and die for was Christianity, but it was a characteristically subjective brand of Christianity that he embraced.

Though Kierkegaard was virtually unknown during his lifetime, his writings have endured and have deeply influenced all subsequent philosophy. His idea of "truth that is true for me" infiltrated popular thought and set the tone for our generation's radical rejection of all objective standards.

Kierkegaard knew how to make irrationalism sound profound. "God does not exist; He is eternal," he wrote. He believed Christianity was full of "existential paradoxes," which he regarded as actual contradictions, proof that truth is irrational.

Using the example of Abraham's willingness to sacrifice Isaac (Gen. 22:1-19), Kierkegaard suggested that God called Abraham to violate moral law in slaying his son. For Kierkegaard, Abraham's willingness to "suspend" his ethical convictions epitomized the leap of faith that is demanded of everyone. Kierkegaard believed the incident proved that "the single individual [Abraham] is higher than the universal [moral law]."[4] Building on that conclusion, the Danish philosopher offered this observation: "Abraham represents faith. . . . He acts by virtue of the absurd, for it is precisely [by virtue of] the absurd that he as the single individual is higher than the universal."[5] "[I] cannot understand Abraham," Kierkegaard declared, "even though in a certain demented sense I admire him more than all others."[6]

It is not difficult to see how such thinking thrusts all truth into the realm of pure subjectivity—even to the point of absurdity or dementia. Everything becomes relative. Absolutes dematerialize.

The difference between truth and nonsense becomes meaningless. All that matters is personal experience.

And one person's experience is as valid as another's—even if everyone's experiences lead to contradictory conceptions of truth. "Truth that is true for me" might be different from someone else's truth. In fact, our beliefs might be obviously contradictory, yet another person's "truth" in no way invalidates mine. Because "truth" is authenticated by personal experience, its only relevance is for the individual who makes the leap of faith. That is existentialism.

Existentialism caught on in a big way in secular philosophy. Friedrich Nietzsche, for example, also rejected reason and emphasized the will of the individual. Nietzsche probably knew nothing of Kierkegaard's works, but their ideas paralleled at the key points. Unlike Kierkegaard, however, Nietzsche never made the leap of faith to Christianity. Instead, he leapt to the conclusion that God is dead. The truth that was "true for him," it seems, turned out to be the opposite of the truth Kierkegaard chose. But their epistemology (the way they arrived at their ideas) was exactly the same.

Later existentialists, such as Martin Heidegger and Jean-Paul Sartre, refined Kierkegaard's ideas while following the atheism of Nietzsche. Heidegger and Sartre both believed that reason is futile and life basically meaningless. Those ideas have been a powerful force in twentieth-century thought. As the world continues to grow more atheistic, more secular, and more irrational, it helps to understand that it is being propelled in that direction by strong existentialist influences.

EXISTENTIALISM INVADES THE CHURCH

But don't get the idea that existentialism's influence is limited to the secular world. From the moment Kierkegaard wedded existentialist ideas with Christianity, neo-orthodox theology was the inevitable outcome.

Neo-orthodoxy is the term used to identify an existentialist variety of Christianity. Because it denies the essential objective basis of truth—the absolute truth and authority of Scripture—neo-orthodoxy must be understood as pseudo-Christianity. Its heyday came in the middle of the twentieth century with the writings of Karl Barth, Emil Brunner, Paul Tillich, and Reinhold Niebuhr. Those men echoed the language and the thinking of Kierkegaard, speaking of the primacy of "personal authenticity," while downplaying or denying the significance of objective truth. Barth, the father of neo-orthodoxy, explicitly acknowledged his debt to Kierkegaard.[7]

Neo-orthodoxy's attitude toward Scripture is a microcosm of the entire existentialist philosophy: the Bible itself is not objectively the Word of God, but it *becomes* the Word of God when it speaks to me individually. In neo-orthodoxy, that same subjectivism is imposed on all the doctrines of historic Christianity. Familiar terms are used, but are redefined or employed in a way that is purposely vague—not to convey objective meaning, but to communicate a subjective symbolism. After all, any "truth" theological terms convey is unique to the person who exercises faith. What the Bible *means* becomes unimportant. *What it means to me* is the relevant issue. All of this resoundingly echoes Kierkegaard's concept of "truth that is true for me."

Thus while neo-orthodox theologians often *sound* as if they are affirming traditional beliefs, their actual system differs radically from the historic understanding of the Christian faith. By denying the objectivity of truth, they relegate all theology to the realm of subjective relativism. It is a theology perfectly suited for the age in which we live.

And that is precisely why it is so deadly.

Francis Schaeffer's 1968 work *The God Who Is There* included a perceptive analysis of Kierkegaard's influence on modern thought and modern theology.[8] Schaeffer named the boundary between rationality and irrationality "the line of despair." He noted that existentialism pushed *secular* thought below the line of despair sometime in the nineteenth century. Religious neo-orthodoxy was simply a johnny-come-lately response of theologians who were jumping on the existentialist bandwagon, following secular art, music, and general culture: "Neo-orthodoxy gave no new answer. What existential philosophy had already said in secular language, it now said in theological language. . . . [With the advent of neo-orthodoxy,] theology too has gone below the line of despair."[9]

Schaeffer went on to analyze how neo-orthodoxy ultimately gives way to radical mysticism:

> Karl Barth opened the door to the existentialistic leap in theology. . . . He has been followed by many more, men like Reinhold Niebuhr, Paul Tillich, Bishop John Robinson, Alan Richardson and all the new theologians. They may differ in details, but their struggle is still the same—it is the struggle of modern man who has given up [rationality]. As far as the theologians are concerned . . . their new system is not open to verification, it must simply be believed.[10]

Such a system, Schaeffer points out, has no integrity. Those who espouse it cannot live with the repercussions of their own illogic. "In practice a man cannot totally reject [rationality], however much his system leads him to it, unless he experiences . . . some form of mental breakdown." Thus people have been forced to an even deeper level of despair: "a level of mysticism with nothing there."[11]

MYSTICISM: IRRATIONALITY GONE TO SEED

Mysticism is the idea that spiritual reality is found by looking inward. Mysticism is perfectly suited for religious existentialism; indeed, it is its inevitable consequence. The mystic disdains rational understanding and seeks truth instead through the feelings, the imagination, personal visions, inner voices, private illumination, or other purely subjective means. Objective truth becomes practically superfluous.

Mystical experiences are therefore self-authenticating; that is, they are not subject to any form of objective verification. They are unique to the person who experiences them. Since they do not arise from or depend upon any rational process, they are invulnerable to any refutation by rational means.

Arthur L. Johnson writes,

The experience convinces the mystic in such a way, and to such a degree, that he simply cannot doubt its value and the correctness of what he believes it "says."

. . . In its crudest form this position says that believing something to be so makes it so. The idea is that ultimate reality is purely mental; therefore one is able to create whatever reality one wishes. Thus the mystic "creates" truth through his experience. In a less extreme form, the view seems to be that there are "alternate realities," one as real as another, and that these "break in upon" the mystic in his experiences. Whatever form is taken, the criterion of truth is again a purely private and subjective experience that provides no means of verification and no safeguard against error. Nevertheless, it is seen by the mystic as being above question by others.

The practical result of all this is that it is nearly impossible to reason with any convinced mystic. Such people are generally beyond the reach of reason.[12]

Mysticism is therefore antithetical to discernment. It is an extreme form of reckless faith.

Mysticism is the great melting pot into which neo-orthodoxy, the charismatic movement, anti-intellectual evangelicals, and even some segments of Roman Catholicism have been synthesized. It has produced movements like the Third Wave (a neo-charismatic movement with excessive emphasis on signs, wonders, and personal prophecies); Renovaré (an organization that blends teachings from monasticism, ancient Catholic mysticism, Eastern religion, and other mystical traditions); the spiritual warfare movement (which seeks to engage demonic powers in direct confrontation); and the modern prophecy movement (which encourages believers to seek private, extrabiblical revelation directly from God). The influx of mysticism has also opened evangelicalism to New-Age concepts like subliminal thought-control, inner healing, communication with angels, channeling, dream analysis, positive confession, and a host of other therapies and practices coming directly from occult and Eastern religions.

The face of evangelicalism has changed so dramatically in the past twenty years that what is called evangelicalism today is beginning to resemble what used to be called neo-orthodoxy. If anything, some segments of contemporary evangelicalism are even more subjective in their approach to truth than neo-orthodoxy ever was.

It could be argued that evangelicalism never successfully resisted neo-orthodoxy. Twenty years ago evangelicals took a heroic stand against neo-orthodox influences on the issue of biblical inerrancy. But whatever victory was gained in that battle is now being sacrificed on the altar of mysticism. Mysticism renders biblical inerrancy irrelevant. After all, if the highest truth is subjective and comes from within us, then it doesn't ultimately matter if the specifics of Scripture are true or not. If the *content* of faith is not the real issue, what does it really matter if the Bible has errors or not?

In other words, neo-orthodoxy attacked the objective inspiration of Scripture. Evangelical mysticism attacks the objective interpretation of Scripture. The practical effect is the same. By embracing existential relativism, evangelicals are forfeiting the very riches they fought so hard to protect. If we can gain meaningful guidance from characters who appear in our fantasies, why should we bother ourselves with what the Bible says? If we are going to disregard or even reject the biblical verdict against homosexuality, what difference does it make if the historical and factual matter revealed in Scripture is accurate or inaccurate? If personal prophecies, visions, dreams, and angelic beings are available to give us up-to-the-minute spiritual direction—"fresh revelation" as it is often called—who cares if Scripture is without error in the whole or in the parts?

Mysticism further nullifies Scripture by pointing people away from the sure Word of God as the only reliable object of faith. Warning of the dangers of mysticism, Schaeffer wrote,

> Probably the best way to describe this concept of modern theology is to say that it is faith in faith, rather than faith directed to an object which is actually there. . . . A modern man cannot talk about the object of his faith, only about the faith itself. So he can discuss the existence of his faith and its "size" as it exists against all reason, but that is all. Modern man's faith turns inward. . . . Faith is introverted, because it has no certain object . . . it is ratio-

nally not open to discussion. *This position, I would suggest, is actually a greater despair and darkness than the position of those modern men who commit suicide.*[13]

The faith of mysticism is an illusion. "Truth that is true for me" is irrelevant to anyone else, because it lacks any objective basis. Ultimately, therefore, existential faith is impotent to lift anyone above the level of despair. All it can do is seek more experiences and more feelings. Multitudes are trapped in the desperate cycle of feeding off one experience while zealously seeking the next. Such people have no real concept of truth; they just *believe*. Theirs is a reckless faith.

MEANWHILE, AT THE OTHER END OF THE SPECTRUM . . .

Mysticism, however, is not the only form of reckless faith that threatens the contemporary church. A new movement has been gaining strength lately. Evangelicals are leaving the fold and moving into Eastern Orthodoxy, Roman Catholicism, and liturgical high-church Protestantism. Rejecting the ever-changing subjectivism of a freewheeling existential Protestantism, they seek a religion with historical roots. Turned off by the shallow silliness that has overrun the evangelical movement, they desire a more magisterial approach. Perhaps sensing the dangers of a religion that points people inward, they choose instead a religion that emphasizes external ceremonies and dogmatic hierarchical authority.

I listened to the taped testimony of one of these converts to Roman Catholicism, a former Protestant minister. He said he had graduated with highest honors from a leading Protestant seminary. He told his audience that as a student he was rabidly anti-Catholic and fully committed to Protestant Reformed doctrine (although he refuted this himself by admitting he had already rejected the crucial doctrine of justification by faith). After college he began to read Roman Catholic writings and found himself drawn to Catholic theology and liturgy. He described his initial resistance to the doctrines of purgatory, the perpetual virginity of Mary, transubstantiation, and prayers to Mary and the saints. All of those doctrines are easily disproved by the Bible.[14] But this man—acknowledging that he could find no warrant anywhere in Scripture for praying to Mary—nevertheless completely changed his outlook on such matters after he tried praying the rosary and received an answer to a very specific prayer. He concluded that it must have been Mary who answered his prayer and immediately began praying regularly to her. Ultimately, he decided the Bible alone was not a sufficient rule of faith for believers, and he put his faith in papal authority and church tradition.

That man's leap of faith may not have been of the existential variety, but it was a blind leap nonetheless. He chose the other extreme of reckless faith, the kind that makes extrabiblical religious tradition the object of one's faith.

This kind of faith is reckless because it subjugates the written Word of God to oral tradition, church authority, or some other human criterion. It is an uncritical trust in an earthly religious authority—the pope, tradition, a self-styled prophet like David Koresh, or whatever. Such faith rarely jettisons Scripture altogether—but by forcing God's Word into the mold of religious tradition, it invalidates the Word of God and renders it of no effect (cf. Matt. 15:6).

The man whose taped testimony I heard is now an apologist for the Roman Catholic Church. He speaks to Catholic congregations and tells them how to counter biblical arguments against Catholicism. At the end of his testimony tape, he deals briefly with the official Catholic attitude toward Scripture. He is eager to assure his listeners that the modern Roman Catholic Church has no objection if Catholic people want to read Scripture for themselves. Even personal Bible *study* is all right, he says—but then hastens to add that it is not necessary to go overboard. "A verse or two a day is enough."

This man, a seminary graduate, surely should be aware that a comment like that seriously understates the importance of the written Word of God. We are commanded to meditate on Scripture day and night (Josh. 1:8; Ps. 1:2). We are to let it fill our hearts at all times (Deut. 6:6-9). We must study it diligently and handle it rightly (2 Tim. 2:15). The Bible alone is able to give us the wisdom that leads

31

to salvation, then adequately equip us for every good work (2 Tim. 3:15-17).

Discernment depends on a knowledge of Scripture. Those who are content to listen gullibly to some voice of human authority rather than hearing God's Word and letting it speak for itself cannot be discerning. Theirs is a reckless, irrational faith.

We identified the inward-looking extreme of reckless faith as *mysticism*. We could call this other variety *rote tradition*. In Isaiah 29:13, that is precisely how God Himself characterized it: "This people draw near with their words and honor Me with their lip service, but they remove their hearts far from Me, and *their reverence for Me consists of tradition learned by rote*" (emphasis added).

Scripture has nothing but condemnation for rote tradition. Barren religious ritual, sacerdotal formalism, or liturgy out of a book are not the same as worship. Real worship, like faith, must *engage the mind*. Jesus said, "The true worshipers . . . worship the Father in spirit and truth; for such people the Father seeks to be His worshipers" (John 4:23).

Did you realize that rote tradition was the very error for which Jesus condemned the Pharisees? He told them,

> "Rightly did Isaiah prophesy of you hypocrites, as it is written, 'This people honors Me with their lips, but their heart is far away from Me. But in vain do they worship Me, teaching as doctrines the precepts of men.' Neglecting the commandment of God, you hold to the tradition of men."
>
> He was also saying to them, "You nicely set aside the commandment of God in order to keep your tradition" (Mark 7:6-9).

Rote tradition is not unlike mysticism in that it also bypasses the mind. Paul said this of the Jews who were so absorbed in their empty religious traditions:

> I bear them witness that they have a zeal for God, but not in accordance with knowledge. For not knowing about God's righteousness, and seeking to establish their own, they did not subject

themselves to the righteousness of God. For Christ is the end of
the law for righteousness to everyone who believes (Rom. 10:2-4).

Their problem was not a lack of zeal. It was not that they were short
on enthusiasm, emotionally flat, or slothful about religious obser-
vances. The issue was that the zeal they displayed was rote tradition,
"not in accordance with *knowledge*." They were not sufficiently discerning, and therefore their faith itself was deficient.

Paul is specific in stating that their ignorance lay in trying to
establish their own righteousness rather than submitting to the righteousness of God. This passage comes at the culmination of Paul's
doctrinal discussion in Romans. In context it is very clear that he was
talking about the doctrine of justification by faith. He had thoroughly
expounded this subject beginning in chapter 3. He said we are "justified as a gift by His grace through the redemption which is in Christ
Jesus" (3:24). Justification is "by faith apart from works of the Law"
(v. 28). "God reckons righteousness apart from works" (Rom. 4:6).

But instead of seeking the perfect righteousness of Christ, which
God reckons to those who believe, the unbelieving Jews had set out
to try to establish a righteousness of their own through works. That
is where rote tradition always leads. It is a religion of works. Thus the
ritualistic, unbelieving Pharisees are an exact parallel to Roman
Catholicism, Eastern Orthodoxy, and most forms of ritual-laden
Protestantism. All of them deny justification by faith.

If the Pharisees or their followers had used the Scriptures as their
standard of truth rather than rabbinical tradition, they would have
known that God justifies sinners by faith. Repeatedly, Jesus said
things to them like "Did you never read in the Scriptures . . . ?"
(Matt. 21:42); "You are mistaken, not understanding the Scriptures,
or the power of God" (22:29); and, "Are you the teacher of Israel, and
do not understand these things?" (John 3:10). What He continually
chided them for was their *ignorance of the Scriptures*. They had set rote
tradition in place of the written Word of God (Matt. 15:6), and they
were condemned for it.

Contrast the way Luke commended the Bereans for their noble-
mindedness: "For they received the word [the New Testament

gospel from the apostles] with great eagerness, examining the Scriptures [the Old Testament books] daily, to see whether these things were so" (Acts 17:11). What made the Bereans worthy of commendation? Their eagerness to be discerning. They rightly refused to blindly accept anyone's teaching (even that of the apostles) without clear warrant from God's Word.

That is what God demands of us.

In the chapters to come, we will look at some passages of Scripture that deal with the issue of discernment. We will also examine some texts that confront the two extremes of reckless faith. And we will deal with some contemporary issues that call for careful biblical discernment.

Spiritual discernment is, I believe, the only antidote to the existentialism of our age. Until Christians regain the will to test everything by the rule of Scripture, reject what is false, and hold fast to what is true, the church will struggle and falter, and our testimony to a world in sin will be impaired.

But if the church will rise up and stand for the truth of God's Word against all the lies of this evil world, then we will begin to see the power of truth that sets people free (John 8:32).

2

The Rise of
Reckless Faith

A FEW SUMMERS AGO I drove across the country to deliver my
son's car to him. He was playing minor-league baseball in
Florida and needed his car for local transportation. The cross-
country trip fit perfectly with some previously scheduled ministry
engagements on my calendar, so I took my assistant, Lance Quinn,
and together we made the journey. As we drove through Lance's
home state of Arkansas, our route took us off the main highways and
through some beautiful rural country. We topped one hill and I
noticed near a very rustic house a homemade sign advertising hand-
sewn quilts. I had hoped to stop somewhere along the way to buy an
anniversary gift for my wife. She likes hand-made crafts and had been
wanting a quilt. So we decided to stop and look.

We went to the door of the old house and knocked. A friendly
woman with a dishtowel answered the door. When we told her we
were interested in quilts, she swung the door open wide and ushered
us in. She showed us into the living room, where she had several
quilts on display.

The television set in the corner was on, tuned in to a religious
broadcast. The woman's husband was lounging in a recliner, half

watching the program and half reading a religious magazine. Around the room were piles of religious books, religious literature, and religious videotapes. I recognized one or two of the books—resources from solid evangelical publishers. The woman left the room to get some more quilts to show us, so the man put aside his magazine and greeted us. "I was just catching up on some reading," he said.

"Are you a believer?" I asked.

"A believer in *what*?" he asked, apparently startled that I would ask.

"A believer in Christ," I said. "I noticed your books. Are you a Christian?"

"Well, sure," he said, holding up the magazine he was reading. I recognized it as the publication of a well-known cult. I took a closer look at the stacks of material around the room. There were a few evangelical best-sellers, materials from several media ministries, a promotional magazine from a leading evangelical seminary, and even some helpful Bible-study aids. But mixed in with all that were stacks of *The Watch Tower* magazines published by the Jehovah's Witnesses, a copy of *Dianetics* (the book by Scientology founder L. Ron Hubbard), a *Book of Mormon*, some literature from the Franciscan brothers, and an incredible array of stuff from nearly every conceivable cult and "ism." I watched as he jotted down the address of the television preacher who was at that moment offering some free literature.

"You read from quite an assortment of material," I observed. "These all represent different beliefs. Do you accept any one of them?"

"I find there's good in all of it," he said. "I read it all and just look for the good."

While this conversation was going on, the woman had come back with a stack of quilts and was ready to show them to us. The first quilt she laid out was a patchwork of all different sizes, colors, and prints of fabric scraps. I looked at it, trying to see some kind of pattern or design in it, but there was none. The color combinations even seemed to clash. The quilt itself was—well, ugly.

I described for her the kind of quilt I was looking for, and she pulled one out that was exactly what I wanted. Her price seemed reasonable, so I told her I would take it.

As she wrapped up my purchase, I couldn't help looking again at that first quilt she had brought out from the back room. Frankly, it was the *least* attractive of all her quilts. But she was obviously quite proud of it, having labored over it for hours. It was evidently her personal favorite—and undoubtedly a genuine piece of folk art. But I couldn't imagine anyone else being attracted to that particular quilt.

Her quilt, I thought, was a perfect metaphor for her husband's religion. Taking bits and pieces from every conceivable source, he was putting together a patchwork faith. He thought of his religion as a thing of beauty, but in God's eyes it was an abomination.

Our generation is exposed to more religious ideas than any people in history. Religious broadcasting and the print media bombard people with all kinds of deviant teachings that claim to be truth. In the area where I live, for example, we are assaulted with everything from Gene Scott—a vulgar, cigar-chomping television preacher whose messages are peppered with profanity—to huge billboards declaring "ISLAM IS TRUTH." The undiscerning person has no means of determining *what* is truth, and many are baffled by the variety.

It is no wonder that people apart from Christ would be confused by such teachings. But why would people who believe the Bible and affirm that Jesus is Lord of all be led astray or confounded by competing doctrines?

Yet many professing Christians *are* perplexed by the lies. The church today is filled with people who lack any ability to differentiate the very worst false doctrines from truth. I constantly encounter Christians who are at a loss to answer the most profound errors they hear from cultists, unorthodox media preachers, or other sources of false doctrine. Too many people are like the man fashioning a patchwork religion, sifting through stacks of religious ideas, looking for what is good in all of it.

This is inexcusable. Scripture warns that the church will be inundated with doctrines of demons, destructive heresies, myths, falsehoods, perverse teachings, commandments of men, human traditions, empty philosophy, vain deceit, speculations, lying spirits, worldly fables, false knowledge, and worldly wisdom. Jesus said false prophets would come as wolves in sheep's clothing (Matt. 7:15). Paul told the elders at Ephesus that savage wolves would enter in, not sparing the flock (Acts 20:29). "And *from among your own selves*," he added, "men will arise, speaking perverse things, to draw away the disciples after them" (v. 30, emphasis added). He wrote Timothy and said, "Evil men and impostors will proceed from bad to worse, deceiving and being deceived" (2 Tim. 3:13). He also wrote, "The Spirit explicitly says that in later times some will fall away from the faith, paying attention to deceitful spirits and doctrines of demons" (1 Tim. 4:1).

Yet the contemporary church is virtually impotent to face such an onslaught. An almost inexhaustible gullibility has destroyed people's will to be discerning. The visible church is shot through with confusion and error. You might think that the televangelist scandals that began in the 1980s would have made people wary, but that does not seem to have been the long-term effect. As soon as one televised charlatan is discredited, someone even more bizarre comes along to fill the time slot—with higher-than-ever audience approval ratings.

In the previous chapter we looked at some of the philosophical errors that underlie the decline of discernment and the rise of reckless faith in the church. Now let's examine some of the *practical* reasons for these trends.

THE WEAKENING OF DOCTRINAL CLARITY

Several of my previous books have documented the decline of any emphasis on sound doctrine in the church. Modern church leaders seem obsessed with methodology, psychology, pragmatics, attendance figures, felt needs, popularity polls, and the like—all to the detriment of biblical doctrine. And when doctrinal understanding declines, real discernment becomes impossible.

Jesus made that very point with the religious leaders of His day. Matthew 16:1-4 records this:

> The Pharisees and Sadducees came up, and testing Him asked
> Him to show them a sign from heaven. But He answered and said

to them, "When it is evening, you say, 'It will be fair weather, for the sky is red.' And in the morning, 'There will be a storm today, for the sky is red and threatening.' Do you know how to discern the appearance of the sky, but cannot discern the signs of the times? An evil and adulterous generation seeks after a sign; and a sign will not be given it, except the sign of Jonah." And He left them, and went away.

Their limited, primitive, non-scientific knowledge of meteorology exceeded their spiritual discernment! As little as they knew about predicting the weather, they were better weathermen than they were discerners. They had no ability to distinguish the "signs of the times"—the great spiritual realities that were unfolding right before their eyes! And Jesus condemned them for it. In effect He said, "I have nothing to offer you." He refused to give them any sign; He simply turned and left them.

How can we explain the biblical illiteracy of the Sadducees and Pharisees? They were extremely religious. The Pharisees in particular were fastidious about insisting on all the details of their law. But in all their spiritual calisthenics, they missed the main message. Consequently they rejected their Messiah. They are proof that generating religious *activity* is no substitute for love of *truth*.

The Jewish leaders adhered to the brand of reckless faith that favors rote tradition. They did not teach people to think biblically, to search the Scriptures thoroughly, to test everything, to discern between truth and error. Instead, they issued a set of rules and told people to live accordingly. Many of their laws and rules were nothing but human inventions added to Moses' law. And like most legalists, the rulers of the Jews were prone to extreme hypocrisy. Jesus denounced them in the strongest language: "You weigh men down with burdens hard to bear, while you yourselves will not even touch the burdens with one of your fingers" (Luke 11:46).

Sometimes the Pharisees are accused of being overly concerned with orthodoxy. But that was not at all where they went astray. Their error was that they became so wrapped up in their own traditions that they *downplayed* the truth of Scripture and distorted sound doctrine.

Far from being theologically orthodox, they had simply invented their own traditions and used a man-made system to nullify the truth of divinely inspired Scripture (Matt. 15:3-6).

It is fashionable today to characterize anyone who is concerned with biblical doctrine as Pharisaical. The biblical condemnation of the Pharisees' legalism has been misread as a denunciation of doctrinal precision. And love of the truth has often been judged inherently legalistic.

But love for truth is *not* the same as legalism. The fact that it has been portrayed that way has sabotaged the very thing the church so desperately needs today. Too many Christians are content to gaze nonchalantly at the surface of scriptural truth without plunging any deeper. They often justify their shallow indifference as a refusal to be legalistic. Conversely, they dismiss as pharisaical narrow-mindedness any attempt to declare the truth authoritatively. Doctrine divides; therefore any concern for doctrinal matters is commonly seen as unchristian. People concerned with discernment and sound doctrine are often accused of fostering a pharisaical, divisive attitude.

But that is exactly backward! True unity is *rooted* in truth. Jesus prayed: "*Sanctify them in the truth*; Thy word is truth. . . . For their sakes I sanctify Myself, that they themselves also may be sanctified in truth. I do not ask in behalf of these alone, but for those also who believe in Me through their word; *that they may all be one*" (John 17:17-21, emphasis added). The unity for which He prayed is preceded by and grows out of sanctification in the truth. Fellowship that ignores or glosses over the crucial doctrines of the faith is not Christian unity; it is ungodly compromise.

As doctrine has been deemphasized, the church has moved from preaching the Word to other activities: drama, music, entertainment—things designed to evoke an emotional response rather than enlighten the mind. The charismatic movement has supplanted doctrine with experience. Psychology has elevated "felt" needs over *real* needs and behavioral theory over revealed truth. All this has accelerated the move away from doctrine and focused the pulpit message on everything *but* the objective truth of Scripture. Preachers have become comedians, storytellers, therapists, showmen, and entertainers rather than powerful envoys of divine truth.

In some circles, this trend has been heralded as a great step forward. David Watson, an influential leader of the evangelical movement in the Church of England until his death in 1984, believed music and drama could be used more effectively than preaching and writing to communicate to unbelievers. He explained why he traveled with a drama and music team: "They are able to communicate the gospel much more effectively than I could with mere words. . . . Most churches rely heavily on the spoken or written word for communication and then wonder why so few people find the Christian faith to be relevant."[1]

What does that mean? That the written word and the spoken word make the Christian faith irrelevant? That our faith is something subjective (a feeling or emotion) that can be better communicated through music, drama, and art forms—rather than by the straightforward proclamation of objective truth?

Recently I watched a televised evangelistic meeting that featured music, celebrity appearances, and a brief message where the preacher told stories, cracked jokes, and played on the emotions of the audience. No reference was made to the issue of sin, no mention of the cross, no call to repentance—in fact, there were only scant references to Scripture, and they had nothing to do with any of the central issues of the gospel. Nothing was said that would remotely challenge the unbelief or sin of non-Christians. Incredibly, however, an invitation was given and people streamed forward to make professions of faith. What were they saying? That they were moved emotionally? That they wanted a religious experience?

Can we really view such a response as evidence of conversion? Can people become Christians on the basis of a message devoid of any gospel truth? Can someone who has never known real conviction of sin trust Christ as Savior in any meaningful sense? Is a walk down the aisle at a religious meeting the same thing as true conversion? Is just any kind of emotional experience as good as genuine repentance?

The state of affairs is such in the church today that multitudes who profess faith in Christ cannot even articulate the most basic issues of the gospel. I once met a man who told me he had been active for nine years in a charismatic businessmen's organization. He had heard that I was critical of the charismatic movement, and he wanted to urge me to be more tolerant. "Life is like a long, dark stairway," he told me. "We all climb the stairs in the dark, feeling our way along. At the top is a door. You knock on the door and just hope Jesus comes and lets you in. Let's not fight each other while we are feeling our way around in the dark."

That man did not believe truth is knowable. He opposed doctrinal clarity because he believed in the final analysis all we can do is make our best guess about what is true, then just hope we get it right. We can't really *know* anything, though. The actual name for that view is *skepticism*, and it is not a Christian position.

On another occasion, I was the guest on a two-hour radio talk show. I had been invited to discuss a book I had written, in which I had stated that psychology has no legitimate role in the process of sanctification. The host was a very pleasant woman whom I had not met before. She was dumbfounded by my opposition to psychology. "You don't mean you think being a Christian solves all the problems of life at once, do you?" she asked.

No, I assured her, but it does solve the core problem—the problem of sin and our resulting alienation from God. Then from conversion on, the process of sanctification conforms us more and more to the image of Christ. Whatever spiritual problems remain after conversion are addressed by the Holy Spirit's sanctifying work through the Word of God. I pointed out that it is actually counterproductive to treat spiritual problems as if they were non-moral, non-spiritual, purely psychological issues.

I went on to say that the first step toward genuine spiritual health is to recognize your sinfulness. Then I gave a brief synopsis of what happens when a person becomes a Christian: You acknowledge that you cannot save yourself. You repent of your sins. You cast yourself on the mercy of God. And you believe in Jesus Christ as God's Son who came into the world and died to pay sin's penalty, then rose again as Lord of all.

That triggered a rather amazing response from her. "Surely you don't believe every person who becomes a Christian must believe all *that*, do you?"

I said, "Well, yes—YES!"

"But I wasn't even aware that I was a sinner when I became a Christian," she said. "That thought never occurred to me. Sin wasn't even an issue in my thinking."

"Then how were you saved, and what were you saved from?" I asked.

This was her reply: "I was into drugs, alcohol, and living with my boyfriend. I had been involved in metaphysics, Science of the Mind, for years. My life just wasn't working. Then one day I simply got Jesus' phone number. That's it."

"You simply got Jesus' phone number?" I asked, hoping for some clarification.

"Yes!" she replied. "Suddenly I just knew He was there, and that He could help me sort out my life. So I gave Him a call."

I pointed out that Jesus Himself said He came to call sinners to repentance, and that it is not those who are whole who need a physician, but those who are sick (Mark 2:17; Luke 5:31). I reiterated that salvation is offered exclusively to people who sense the guilt of their sin—those who labor and are heavy-laden under the weight of sin (Matt. 11:28-30).

She broke for a commercial, then changed the subject.

After the program ended, I reiterated the content of the gospel for her and urged her to begin filling her mind with the *content* of Scripture. Her Christianity was nothing more than a feeling, altogether subjective. She couldn't even communicate the gospel clearly to her listening audience. She was spreading reckless faith.

What is left for the church if we can't even get our doctrine clear at the level of the gospel? Is it not obvious that such doctrinal shallowness undermines people's ability to discern?

That is precisely why Paul told Timothy, "Be diligent to present yourself approved to God as a workman who does not need to be ashamed, handling accurately the word of truth" (2 Tim. 2:15). The contemporary assault on doctrine is a rejection of this command. It is ultimately a denial of God Himself. Or, as Christian philosopher

Gordon Clark wrote, "Since God is truth, a contempt for truth is equally a contempt for God."[2]

Again, emphatically, none of this suggests that love and unity are unimportant. We must be loving. We must seek unity. We must reflect the long-suffering of God and the meekness of our Savior. But all of that must be built on a foundation of non-negotiable truth.

A few years ago a man sent me his doctoral dissertation. He was analyzing preaching styles and had used me as an example of expository preaching (preaching that aims to set forth the *meaning* of a passage of Scripture). In his final assessment he concluded that the expository preaching model is "biblical but not relevant." How can anything be both biblical and irrelevant? What does this say about our attitude toward the Word of God?

When doctrine declines, people's thinking grows fuzzy. People who are confused about the truth have absolutely no hope of being careful discerners. When doctrine is relegated to secondary status, it is inevitable that discernment will wane.

THE DISPARAGEMENT OF STRONG CONVICTIONS

A closely related second reason for the low level of discernment in the church today is the reluctance to take a definitive stand on any issue. Those with any convictions at all are supposed to hold those beliefs with as much slack as possible. Dogmatism is not permitted. To pronounce anything *true* and call its antithesis *error* is to challenge society's only remaining dogma. Refuse to equivocate on any point of principle or doctrine, and you will be labeled too narrow. Zeal for the truth has become politically incorrect.

In the secular world it is often thought uncouth to voice any opinion at all on spiritual, moral, or ethical matters. A plethora of Phil Donahue-style talk shows exist to remind us of this fact, and they do so by parading in front of us the most bizarre and extreme advocates of every radical "alternative lifestyle" imaginable. We are not supposed to condemn these people; the whole point is to broaden our minds and raise our level of tolerance. Anyone who responds negatively is viewed with the same contempt that used to be reserved for bigots and religious hypocrites.

The other day one of these programs broadcast a show featuring bearded lesbians. A petite woman was seated on the stage sporting a thick black beard and full moustache. All her other physical attributes, her voice, and her clothing were fully feminine. She declared that she was proud of the beard and really didn't care what anyone else thought of it. Besides, her lesbian lover found facial hair attractive. She said she was actually taking hormones to make her beard grow even thicker.

A teenage girl in the audience timidly stated that she thought it was unfortunate that the bearded woman was purposely alienating herself from mainstream society. She suggested that the woman might really be happier if she stopped the hormone treatments and underwent electrolysis instead.

At that the studio audience turned disagreeable. Several people booed the teenage girl. Another woman from the audience, her voice choked with emotion, scolded the teenager: "How *dare* you criticize this beautiful creature! Who are you to tell her how she should look? Society shouldn't impose arbitrary standards on people. Everyone should be free to be whatever they want to be."

The audience responded with sustained applause. The bearded woman grinned triumphantly. And the teenage girl sat down in shame.

The culture around us has declared war on all standards, and the church is unwittingly following suit. It has become quite popular among Christians to assert that almost nothing is really black and white. Virtually all issues of right and wrong, true and false, good and bad are painted in shades of gray. Many Christians assume this is the proper way of understanding truth. It is, once again, a capitulation to the relativism of an existential culture.

Any tone of certainty is offensive to some people. A few years ago I did a live radio interview where listeners were invited to phone in. One caller told me, "You seem like a lot nicer person than I thought you were by listening to your sermons." He meant it kindly, and I took it in that spirit. But I was curious to know what he had heard in my preaching that he interpreted as not nice. (When I preach, I am certainly not mean or hateful. Besides, if I ever did say anything unkind or malicious, our staff would edit it out of the tape. So I asked what he meant.)

"I don't know," he said. "In your sermons, you sound so opinionated, so dogmatic. But this afternoon you're more conversational. You just sound nicer." Like many people today, he thought of dialogue as "nicer" than a sermon.

I once met a pastor who cringed every time anyone used the word *preaching*. "I don't preach," he would insist. "I *share*." Somehow "sharing" seemed more polite to him than "preaching."

That is the mood of this generation. It reflects the philosophy and the culture of existentialism. It is no accident that the church has moved away from emphatically proclaiming truth. That shift is an accommodation to the unbelieving spirit of our age. Narrowness and dogmatism are unacceptable in a society that views truth as a personal matter. After all, existentialism rules out any universal truth. And that makes strong conviction seem haughty and inappropriate.

Compromise is therefore what drives this pragmatic age. In most people's minds, the very word *compromise* is rich with positive connotations. Obviously, in the realm of social and political discourse, compromise can certainly be helpful, even constructive. Compromise lubricates the political machinery of secular government. The art of compromise is the key to successful negotiations in business. And even in marriage, small compromises are often necessary for a healthy relationship.

But when it comes to biblical issues, moral principles, theological truth, divine revelation, and other spiritual absolutes, compromise is *never* appropriate.

The church, caught up in the existentialism of our age, is losing sight of that reality. In recent years evangelicals have embraced compromise as a tool for church growth, a platform for unity, and even a test of spirituality. Take an uncompromising stance on almost any doctrinal or biblical issue, and a chorus of voices will call you obstinate, unkind, heartless, contentious, or unloving, no matter how irenically you frame your argument.

Did I say "argument"? Many people have the false idea that Christians are never supposed to be argumentative. We're not supposed to engage in polemics. I hear this frequently: "Why don't you just state truth in positive terms and ignore the views you disagree with? Why not steer clear of controversy, forget the negatives, and present everything affirmatively?"

I first began to realize the force of this trend more than a decade ago. A well-known pastor published an excellent devotional book in which he incidentally pointed out the fallacy of presenting Christ's lordship only as an option to be considered after conversion. The entire book devoted a few scant paragraphs to the so-called "lordship controversy," but in that context, the pastor cited an eminent seminary professor whose writings have contributed greatly to widespread confusion on the issue. The pastor was very objective and wrote with a charitable tone, but he took an opposing view.

Shortly after the book came out, I was expressing my appreciation to the publisher. To my surprise, the editor responsible for the book told me he was sorry they had published it. When I probed, he told me the company had been hit with some highly placed criticism about the book. Friends of the seminary professor were outraged that he had been named in a footnote by someone who disagreed with him. Even the book's editor said, "I see now that the pastor was very unkind to the seminary professor."

I went back and re-read the offending passage carefully. The pastor's inflection was as thoroughly benevolent as I had recalled. Nothing in it could reasonably be construed as unfair or ungracious. It was certainly not "unkind." The pastor had correctly cited a published work. He had adequately and straightforwardly represented the professor's teaching. He was simply expressing an honest but crucial disagreement.

Unfortunately, it is no longer permissible to deal with biblical issues in an uncompromising fashion. Those who dare to take an unpopular stand, declare truth in a definitive way—or worst of all, express disagreement with someone else's teaching—will inevitably be marked as troublesome. Compromise has become a virtue while devotion to truth has become offensive.

Martyn Lloyd-Jones called the modern distrust of polemics "very loose and very false and very flabby thinking. . . . The attitude of many seems to be, 'We do not want these arguments. Give us the simple message, the simple gospel. Give it to us positively, and do not bother about other views.'"[3]

Lloyd-Jones responded to those sentiments: "It is important that we should realize that if we speak like that we are denying the Scriptures. The Scriptures are full of arguments, full of polemics."[4] He went on:

> Disapproval of polemics in the Christian Church is a very serious matter. But that is the attitude of the age in which we live. The prevailing idea today in many circles is not to bother about these things. As long as we are all Christians, anyhow, somehow, all is well. Do not let us argue about doctrine, let us all be Christians together and talk about the love of God. That is really the whole basis of ecumenicity. Unfortunately, that same attitude is creeping into evangelical circles also and many say that we must not be too precise about these things. . . . If you hold that view you are criticizing the Apostle Paul, you are saying that he was wrong, and at the same time you are criticizing the Scriptures. The Scriptures argue and debate and dispute; they are full of polemics.[5]

Lloyd-Jones added this helpful qualifier:

> Let us be clear about what we mean. This is not argument for the sake of argument; this is not a manifestation of an argumentative spirit; this is not just indulging one's prejudices. The Scriptures do not approve of that, and furthermore the Scriptures are very concerned about the spirit in which one engages in discussion. No man should like argument for the sake of argument. We should always regret the necessity; but though we regret and bemoan it, when we feel that a vital matter is at stake we must engage in argument. We must "earnestly contend for the truth," and we are called upon to do that by the New Testament.[6]

Obviously not *every* issue is cast in black and white. There are many questions to which Scripture does not explicitly speak. For example, should Christians watch television? Nothing in Scripture forbids it. But clearly television poses certain dangers for the Christian. And there *are* principles in Scripture that can help us discern what kinds of things we should watch and how we should interact with what we see. But there is no express rule given to govern how much or how little television we should watch. It is a gray area.

But many of the issues being compromised among Christians today are *not* questionable. These are *not* gray areas. There is no room for compromise here. Scripture speaks very clearly against homosexuality, for example. The Christian position on adultery is not at all vague. The question of whether a believer ought to marry an unbeliever is spelled out with perfect clarity. Scripture quite plainly forbids any Christian to take another Christian to court. Selfishness and pride are explicitly identified as sins.

Yet in recent weeks I have seen every one of those issues treated as a gray area—on Christian radio, on Christian television, and in Christian literature. People want all such matters to be negotiable. And too many Christian leaders willingly oblige. They hesitate to speak with authority on matters where Scripture is plain. The lines of distinction between truth and error, wisdom and foolishness, and church and world are being obliterated.

The truth is that far more things are black-and-white issues than most people realize. Most of the truths of God's Word are explicitly contrasted with opposing ideas. Jay Adams calls this the principle of *antithesis*, and he points out that it is fundamental to genuine discernment:

In the Bible, where antithesis is so important, discernment—the ability to distinguish God's thoughts and God's ways from all others—is essential. Indeed, God says that "the wise in heart will be called discerning" (Proverbs 16:21).

From the Garden of Eden with its two trees (one allowed, one forbidden) to the eternal destiny of the human being in heaven or in hell, the Bible sets forth two, and only two, ways: God's way, and all others. Accordingly, people are said to be saved or lost. They belong to God's people or the world. There was Gerizim, the mount of blessing, and Ebal, the mount of cursing. There is the narrow way and the wide way, leading either to eternal life or to destruction. There are those who are against and those who are with us, those within and those without. There is life and death, truth and falsehood, good and bad, light and darkness, the kingdom of God and the kingdom of Satan, love and hatred, spiritual wisdom and the wisdom of the world. Christ is said to be the way, the truth, and the life, and no one may come to the Father but by Him. His is the only name under the sky by which one may be saved.[7]

Adams suggests that such antithetical teaching is found "on nearly every page of the Bible."[8] "People who study the Bible in depth develop antithetical mindsets: They think in terms of contrasts or opposites."[9] He believes that the Old Testament laws distinguishing between clean and unclean animals have a distinct purpose. Regulations governing choices in clothing, health care, and other matters of daily life were not arbitrary, but were meant to cause God's people to think constantly about the difference between God's ways and the world's way—"to develop in God's people an antithetical mentality."[10]

I agree. All truth sets itself against error. Where Scripture speaks, it speaks with authority. It speaks definitively. It speaks decisively. It calls for absolute conviction. It demands that we submit to God and resist the devil (James 4:7). It urges us to discern between the spirit of truth and the spirit of error (1 John 4:6). It commands us to turn away from evil and do good (1 Peter 3:11). It calls us to reject the broad way that seems right to the human mind (Prov. 14:12; 16:25) and follow the narrow way prescribed by God (Matt. 7:13-14). It tells us that our ways are not God's ways, nor are our thoughts His thoughts (Isa. 55:8). It orders us to protect the truth and reject lies (Rom. 1:25). It declares that no lie is of the truth (1 John 2:21). It guarantees that the righteous shall be blessed and the wicked perish (Ps. 1:1, 6). And it reminds us that "friendship with the world is hostility toward God" (James 4:4).

Discernment demands that where Scripture speaks with clarity, a hard line must be drawn. Christ is against human philosophy, against empty deception, against human tradition, and against the elementary principles of this world (Col. 2:8). Those things cannot be integrated with true Christian belief; they must be repudiated and steadfastly resisted. Scripture demands that we make a definitive choice: "How long will you hesitate between two opinions? If the Lord is God, follow Him; but if Baal, follow him" (1 Kings 18:21). "Choose for yourselves today whom you will serve . . . but as for me and my house, we will serve the Lord" (Josh. 24:15).

The modern canonization of compromise represents a detour down a dead-end alley. Both Scripture and church history reveal the danger of compromise. Those whom God uses are invariably men and women who swim against the tide. They hold strong convictions with great courage and refuse to compromise in the face of incredible opposition. David stubbornly refused to tremble before Goliath; he saw Goliath as an affront to God. While all Israel cowered in fear, David stood alone before the enemy. Daniel, Shadrach, Meshach, and Abed-nego all courageously refused the easy path of compromise. It would surely have cost them their lives if God had not sovereignly intervened. Yet they never wavered.

Where are the men and women today with the courage to stand alone? The church in our age has abandoned the confrontive stance. Instead of overturning worldly wisdom with revealed truth, many Christians today are obsessed with finding areas of agreement. The goal has become *integration* rather than *confrontation*. As the church absorbs the values of secular culture, it is losing its ability to differentiate between good and evil. What will happen to the church if everyone proceeds down the slippery path of public opinion?

It is interesting to speculate what the church would be like today if Martin Luther had been prone to compromise. The pressure was heavy on him to tone down his teaching, soften his message, and stop poking his finger in the eye of the papacy. Even many of his friends and supporters urged Luther to come to terms with Rome for the sake of harmony in the church. Luther himself prayed earnestly that the effect of his teaching would not just be divisive—but that the truth would triumph. When he nailed his Ninety-five Theses to the door, the last thing he wanted to do was split the church.

Yet sometimes division is fitting, even healthy. Especially in times like Luther's—and like ours—when the visible church seems full of counterfeit Christians, it is right for the true people of God to declare themselves. There is no room for compromise. ⤸

Discernment demands that we hold biblical convictions with the most fervent tenacity. Titus 1:9 says a basic requirement for every elder is that he be the kind of man who "[holds] fast the faithful word which is in accordance with the teaching, that he may be able both to exhort in sound doctrine and to refute those who contradict." It is thus mandated by God that we take issue with error. We must refute those who contradict, or we do not fulfill our divine calling.

In other words, truly biblical ministry *must* hold forth truths that are absolute. We must take an unmovable stance on all issues where the Bible speaks plainly. What if people don't like such dogmatism? It is necessary anyway. Sound doctrine divides, it confronts, it separates, it judges, it convicts, it reproves, it rebukes, it exhorts, it refutes error. None of those things is very highly esteemed in modern thought. But the health of the church depends on our holding firmly to the truth, for where strong convictions are not tolerated, discernment cannot survive.

A REFUSAL TO SHUN THE WORLD

We have already hinted at another factor contributing to the decline of discernment in the contemporary church. It is a preoccupation with image and influence. Many Christians have the misconception that to win the world to Christ we must first win the world's favor. If we can get the world to like us, they will embrace our Savior. That is the philosophy behind the user-friendly church movement, which I have evaluated in an earlier book.[11]

The express design of this user-friendly philosophy is to make unconverted sinners feel comfortable with the Christian message. People won't come to hear the Gospel proclaimed? Give them something they want. Put on a show. Entertain them. Avoid sensitive subjects like sin and damnation. Accommodate their worldly desires and felt needs. Slip in the Gospel in small, diluted doses. The whole point is to make the church a place where non-Christians can enjoy themselves. The strategy is to tantalize non-Christians rather than confront their unbelief. That is altogether incompatible with sound doctrine. It is compromise with the world. James called it spiritual adultery (James 4:4).

Look at the effect of this philosophy on the church. In order to entice sinners, preaching has been replaced with entertainment. The preacher who once took his stand for truth and made the biblical message clear is now asked to take his seat. He's a problem. He's an embarrassment. He's an offense to non-Christians.

But if the truth cannot be fearlessly proclaimed in the church, what place is there for truth at all? How can we build a generation of discerning Christians if we are terror-struck at the thought that non-Christians might not like hearing the unvarnished truth?

And since when has it been legitimate for the church to woo the world? Didn't the apostle John write, "Do not marvel, brethren, if the world hates you" (1 John 3:13)? And did not Jesus say, "The world . . . hates Me because I testify of it, that its deeds are evil" (John 7:7)? Biblical Christians have always understood that they must shun the world. Here are our Lord's own words:

> If the world hates you, you know that it has hated Me before it
> hated you. If you were of the world, the world would love its own;
> but because you are not of the world, but I chose you out of the
> world, therefore the world hates you. Remember the word that I
> said to you, "A slave is not greater than his master." If they per-
> secuted Me, they will also persecute you; if they kept My word,
> they will keep yours also. But all these things they will do to you
> for My name's sake, because they do not know the One who sent
> Me (John 15:18-21).

Does that sound like it gives any latitude for an evangelistic strategy that soft-pedals the offense of the cross?

The apostle Paul frankly would have had no patience for such tac-

tics. He never sought to win the world through intellectual acceptance, personal popularity, image, status, reputation, or things of that
sort. He wrote, "We have become as the scum of the world, the dregs
of all things, even until now" (1 Cor. 4:13). Is the contemporary
church right to attempt a "more sophisticated" approach? Dare we
set ourselves apart from the godly men of the past, all of whom had
to fight for the truth?

Charles Spurgeon said,

> We want again Luthers, Calvins, Bunyans, Whitefields, men fit to
> mark eras, whose names breathe terror in our [foes'] ears. We have
> dire need of such. Whence will they come to us? They are the
> gifts of Jesus Christ to the Church, and will come in due time. He
> has power to give us back again a golden age of preachers, a time
> as fertile of great divines and mighty ministers as was the Puritan
> age, and when the good old truth is once more preached by men
> whose lips are touched as with a live coal from off the altar, this
> shall be the instrument in the hand of the Spirit for bringing
> about a great and thorough revival of religion in the land.
>
> I do not look for any other means of converting men beyond
> the simple preaching of the gospel and the opening of men's ears
> to hear it. *The moment the Church of God shall despise the pulpit, God will
> despise her.*[12]

And, we might add, the moment any church sets out to make friends
with the world, that church sets itself at enmity with God (James
4:4).

In practical terms, the movement to accommodate the world has
diminished Christians' confidence in divinely revealed truth. If we
can't trust the preaching of God's Word to convert the lost and build
the church, how can we trust the Bible at all—even as a guide for our
daily living? People are learning from the example of some of their
church leaders that faithfulness to the Word of God is optional.

Furthermore, as biblical preaching continues to diminish, ignorance of Scripture grows. An increase in biblical illiteracy leads
inevitably to the rise of reckless faith.

We cannot avoid being an offense to the world and still remain faithful to the gospel. The gospel is inherently offensive. Christ Himself is offensive to unbelievers. He is an offense to all in error. He is an offense to all who reject the truth. He is "'a stone of stumbling and a rock of offense'; for they stumble because they are disobedient to the word, and to this doom they were also appointed" (1 Peter 2:8). The message of the cross is also a stumbling block (Gal. 5:11)—"For the word of the cross is to those who are perishing foolishness" (1 Cor. 1:18).

"But to us who are being saved [the message of the cross] is the power of God." Paul wrote, "May it never be that I should boast, except in the cross of our Lord Jesus Christ, through which the world has been crucified to me, and I to the world" (Gal. 6:14).

Christians today do not speak in such terms. Few today have any concept of being crucified to the world. The word *worldliness* has lost its evil connotation. When did you last hear anyone call worldliness a sin?

James's words are worth citing once more: "Whoever wishes to be a friend of the world makes himself an enemy of God" (James 4:4). Church history confirms this again and again. Making friends with the world is a fast track to apostasy. Look what has happened in the major denominations. For several decades the denominational meetings of United Methodists, Episcopalians, and many Presbyterian groups have been wholly dominated by discussions of how to be "relevant" in the modern world. This has led them to alter their theology, to adopt radical leftist politics, to adapt their morality, to vote in new ethical precepts, and to abandon virtually every doctrinal position they ever stood for. This accommodation to the world has advanced to the point where some of these groups no longer deserve to be called Christian. In recent years most of the oldest denominational groups have rejected the biblical standard regarding the ordination of women; they have accepted homosexuality as a legitimate lifestyle; and they have even declared that Scripture does not give us a reliable historical record of the life of Christ. The seeds of that same apostasy are being sown today among evangelicals by those who are urging the church to adapt herself to the world.

In true Christianity, of course, truth is unchanging. The Word of

God is settled forever in heaven (Ps. 119:89). Jesus Christ is the same yesterday, today, and forever (Heb. 13:8). God Himself does not change (Mal. 3:6). How could we ever view truth as transient, pliable, or adaptable?

This unchanging view of truth is essential for true discernment. When the church loses its commitment to the inflexibility of truth, it loses its will to discern. It forfeits precise theology, precise morals, and precise conduct.

Right thinking and right living therefore demand careful discipline and an unyielding commitment to the truth. Discernment does not survive in an atmosphere of doctrinal confusion. It will not survive where relativism is tolerated. And it cannot survive if we compromise with the world.

A FAILURE TO INTERPRET SCRIPTURE CAREFULLY

Another basic factor leading to the decline of discernment is a widespread failure to interpret Scripture properly. *Hermeneutics*—Bible interpretation—is an exacting science. Good preaching depends on careful hermeneutics. But too much modern preaching ignores the *meaning* of Scripture altogether. Pulpits are filled with preachers who are unwilling to do the hard work necessary to interpret Scripture properly. They pad their messages with stories, anecdotes, and clever outlines—all of which disguise the weakness or lack of biblical content.

Some have even gone so far as to suggest that a preoccupation with the meaning of Scripture is unhealthy. A book that rose to the top of the Christian best-sellers list a few years ago included a warning to readers that they should be wary of preachers whose emphasis is on *explaining* Scripture rather than *applying* it.

Certainly application is crucial, but careful interpretation must always come first. To attempt to apply the Word without understanding it is sheer folly. We must be diligent workmen, handling accurately the Word of Truth (2 Tim. 2:15).

I cringe when I hear a novice wrench a verse out of context and impose on it a meaning that is totally unwarranted—or even contradictory to the intended sense of the text. Unfortunately, the standard has sunk so low today that even well-known Christian leaders can twist and contort Scripture beyond recognition, and yet no one seems to notice. One man who pastors a church of several thousand people recently appeared on nationwide television preaching a message on Acts 26:2, Paul's defense before Agrippa. Paul said, "I think myself happy, king Agrippa, because I shall answer for myself this day before thee touching all the things whereof I am accused of the Jews" (KJV). This man pulled out the phrase "I think myself happy," and preached a sermon on the importance of positive thinking in the midst of adversity! But Paul was not telling Agrippa anything about positive thinking; he was saying, "I consider myself fortunate" (NASB) to be able to make a defense. That preacher had corrupted the intent of Paul's inspired words because he was using the verse out of context to teach an unbiblical doctrine.

Another preacher preached a sermon from Mark 2, which tells about some men who brought their paralyzed friend to Jesus and lowered him through the roof of the house so he could be healed. Mark 2:4 says, "They could not come nigh unto him for the press" (KJV). This man took that phrase as his text and waxed eloquent, sermonizing for more than a half hour about how the press—the news media—are still keeping people from Jesus even to this day! But that verse has nothing to do with the news media. "The press" in that verse refers to the dense crowd. The whole sermon was based on an utter corruption of the meaning of the text.

Bible interpretation is a skill that requires rigorous training, understanding the meaning in the original languages, a working knowledge of grammar and logic, a grasp of historical settings, competence in theology, and a broad understanding of the whole of Scripture. Those who lack expertise in Greek and Hebrew must be all the more careful, checking commentaries, dictionaries, and other study helps to analyze the text as carefully as possible.

In this age of existentialism, many people have the impression that Bible interpretation is a subjective exercise. Perhaps you have been to a "Bible study" where the method of exploring a text was to go around the room and ask everyone, "What does this verse mean to *you*?" That is a sure path to confusion and a formula for reckless faith.

Even though the Bible itself commands us to be diligent and careful workmen, handling the Word with great care, there are some Christians who believe objective study is unnecessary. They suggest that we can just read the Bible and somehow Jesus will tell us what it means. Somehow the message just rises up from within, mystically. They will usually cite 1 John 2:27: "As for you, the anointing which you received from Him abides in you, and you have no need for anyone to teach you; but as His anointing teaches you about all things, and is true and is not a lie, and just as it has taught you, you abide in Him."

If that verse meant what some people suggest it means, it would eliminate the need for interpretation at all. It would also nullify the need for gifted pastors and teachers to equip the saints (Eph. 4:11-12). It would cancel any need for the gift of teaching (Rom. 12:6-7). It therefore cannot mean that instruction and diligent study are unnecessary as we approach the Word of God. So what was the apostle John saying? He was attacking an embryonic form of Gnosticism. Gnosticism taught that there is a secret knowledge that is not even contained in Scripture. If you weren't initiated by some "enlightened" person into that secret knowledge, according to the Gnostics, you had not arrived spiritually. John was attacking that claim, saying that real spiritual enlightenment cannot be given by one person to another. He was *not* attacking study or learning. He was *not* advocating a subjective, mystical, existential approach to Bible interpretation.

Now and then you will hear someone say, "I don't read commentaries and books *about* the Bible. I limit my study to the Bible itself." That may sound very pious, but is it? Isn't it actually presumptuous? Are the written legacies of godly men of no value to us? Can someone who ignores study aids understand the Bible just as well as someone who is familiar with the scholarship of other godly teachers and pastors?

One textbook on hermeneutics answers the question this way:

Suppose we select a list of words from Isaiah and ask a man who claims he can by-pass the godly learning of Christian scholarship if he can out of his own soul or prayer give their meaning or significance: Tyre, Zidon, Chittim, Sihor, Moab, Mahershalahashbas, Calno, Carchemish, Hamath, Aiath, Migron, Michmash, Geba, Anathoth, Laish, Nob, and Gallim. He will find the only light he can get on these words is from a commentary or a Bible dictionary.[13]

Good answer. It reveals the utter folly of thinking objective study is unnecessary. The person who is not a diligent student *cannot* be an accurate interpreter of God's Word. Scripture indicates that such a person is *not* approved by God and should be ashamed of himself (2 Tim. 2:15).

People do not usually accept false doctrine purposely. They err because of laziness, ineptness, carelessness, foolishness in handling the Scripture. In 2 Timothy 2:17-18, Paul mentions "Hymenaeus and Philetus, men who have gone astray from the truth saying that the resurrection has already taken place, and thus they upset the faith of some."

The Greek verb translated "gone astray" is *astocheō*, which literally means, "to miss the mark." It suggests that Hymenaeus and Philetus were aiming at the truth; they just missed it. They weren't trying to devise error, but being careless and unskilled in handling the truth, they turned to "worldly and empty chatter" (2 Tim. 2:16), which led them to conclude that the resurrection had already taken place. And their error, absurd as it was, had already upset the faith of others.

That is precisely why in verse fifteen Paul urged Timothy to be a diligent student of the Word of Truth.

What Paul was calling for is exactly the opposite of the shoot-from-the-hip ad-libbing that takes place in many contemporary pulpits. You can see this daily on religious television. It is one of the chief reasons some of the celebrity televangelists come up with so many novel doctrines. I'm convinced many of them improvise their theology as they speak.

That is a dangerous, deadly approach. It tends to corrupt God's Word. It perverts the truth, and it subverts people's ability to differentiate between sound doctrine and error. How can we be discerning if we don't even know how to interpret Scripture rightly? And without an accurate understanding of Scripture, we can't even establish principles for discernment.

THE NEGLECT OF CHURCH DISCIPLINE

Yet another reason for the decline of discernment and the rise of reckless faith is the almost universal failure of churches to follow Jesus' instructions in Matthew 18 on how to deal with sinning church members. Sadly, few Christians obey Christ in this crucial area of confronting sin in individual lives.

Jesus said,

> If your brother sins, go and reprove him in private; if he listens to you, you have won your brother. But if he does not listen to you, take one or two more with you, so that by the mouth of two or three witnesses every fact may be confirmed. And if he refuses to listen to them, tell it to the church; and if he refuses to listen even to the church, let him be to you as a Gentile and a tax-gatherer (Matt. 18:15-17).

If you see a brother in sin, go to him. Confront him. Try to lift him up, build him up, strengthen him. Urge him to repent. If he refuses to repent, he must ultimately be put out of the church. Paul said "not even to eat with such a one" (1 Cor. 5:11). This is not to suggest you should treat him like an enemy, but rather that you love him enough to seek his repentance by whatever means possible. Paul even instructed the Corinthians "to deliver such a one to Satan for the destruction of his flesh, that his spirit may be saved in the day of the Lord Jesus" (v. 5).

The church must hold up a high and holy standard. A very clear line must be drawn between the world and the church. Known and open sin cannot be tolerated. As soon as the church stops dealing with sin seriously, the world mingles with the church and the difference is obliterated. Christians are not supposed to be able to go on sinning and remain unchallenged by one another.

Why do you think the Lord struck Ananias and Sapphira dead in front of the whole congregation? It was so that the rest would be fearful of sinning (Acts 5:1-11; cf. 1 Tim. 5:20).

As we noted earlier, today's experts argue instead that the church should seek to make sinners comfortable so they will want to attend. I even heard one pastor advocate a no-confrontation policy. He said that when new people come to the church, if they are living in adultery, practicing homosexuality, or conducting themselves sinfully—even in a flagrant way—no one should confront them about those sins until they feel comfortable and accepted for who they are. He said he believes most people will just grow out of their sinful lifestyles as they become more involved in the church.

But what are we to conclude when someone living in open sin can sit in church and feel comfortable? Is that church proclaiming what it's supposed to proclaim? I can't imagine that a practicing homosexual would have sat comfortably under Paul's teaching in Ephesus or Corinth.

The primary message of the church should *not* be, "We're a nice place; you'll like us." Instead, the message should be, "This is a holy place where sin is despised." Wasn't that, after all, the very point of the Ananias and Sapphira episode?

We can't lower the biblical standard. We can't accumulate sinning Christians or sinning non-Christians. We must purge and discipline and sift and purify. First Peter 4:17 says, "It is time for judgment to begin with the household of God." And Paul wrote, "Do you not judge those who are within the church?" (1 Cor. 5:12). "If we judged ourselves rightly, we should not be judged" (11:31).

The church that tolerates sin destroys its own holiness and subverts the discernment of its own members. How can the lines be drawn in people's thinking when a church refuses to regulate behavior? If the goal is to make everyone feel all right, tolerance and compromise must rule. Discernment and discrimination are then ruled out.

Jay Adams has written:

Lack of discernment and lack of church discipline walk side by side. Not only does the same mentality lead to both lacks, but by rejecting discipline one naturally downplays the very concerns that make him discerning. When churches reacted to the abuse of church discipline that was all too common in the eighteenth and nineteenth centuries by virtually eliminating church discipline, the broken dike cleared the way for the liberal takeover of the church and allowed the ways of the world to flood in.[14]

Adams calls the collapse of church discipline the most obvious reason for the decline of discernment in the church. As he points out, "Discipline, by its very nature, requires discernment."[15]

But in an undiscerning church, discipline is neglected. And where discipline is neglected, discernment declines further and further.

A LACK OF SPIRITUAL MATURITY

One more factor in the abysmal lack of discernment today is a growing deterioration of the overall level of spiritual maturity in today's church. As knowledge of God's truth ebbs, people follow more popular views, seeking feelings and experiences. They are hungry for miracles, healings, and spectacular wonders. They grope for easy and instant solutions to the routine trials of life. They turn quickly from the plain truth of God's Word to embrace doctrines fit only for the credulous and naive. They chase personal comfort and success. Christianity today may be shallower than at any time in history.

A survey released by the Barna Research Group in February of 1994 revealed that half of all people who described themselves as "born-again" had no clue what John 3:16 refers to. Large percentages of professing Christians were also at a loss to explain terms such as "The Great Commission," or "the Gospel." Many defined "Gospel" simply as "a style of music."[16]

Spiritual ignorance and biblical illiteracy are commonplace. That kind of spiritual shallowness is a direct result of shallow teaching. Solid preaching with deep substance and sound doctrine is essential for Christians to grow. But churches today often teach only the barest basics—and sometimes less than that.

Churches are therefore filled with baby Christians—people who are spiritual infants. That is a fitting description, because the characteristic that is most descriptive of an infant is selfishness. Babies are completely self-centered. They scream if they don't get what they want when they want it. They are aware of only their own needs and desires. They never say thanks for anything. They can't help others; they can't *give* anything. They can only receive. And certainly there is nothing wrong with that when it occurs in the natural stage of infancy. But to see a child whose development is arrested so he never gets beyond the stage of helpless selfishness—that is a tragedy.

And that is exactly the spiritual state of multitudes in the church today. They are utterly preoccupied with self. They want their own problems solved and their own comfort elevated. Their spiritual development is arrested, and they remain in a perpetual state of selfish helplessness. It is evidence of a tragic abnormality.

Arrested infancy means people do not discern. Just as a baby crawls along the floor, putting anything it finds in its mouth, spiritual babies don't know what is good for them and what isn't. Immaturity and lack of discernment go together; they are virtually the same thing.

The tendency to stall in a state of immaturity also existed in New Testament times. Paul repeatedly appealed to Christians to grow up spiritually. In Ephesians 4:14-15, he wrote, "We are no longer to be children, tossed here and there by waves, and carried about by every wind of doctrine, by the trickery of men, by craftiness in deceitful scheming; but speaking the truth in love, we are to *grow up* in all aspects into Him, who is the head, even Christ" (emphasis added).

How do we grow spiritually? By "speaking the truth in love" to one another. We grow under the truth. It is the same truth by which we are sanctified, conformed to the image of Christ, made to be mature spiritually (John 17:17, 19). As we absorb the truth of God's Word, we grow up and are built up. We might say accurately that the process of spiritual growth *is* a process of training for discernment.

Hebrews 5:12—6:1 underscores all this:

> Though by this time you ought to be teachers, you have need again for someone to teach you the elementary principles of the oracles of God, and you have come to need milk and not solid food. For everyone who partakes only of milk is not accustomed to the word of righteousness, for he is a babe. But solid food is for the mature, who because of practice have their senses trained to discern good and evil. Therefore leaving the elementary teaching about the Christ, let us press on to maturity.

The writer of Hebrews told his readers, "You're babies. You've been around long enough to be teachers, but instead I have to feed you milk. I have to keep giving you elementary things. You can't take solid food. You're not accustomed to the rich things of the Word—and that is tragic."

Notice in verse fourteen he states that discernment and maturity go hand in hand: "solid food is for the mature, who because of practice have their senses trained to discern good and evil." Knowing and understanding the Word of righteousness—taking in solid food—trains your senses to discern good and evil.

The word "senses" is not a reference to the feelings, emotions, or other subjective sensory mechanisms. The writer of this epistle is explicitly encouraging his readers to exercise their *minds*. Those who "because of practice have their senses trained to discern" are the wise, the understanding, people who thrive on the solid food of the Word of God. As we have seen from the beginning, discernment results from a carefully disciplined mind. Discernment is not a matter of feelings, nor is it a mystical gift. Notice from the wisdom literature of the Old Testament how closely discernment is linked with a seasoned, developed, biblically informed mind.

- Psalm 119:66: "Teach me good discernment and knowledge, for I believe in Thy commandments."
- Proverbs 2:2-5: "Make your ear attentive to wisdom, incline your heart to understanding; for if you cry for discernment, lift your voice for understanding; if you seek her as silver, and search for her as for hidden treasures; then you will discern the fear of the Lord, and discover the knowledge of God."

- Proverbs 10:13: "On the lips of the discerning, wisdom is found."
- Proverbs 16:21: "The wise in heart will be called discerning."

The path to discernment is the way of spiritual maturity. And the only means to spiritual maturity is mastery of the Word of God.

Most people are discerning about things that are important to them. People who regard a healthy diet as crucial watch carefully what they eat. They read the fine print on the package to see how many grams of fat it has and what percentages of the daily required nutrients are offered. People who work with pesticides or dangerous chemicals must be very discerning. They study the procedures and the precautions very carefully to avoid any potentially lethal exposure. People who make investments in the stock market usually practice discernment. They study the cryptic newspaper listings on the stock market and watch the ticker tape. Lawyers are very discerning with contracts. They have to figure out the legal jargon and make sure they understand what they are signing. People who undergo delicate surgery are usually very discerning. They try to find the doctor with the finest skills—or at least verify that he or she has plenty of experience in whatever procedure is to be done. I know many people who are very discerning sports enthusiasts. They watch a football game and can assess any offense, any defense, any play. They often feel they are *more* discerning than whoever is calling the actual plays. They study statistics and averages and take it all very seriously.

Do you realize those are essentially the same skills that are required in spiritual discernment? Careful thought, keen interest, thorough analysis, close observation—together with alertness, attentiveness, thoughtfulness, and above all, a love of truth. All of us have those skills to some degree, and we use them in whatever field of endeavor is important to us.

Yet what could be *more* important than spiritual discernment?

There is no valid explanation for why contemporary Christians are so *un*discerning—but it reveals a spiritual apathy that is deadly evil.

Can the church regain her ability to be discerning? Only by growing up spiritually. That means confronting the spirit of a relativistic age and diligently applying ourselves to the unfailing Word of God. We cannot gain discernment overnight, or through a mystical experience. Understanding the problem is not the answer. Discernment will come only as we train our minds to be understanding in the truth of God's Word and learn to apply that truth skillfully to our lives. In the following chapter we will look at the practical means of accomplishing that goal.

3

The Biblical Formula
for Discernment

D O DISCERNMENT AND DIVISIVENESS go hand in hand? Is it
true that the term *discernment* is often employed as a cover
for a contentious or critical spirit?

Let's acknowledge that there *are* unscrupulous people who under
the guise of "biblical discernment" engage in unbrotherly criticism.
Their tactics often include innuendo, character assassination, guilt by
association, and other dishonest methods. They weave conspiracy
theories, sensationalize their attacks against others, and favor personal slurs rather than substantive doctrinal analysis. Militant fundamentalism has made this type of criticism its specialty. As a
consequence this movement has steadily lost its influence, forfeited
its credibility, and fragmented into tiny, warring factions. My appeal
for discernment is *not* a call to that sort of factious attitude.

Undoubtedly the prevalence of a hypercritical attitude among
some fundamentalists has caused a backlash that has only accelerated
the decline of discernment in the church. We rightfully deplore a
pugnacious spirit. No true Christian wants to be contentious. No one
who has the mind of Christ *enjoys* conflict. Obviously, harmony is
preferable to discord. But when some crucial truth is at stake, how do

we display the mind of Christ? Certainly not by allowing the error to go unchallenged. If we truly are to be like our Savior, we must both proclaim truth *and* condemn error in precise and unambiguous language (see Matt. 23).

That means we must learn to discriminate. In modern usage, the word *discrimination* carries powerful negative connotations. But the word itself is not negative. *Discriminate* simply means "to make a clear distinction." We used to call someone "a discriminating person" if they exercised keen judgment. "Discrimination" signified a positive ability to draw the line between good and evil, true and false, right and wrong. In the heyday of the American civil rights movement the word was widely applied to racial bigotry. And, indeed, people who make unfair distinctions between races are guilty of an evil form of discrimination.

Unfortunately, the word itself took on that negative connotation and the sinister implication is often transferred to anyone who tries to discriminate in any way. To view homosexuality as immoral (1 Cor. 6:9-10; 1 Tim. 1:9-10) is condemned now by the politically correct as an unacceptable form of discrimination. To suggest that wives ought to submit to their own husbands (Eph. 5:22; Col. 3:18) is now classified as unfair discrimination. To suggest that children ought to obey their parents (Eph. 6:1) is also labeled unjust discrimination by some. Anyone who "discriminates" in these ways risks becoming a target of lawsuits by the ACLU.

The idea of discrimination itself has fallen out of favor. We are not supposed to draw lines. We are not supposed to discriminate. That is the spirit of this age, and unfortunately, it has crept into the church.

If we are going to be discerning people, we must develop the skill of discriminating between truth and error, good and bad. The original languages of Scripture convey this very idea. The main Hebrew word for "discernment" is *bin*. The word and its variants are used hundreds of times in the Old Testament. It is often translated "discernment," "understanding," "skill," or "carefulness." But in the original language it conveys the same idea as our word *discrimination*. It entails the idea of making distinctions. Jay Adams points out that the word *bin* "is related to the noun *bayin*, which means 'interval' or 'space between,' and the preposition *ben*, 'between.' In essence it means to separate things from one another at their points of difference in order to distinguish them."[1] *Discernment*, then, is a synonym for *discrimination*. In fact, the Greek verb translated "discern" in the New Testament is *diakrinō*. It means, "to make a distinction," and is literally translated that way in Acts 15:9.

So discernment is the process of making careful distinctions in our thinking about truth. The discerning person is the one who draws a clear contrast between truth and error. This is the principle of antithesis we discussed in chapter 2. Discernment is black-and-white thinking—the conscious refusal to color every issue in shades of gray. No one can be truly discerning without developing skill in separating divine truth from error.

Does Scripture tell us *how* to be discerning? It certainly does. Paul sums up the process in 1 Thessalonians 5:21-22: "Examine everything carefully; hold fast to that which is good; abstain from every form of evil." There, in three straightforward commands, he spells out the requirements of a discerning mind.

JUDGE EVERYTHING

Let's quickly set the context for this passage. Starting with verse sixteen, Paul lists some very brief reminders to the Thessalonian Christians. These might be thought of as the basics of Christian living: "Rejoice always; pray without ceasing; in everything give thanks; for this is God's will for you in Christ Jesus. Do not quench the Spirit; do not despise prophetic utterances." (A "prophetic utterance," as we shall note, is the equivalent of a sermon today.) Rejoicing, prayer, contentment, responsiveness to the preaching of God's Word—those are all primary duties of every Christian.

Another duty is discernment. "Examine everything carefully" (v. 21) is a call to discernment. It is significant that Paul sets discernment in a context of very basic commands. It is as crucial to the effective Christian life as prayer and contentment.

That may surprise some Christians who see discernment as uniquely a pastoral responsibility. It is certainly true that pastors and elders have an even greater duty to be discerning than the average lay person. Most of the calls to discernment in the New Testament are issued to church leaders. In 1 Timothy 4:6-7, for example, Paul told Timothy: "[Be] constantly nourished on the words of the faith and of the sound doctrine which you have been following. But have nothing to do with worldly fables fit only for old women." "Worldly fables fit only for old women" was an epithet Paul applied to the philosophy of his day. He was urging Timothy to know the difference between the truth of God and the nonsense of the world. If Timothy couldn't tell the difference between sound doctrine and dangerous philosophy, he would not be able to protect the flock. Just a few verses later, Paul added, "give attention to the public reading of Scripture, to exhortation and teaching" (v. 13). And then, "pay close attention to yourself and to your teaching; persevere in these things" (v. 16).

Throughout his epistles to Timothy, Paul repeatedly commanded the pastor to pay close attention to sound doctrine, preach the Word, preach and teach these things, guard the truth, and so on. Paul also charged Timothy to avoid empty talk, shun worldly wisdom, turn away from false teachers, and rebuke those who oppose the truth. Timothy needed to stay alert to the differences between the truth and lies, to separate the truth from falsehoods and half-truths. Paul was commanding him as a pastor of the flock to be discerning.

Every elder is required to be skilled in teaching truth and able to refute unsound doctrine (Titus 1:9). As a pastor, I am constantly aware of this responsibility. Everything I read, for example, goes through a grid of discrimination in my mind. If you were to look through my library, you would instantly be able to identify which books I have read. The margins are marked. Sometimes you'll see approving remarks and heavy underlining. Other times you'll find question marks—or even red lines through the text. I constantly strive to separate truth from error. I read that way, I think that way, and of course I preach that way. My passion is to know the truth and proclaim it with authority. That should be the passion of every elder, because everything we teach affects the hearts and lives of those who hear us. It is an awesome responsibility. Any church leader who does not feel the burden of this duty ought to step down from leadership.

But discernment is not *only* the duty of pastors and elders. The same careful discernment Paul demanded of pastors and elders is also the duty of every Christian. First Thessalonians 5:21 is written to the *entire church*: "Examine everything carefully."

The Greek text is by no means complex. The word "carefully" has been added by the translators to make the sense clear. If we translate the phrase literally, we find it simply says, "Examine everything." But the idea conveyed by our word *carefully* is included in the Greek word translated "examine," *dokimazō*. This is a familiar word in the New Testament. Elsewhere it is translated "analyze," "test," or "prove." It refers to the process of testing something to reveal its genuineness, such as in the testing of precious metals. Paul is urging believers to scrutinize everything they hear to see that it is genuine, to distinguish between the true and the false, to separate the good from the evil. In other words, he wants them to examine everything *critically*. "Test everything," he is saying. "Judge everything."

Wait a minute. What about Matthew 7:1: "Do not judge lest you be judged"? Typically someone will quote that verse and suggest that it rules out any kind of critical or analytical appraisal of what others believe. Was Jesus forbidding Christians from judging what is taught in His name?

Obviously not. The spiritual discernment Paul calls for is different from the judgmental attitude Jesus forbade. In Matthew chapter 7, Jesus went on to say,

> In the way you judge, you will be judged; and by your standard of measure, it will be measured to you. And why do you look at the speck that is in your brother's eye, but do not notice the log that is in your own eye? Or how can you say to your brother, "Let me take the speck out of your eye," and behold, the log is in your own eye? You hypocrite, first take the log out of your own eye, and then you will see clearly to take the speck out of your brother's eye (vv. 2-5).

Obviously, what Jesus condemned was the hypocritical judgment of those who held others to a higher standard than they themselves were willing to live by. He was certainly not suggesting that *all* judgment is forbidden. In fact, Jesus indicated that taking a speck out of your brother's eye is the *right* thing to do—if you first get the log out of your own eye.

Elsewhere in Scripture we are forbidden to judge others' motives or attitudes. We are not "able to judge the thoughts and intentions of the heart" (Heb. 4:12). That is a divine prerogative. Only God can judge the heart, because only God can see it (1 Sam. 16:7). He alone knows the secrets of the heart (Ps. 44:21). He alone can weigh the motives (Prov. 16:2). And He alone "will judge the secrets of men through Christ Jesus" (Rom. 2:16). That is not our role. "Therefore do not go on passing judgment before the time, but wait until the Lord comes who will both bring to light the things hidden in the darkness and disclose the motives of men's hearts" (1 Cor. 4:5).

What is forbidden is hypocritical judging and judging others' thoughts and motives. But other forms of judgment are explicitly commanded. Throughout Scripture the people of God are urged to judge between truth and error, right and wrong, good and evil. Jesus said, "Judge with righteous judgment" (John 7:24). Paul wrote to the Corinthian believers, "I speak as to wise men; you judge what I say" (1 Cor. 10:15). Clearly, God *requires* us to be discriminating when it comes to matters of sound doctrine.

We are also supposed to judge one another with regard to overt acts of sin. Paul wrote, "Do you not judge those who are within the church? But those who are outside, God judges. Remove the wicked man from among yourselves" (1 Cor. 5:12-13). That speaks of the same process of discipline outlined by Jesus Himself in Matthew 18:15-20.

At least one other kind of judgment is expressly required of every believer. We must examine and judge our own selves: "If we judged ourselves rightly, we should not be judged" (1 Cor. 11:31). This calls for a careful searching and judging of our own hearts. Paul called for this self-examination every time we partake of the Lord's Supper (v. 28). All other righteous forms of judgment depend on this honest self-examination. That is what Jesus meant when He said, "First take the log out of your own eye" (Luke 6:42).

Clearly, then, the command in 1 Thessalonians 5:21, "Examine everything," in no way contradicts the biblical strictures against being judgmental. The discernment called for here is *doctrinal* discernment. The conjunction at the beginning of this verse—*"but* examine everything"—ties it to the "prophetic utterances" mentioned in verse twenty.

As suggested earlier, a "prophetic utterance" was not necessarily a new revelation. The gift of prophecy in the New Testament has to do more with *proclaiming* the Word of God than with *obtaining* it. A "prophet" is simply one who declares divine truth with authority. Thus 1 Corinthians 14:3-4 says, "One who prophesies speaks to men for edification and exhortation and consolation. . . . [He] edifies the church." In modern terminology, the New Testament gift of prophecy is simply *preaching*. Paul was calling the Thessalonian believers to judge all the preaching they heard and avoid everything that didn't measure up to the standard of revealed truth. He was suggesting that they should measure everything according to God's revealed Word and thus discern between truth and error.

The unusually gullible Thessalonians seemed to have a problem in this regard. Like many today, they were eager to believe whatever was preached in the name of Christ. They were undiscriminating. They were prone to be like "children, tossed here and there by waves, and carried about by every wind of doctrine, by the trickery of men, by craftiness in deceitful scheming" (Eph. 4:14). Luke contrasted the Thessalonians with the more discerning church at Berea. The Bereans "were more noble-minded than those in Thessalonica, for they received the word with great eagerness, examining the Scriptures daily, to see whether these things were so" (Acts 17:11). Evidently the Thessalonians were lacking in discernment from day one.

Paul addresses this continual lack of discernment in both his Thessalonian epistles. There is evidence in the first epistle, for example, that someone had confused the Thessalonians about the return of Christ. They were going through a time of severe persecution, and apparently some of them thought they had missed the Second Coming. In chapter 3 we learn that Paul had sent Timothy from Athens specifically to strengthen and encourage them in their faith (v. 2). They were unaccountably confused about why they were being persecuted. Paul had to remind them, "you yourselves know that we have been destined for this. For indeed when we were with you, we kept telling you in advance that we were going to suffer afflic-tion; and so it came to pass" (vv. 3-4). Evidently someone had also taught them that believers who died before the Second Coming of Christ would miss that event entirely. They were in serious confu-sion. Chapters 4 and 5 contain Paul's efforts to correct that confusion. He tells them that the dead in Christ will rise and be caught up with the living (4:16-17). And he assures them that although that day will come like a thief in the night (5:2), they need not fear being caught off guard (vv. 3-6).

Incredibly, shortly after this, Paul had to write a second epistle, *again* assuring the Thessalonians that they had not missed some great event on the prophetic calendar. Someone, it seems, had sent them a counterfeit epistle claiming to be from Paul and suggesting that the day of the Lord had come already. They should not have been duped by such a ploy, because Paul had written so plainly in his first epistle. He wrote them again: "Now we request you, brethren, with regard to the coming of our Lord Jesus Christ, and our gathering together to Him, that you may not be quickly shaken from your composure or be disturbed either by a spirit or a message or a letter as if from us, to the effect that the day of the Lord has come. Let no one in any way deceive you" (2 Thess. 2:1-3). There was no excuse for their chronic gullibility.

Why were they so vulnerable to false teaching? Surely it was pre-cisely because they lacked the discernment exemplified by the Bereans. The Thessalonians did not examine everything in light of God's Word. If they had, they would not have been so easily hood-winked. And that is why Paul urged them, "Examine all things."

It is fair to point out that the Thessalonians were at a disadvan-tage compared to Christians today. They did not have all the written books of New Testament Scripture. Paul wrote these two epistles to Thessalonica very early in the New Testament era—about A. D. 51. The two letters were probably written only a few months apart and are among the very earliest of all the New Testament writings. The Thessalonians' primary source of authoritative gospel truth was Paul's teaching. As an apostle, Paul taught with absolute authority. When he taught them, his message *was* the Word of God, and he commended them for recognizing that: "And for this reason we also constantly thank God that when you received from us the word of God's message, you accepted it not as the word of men, but for what it really is, the word of God, which also performs its work in you who believe" (1 Thess. 2:13). Elsewhere he said that the commandments he gave them were "by the authority of the Lord Jesus" (4:2).

The *substance* of what he taught them represented the same body of truth that is available to us in the New Testament Scriptures. How do we know? Paul himself said so. Even as he was recording his inspired epistle to them, he reminded them, "Do you not remember that while I was still with you, I was telling you these things?" (2 Thess. 2:5). The written Word simply confirmed and recorded for all time the authoritative truth he had already taught them in person. These epistles were a written reminder of what they had already heard from Paul's own mouth (1 Thess. 4:2).

Second Thessalonians 2:15 confirms this: "Stand firm and hold to the traditions which you were taught, whether by word of mouth or by letter from us." There he declares, first of all, that his epistles to them are authoritative, inspired truth. This verse is a clear statement that Paul himself regarded these epistles as inspired Scripture.

But notice also that this verse joins the apostolic "traditions" with the written Word of God. The "traditions" necessary for Christians to be discerning are recorded for all ages in the text of Scripture. Those who claim that apostolic tradition is *other* truth *in addition to* Scripture often attempt to use this verse for support. Note, however, that Paul is not saying "the traditions [they] were taught" are *different* from the written Scriptures. Rather he links the two, affirming that the written Word of God is the only permanent and authoritative record of the apostolic tradition. He is specifically suggesting that the Thessalonians should not trust "word of mouth" or letters pretending to be from apostolic sources. Only what they had heard firsthand from Paul's own lips or read in authentic letters from him were they to treat as authoritative divine truth. That is why Paul usually signed his epistles "with [his] own hand" (1 Cor. 16:21; Gal. 6:11; Col. 4:18; 2 Thess. 3:17; Philem. 19).

With this in mind, 2 Thessalonians 2:15 cannot be used to support the claim that extrabiblical, spiritually binding "apostolic tradition" is passed down verbally through popes and bishops. Paul's whole point was that the Thessalonians should treat as authoritative only what they had heard from his own mouth or received from his own pen. That body of truth—the Word of God—was to be the measuring stick they used to examine all things. Two other verses confirm this. In 2 Thessalonians 3:6 Paul writes, "now we command you, brethren, in the name of our Lord Jesus Christ, that you keep aloof from every brother who leads an unruly life and not according to the tradition which you received from us." And in verse fourteen he adds, "if anyone does not obey our instruction in this letter, take special note of that man and do not associate with him, so that he may be put to shame."

Therefore, Paul is affirming that the Bible is the only reliable criterion by which believers in this age can evaluate any message claiming to be truth from God.

CLING TO WHAT IS GOOD

The testing of truth Paul calls for is not merely an academic exercise. It demands an active, twofold response. First there is a positive response to whatever is good: "Hold fast to that which is good" (1 Thess. 5:21). This is an echo of Romans 12:9: "Abhor what is evil; cling to what is good." The expressions "hold fast" and "cling to" speak of jealously safeguarding the truth. Paul is calling for the same careful watchfulness he demanded of Timothy every time he wrote him: "O Timothy, guard what has been entrusted to you" (1 Tim. 6:20); and "Retain the standard of sound words which you have heard from me. . . . Guard, through the Holy Spirit who dwells in us, the treasure which has been entrusted to you" (2 Tim. 1:13-14). In other words, the truth is given to our custody, and we are charged with guarding it against every possible threat.

This describes a militant, defensive, protective stance against anything that undermines the truth or does violence to it in any way. We must hold the truth securely; defend it zealously; preserve it from all threats. To placate the enemies of truth or lower our guard is to violate this command.

"Hold fast" also carries the idea of embracing something. It goes beyond bare assent to "that which is good" and speaks of loving the truth wholeheartedly. Those who are truly discerning are passionately committed to sound doctrine, to truth, and to all that is inspired by God.

Every true Christian has this quality to some degree. Paul even defined salvation as "the love of the truth" (2 Thess. 2:10), and he told the Corinthians they proved their salvation by holding fast to the gospel he had delivered (1 Cor. 15:2). Those who utterly fail to hold fast to the saving message are those who have "believed in vain"; that is, their faith was empty to begin with. The apostle John said something similar: "They went out from us, but they were not really of us; for if they had been of us, they would have remained with us; but they went out, in order that it might be shown that they all are not of us" (1 John 2:19). All true believers hold fast to the Gospel.

Paul was urging the Thessalonians to nurture and cultivate their love for truth, to let it rule their thinking. He wanted them to foster a conscious commitment to *all* truth; a faithfulness to sound doctrine; a pattern of holding fast to all that is good.

The attitude this calls for is incompatible with the suggestion that we should lay doctrine aside for the sake of unity. It cannot be reconciled with the opinion that hard truths should be downplayed to make God's Word more palatable for unbelievers. It is contrary to the notion that personal experience takes precedence over objective truth. God has given us His truth objectively in His Word. It is a treasure that we should protect at all costs.

This is the opposite of reckless faith. Paul leaves no room for rote tradition. He makes no place for a blind, irrational faith that refuses to consider the authenticity of its object and just accepts at face value everything that claims to be true. He rules out the kind of "faith" that is driven by feelings, emotion, and the human imagination. Instead, we are to identify "that which is good" by examining everything carefully, objectively, rationally—using Scripture as our standard.

No human teacher, no personal experience, no strong feeling is exempt from this objective test. Jay Adams writes, "If inspired prophecies in the apostolic age had to be subjected to testing . . . then surely the teachings of men today should also be put to the test."[2] Indeed, if the words of prophets in apostolic times needed to be examined and evaluated, then surely we ought to subject the words of self-proclaimed "prophets" and preachers today to even more intense scrutiny in the bright light of the completed New Testament. The same is true of every subjective experience and every emotion. Experience and feelings—no matter how powerful—do not determine what is true. Rather, those things themselves must be subjected to the test.

"That which is good" is truth that accords with God's Word. The word "good" is *kalos*, meaning something that is inherently good. It isn't just something that is fair to look at, lovely or beautiful in appearance. This speaks of something good in itself—genuine, true, noble, right, and good. In other words, "that which is good" does not refer to that which is entertaining. It does not refer to that which garners accolades from the world. It does not refer to that which is satisfying to the flesh. It refers to that which is good, true, accurate, authentic, dependable—that which is in agreement with the infallible Word of God.

When you find such truth, embrace it and guard it like a treasure.

SHUN WHAT IS EVIL

The other side of Paul's command is a negative response to evil: "Abstain from every form of evil" (1 Thess. 5:22). The word translated "abstain" is a very strong verb, *apechō*, meaning "hold oneself back," "keep away from," "shun." It is the same word used in 1 Thessalonians 4:3, "abstain from sexual immorality," and 1 Peter 2:11, "abstain from fleshly lusts." It calls for a radical separation from "every form of evil." This would include evil behavior, of course. But in this context, the primary reference seems to be evil teaching—

false doctrine. Having examined everything in light of God's Word, when you identify something that does not measure up—something that is evil, untrue, erroneous, or contrary to sound doctrine—shun it.

Scripture does not give believers permission to expose themselves to evil. Some people believe the only way to defend against false doctrine is study it, become proficient in it, and master all its nuances—then refute it. I know people who study the cults more than they study sound doctrine. Some Christians immerse themselves in the philosophy, entertainment, and culture of society. They feel such a strategy will strengthen their witness to unbelievers.

But the emphasis of that strategy is all wrong. Our focus should be on knowing the *truth*. Error is to be shunned.

Granted, we cannot recede into a monastic existence to escape exposure to every evil influence. But neither are we supposed to be experts about evil. The apostle Paul wrote, "I want you to be wise in what is good, and innocent in what is evil" (Rom. 16:19).

Federal agents don't learn to spot counterfeit money by studying the counterfeits. They study genuine bills until they master the look of the real thing. Then when they see bogus money they recognize it. Detecting a spiritual counterfeit requires the same discipline. Master the truth to refute error. Don't spend time studying error; shun it. Study truth. Hold fast the faithful Word. Then you will be able both to exhort in sound doctrine and to refute those who contradict (Titus 1:9). As Paul wrote elsewhere, "Do not be overcome by evil, but overcome evil with good" (Rom. 12:21).

In the King James Version, 1 Thessalonians 5:22 is translated "abstain from all *appearance* of evil." The word translated "appearance" is *eidos*, literally "that which is seen." The *New American Standard Bible* translation, "every *form* of evil," gives the better sense. We are to reject evil however it appears, to shun every manifestation of it.

This explicitly rules out *syncretism*. Syncretism is the practice of blending ideas from different religions and philosophies. Remember the man I described at the beginning of chapter 2. He devoured materials from every cult and denomination, looking for good in all of it. Whatever he deemed good, he absorbed for his belief system. He was designing his own unique religion based on syncretism.

That man might attempt to use 1 Thessalonians 5:21 to justify his methodology: "Examine everything carefully; hold fast to that which is good." That is, after all, precisely what he thought he was doing. But what he was really doing is actually the opposite of what this passage demands. Verse 21 is balanced by verse 22: "Abstain from every form of evil."

The only proper response to false teaching is to shun it. Erroneous doctrine is no place to look for truth. There is usually *some* point of truth even in rank heresy. But it is truth out of balance, corrupted truth, truth mixed with lies and therefore rendered dangerous. Shun it.

Integration is a popular term today. There is a widespread movement among evangelicals to integrate ideas from Freudian psychology into counseling methods used by the church. Self-esteem theory, secular "twelve-step" recovery techniques, and a host of other faddish therapies are all being "integrated" with what Scripture teaches about how to address the problem of sin. These methods seem so sophisticated, so progressive. But all such therapies are based on humanistic ideas that are contrary to Scripture. They deny human depravity. They undermine the Holy Spirit's role in sanctification. To attempt to integrate them with biblical teaching does extreme violence to the biblical position. *Integration* turns out to be simply another word for syncretism. And "Christian psychology" that uses this humanistic integration is nothing but classic religious syncretism. It contradicts 1 Thessalonians 5:22: "Abstain from every form of evil."

Satan is subtle. He often sabotages the truth by mixing it with error. Truth mixed with error is usually far more effective and far more destructive than a straightforward contradiction of the truth. If you think everything you read or hear on Christian radio and television is reliable teaching, then you are a prime target for reckless faith. If you think everyone who *appears* to love the truth really does, then you don't understand the wiles of Satan. "Satan disguises himself as an angel of light," Paul wrote. "Therefore it is not surprising if his servants also disguise themselves as servants of righteousness" (2 Cor. 11:14-15).

Satan also disguises his lies as truth. He doesn't always wage war openly against the Gospel. He is much more likely to attack the church by infiltrating with subtle error. He uses the Trojan horse stratagem by placing his false teachers *in the church*, where they can "secretly introduce destructive heresies" (2 Peter 2:1). He puts his lies in the mouth of someone who claims to speak for Jesus Christ— someone likable and appealing—then he spreads his perverse lies in the church where they can draw away Christ's disciples (Acts 20:30). He attaches Bible verses to his lies (Matt. 4:6). He uses deception and hypocrisy. He disguises falsehood as truth. He loves syncretism. It makes evil *look* good.

That's why we are to examine *everything* carefully, and shun whatever is unsound, corrupt, or erroneous. It is deadly. Millions in the church today are being overwhelmed by the Trojan-horse ploy calling for the integration of secular ideas with biblical truth. Others are easily duped by anything labeled Christian. They don't examine everything. They don't hold fast to the truth. And they won't shun evil. They are left vulnerable to false doctrine and have no defense against reckless faith.

A RECIPE FOR DISCERNMENT

We cannot simply flow with the current of our age. We cannot elevate love by downplaying truth. We cannot promote unity by repressing sound doctrine. We cannot learn to be discerning by making an idol out of tolerance. By adopting those attitudes, the church has opened her gates to all of Satan's Trojan horses.

God gives us the truth of His Word, and He commands us to guard it and pass it on to the next generation. Frankly, the current generation is failing miserably in this task. Our failure to discern has all but erased the line between biblical Christianity and reckless faith. The church is filled with doctrinal chaos, confusion, and spiritual anarchy. Few seem to notice, because Christians have been conditioned by years of shallow teaching to be broad-minded, superficial, and non-critical. Unless there is a radical change in the way we view truth, the church will continue to wane in influence, become increasingly worldly, and move further and further into the realms of reckless faith.

How can we cultivate discernment? What needs to happen if the church is going to reverse the trends and recover a biblical perspective?

Desire Wisdom

Step one is desire. Proverbs 2:3-6 says, "cry for discernment, lift your voice for understanding; if you seek her as silver, and search for her as for hidden treasures; then you will discern the fear of the Lord, and discover the knowledge of God. For the Lord gives wisdom; from His mouth come knowledge and understanding."

If we have no desire to be discerning, we won't be discerning. If we are driven by a yearning to be happy, healthy, affluent, prosperous, comfortable, and self-satisfied, we will never be discerning people. If our feelings determine what we believe, we cannot be discerning. If we subjugate our minds to some earthly ecclesiastical authority and blindly believe what we are told, we undermine discernment. Unless we are willing to examine all things carefully, we cannot hope to have any defense against reckless faith.

The desire for discernment is a desire born out of humility. It is a humility that acknowledges our own potential for self-deception ("The heart is more deceitful than all else and is desperately sick; who can understand it?"—Jer. 17:9). It is a humility that distrusts personal feelings and casts scorn on self-sufficiency ("On my own behalf I will not boast, except in regard to my weaknesses"—2 Cor. 12:5). It is a humility that turns to the Word of God as the final arbiter of all things (". . . examining the Scriptures daily, to see whether these things [are] so"—Acts 17:11).

No one has a monopoly on truth. I certainly do not. I don't have reliable answers within myself. My heart is as susceptible to self-deception as anyone's. My feelings are as undependable as everyone else's. I am not immune to Satan's deception. That is true for all of us. Our only defense against false doctrine is to be discerning, to distrust our own emotions, to hold our own senses suspect, to examine all things, to test every truth-claim with the yardstick of Scripture, and to handle the Word of God with great care.

The desire to be discerning therefore entails a high view of Scripture linked with an enthusiasm for understanding it correctly. God requires that very attitude (2 Tim. 2:15)—so the heart that truly loves Him will naturally burn with a passion for discernment.

Pray for Discernment

Step two is prayer. Prayer, of course, naturally follows desire; prayer is the expression of the heart's desire to God.

When Solomon became king after the death of David, the Lord appeared to him in a dream and said, "Ask what you wish me to give you" (1 Kings 3:5). Solomon could have requested anything. He could have asked for material riches, power, victory over his enemies, or whatever he liked. But Solomon asked for discernment: "Give Thy servant an understanding heart to judge Thy people to discern between good and evil" (v. 9). Scripture says, "it was pleasing in the sight of the Lord that Solomon had asked this thing" (v. 10).

Moreover, the Lord told Solomon,

> Because you have asked this thing and have not asked for your-self long life, nor have asked riches for yourself, nor have you asked for the life of your enemies, but have asked for yourself discernment to understand justice, behold, I have done according to your words. Behold, I have given you a wise and discerning heart, so that there has been no one like you before you, nor shall one like you arise after you. And I have also given you what you have not asked, both riches and honor, so that there will not be any among the kings like you all your days. And if you walk in My ways, keeping My statutes and commandments, as your father David walked, then I will prolong your days (vv. 11-14).

Notice that God commended Solomon because his request was completely *unselfish*: "Because you have asked this thing and have not asked for yourself." Selfishness is incompatible with true discernment. People who desire to be discerning must be willing to step outside themselves.

Modern evangelicalism, enamored with psychology and self-esteem, has produced a generation of believers so self-absorbed that they *cannot* be discerning. People aren't even interested in discernment. All their interest in spiritual things is focused on self. They are interested only in getting their own felt needs met.

Solomon did not do that. Although he had an opportunity to ask for long life, personal prosperity, health and wealth—he bypassed all of that and asked for discernment instead. Therefore God also gave him riches, honor, and long life for as long as he walked in the ways of the Lord.

James 1:5 promises that God will grant the prayer for discernment generously: "If any of you lacks wisdom, let him ask of God, who gives to all men generously and without reproach, and it will be given to him."

Obey the Truth

Someone will point out that with all his abundance of wisdom, Solomon was nevertheless a dismal failure at the end of his life (1 Kings 11:4-11). "His heart was not wholly devoted to the Lord his God, as the heart of David his father had been" (v. 4). Scripture records this sad assessment of the wisest man who ever lived:

> King Solomon loved many foreign women along with the daughter of Pharaoh: Moabite, Ammonite, Edomite, Sidonian, and Hittite women, from the nations concerning which the Lord had said to the sons of Israel, "You shall not associate with them, neither shall they associate with you, for they will surely turn your heart away after their gods." Solomon held fast to these in love. And he had seven hundred wives, princesses, and three hundred concubines, and his wives turned his heart away. For it came about when Solomon was old, his wives turned his heart away after other gods. . . . For Solomon went after Ashtoreth the goddess of the Sidonians and after Milcom the detestable idol of the Ammonites. And Solomon did what was evil in the sight of the Lord, and did not follow the Lord fully, as David his father had

done. Then Solomon built a high place for Chemosh the detestable idol of Moab, on the mountain which is east of Jerusalem, and for Molech the detestable idol of the sons of Ammon. Thus also he did for all his foreign wives, who burned incense and sacrificed to their gods.

Now the Lord was angry with Solomon because his heart was turned away from the Lord (vv. 1-9).

But Solomon did not suddenly fail at the end of his life. The seeds of his demise were sown at the very beginning. First Kings 3, the same chapter that records Solomon's request for discernment, also reveals that Solomon "formed a marriage alliance with Pharaoh king of Egypt" (v. 1). Verse three tells us, "Solomon loved the Lord, walking in the statutes of his father David, except he sacrificed and burned incense on the high places."

From the very beginning his obedience was deficient. Surely with all his wisdom he knew better, but he tolerated compromise and idolatry among the people of God (v. 2)—and even participated in some of the idolatry himself!

Discernment is not enough apart from obedience. What good is it to know the truth if we fail to act accordingly? That is why James wrote, "Prove yourselves doers of the word, and not merely hearers who delude themselves" (James 1:22). Failure to obey is self-delusion; it is not true discernment, no matter how much intellectual knowledge we may possess. Solomon is biblical proof that even true discernment can give way to a destructive self-delusion. Disobedience inevitably undermines discernment. The only way to guard against that is to be doers of the Word and not hearers only.

Follow Discerning Leaders

Fourth in our series of steps toward biblical discernment is this: emulate those who demonstrate good discernment. *Do not* follow the leadership of people who are themselves "tossed here and there by waves, and carried about by every wind of doctrine" (Eph. 4:14). Find and follow leaders who display an ability to discern, to analyze and refute error, to teach the Scriptures clearly and accurately. Read from authors who prove themselves careful handlers of divine truth. Listen to preachers who rightly divide the Word of Truth. Expose yourself to the teaching of people who think critically, analytically, and carefully. Learn from people who understand where error has attacked the church historically. Place yourself under the tutelage of those who serve as watchmen of the church.

I do this myself. There are certain authors who have demonstrated skill in handling the Word and whose judgment I have come to trust. When I encounter a difficult issue—whether it is a theological problem, an area of controversy, a new teaching I have never heard before, or whatever—I turn to these authors first to see what they have to say. I wouldn't seek help from an unreliable source or a marginal theologian. I want to know what those who are skilled in exposing error and gifted in presenting truth have to say.

There have been outstanding men of discernment in virtually every era of church history. Their writings remain as an invaluable resource for anyone who wishes to cultivate discernment. Martyn Lloyd-Jones and J. Gresham Machen are just two of many from this present century who have distinguished themselves in the battle for truth. Charles Spurgeon, Charles Hodge, or scores of other writers from the nineteenth century have left a rich legacy of written material to help us discern between truth and error. In the century before that, Thomas Boston, Jonathan Edwards, and George Whitefield battled for truth as did many others like them. The preceding era was the Puritan age—the sixteenth and seventeenth centuries, which gave us what is undoubtedly the richest catalog of resources for discernment. Before that the Reformers fought valiantly for the truth of God's Word against the traditions of men. Virtually every era before the Reformation also had godly men of discernment who stood against error and defended the truth of God's Word. Augustine, for example, preceded John Calvin by more than a thousand years, but he fought exactly the same theological battles and proclaimed precisely the same doctrines. Calvin and the Reformers drew heavily on Augustine's writings as they framed their own arguments against error. In A. D. 325 a contemporary of Augustine, Athanasius, took a decisive stand against *Arianism*, the very same error that is perpetuated by modern-day Jehovah's Witnesses. His writings stand today as the definitive response to that error.

Much of the written legacy these spiritual giants left is still available today. We can all learn from these men of discernment—and we would do well to emulate the clarity with which they spoke the truth against error.

Those who can expose and answer the errors of false teachers are set in the body of Christ to assist us all to think critically and clearly. Learn from them.

Depend on the Holy Spirit

As important as human examples are, however, the Spirit of God is ultimately the true Discerner. It is His role to lead us into all truth (John 16:13). First Corinthians 2:11 says, "The thoughts of God no one knows except the Spirit of God." Paul goes on to write,

> We have received . . . the Spirit who is from God, that we might know the things freely given to us by God, which things we also speak, not in words taught by human wisdom, but in those taught by the Spirit, combining spiritual thoughts with spiritual words. But a natural man does not accept the things of the Spirit of God; for they are foolishness to him, and he cannot understand them, because they are spiritually appraised. But he who is spiritual appraises all things, yet he himself is appraised by no man (vv. 12-15).

So discernment ultimately depends on the Holy Spirit. As we are filled with and controlled by the Spirit of God, He makes us discerning.

Study the Scriptures

Finally, we return to the point we have touched on repeatedly. It cannot be overemphasized: True discernment requires diligent study of the Scriptures. None of the other steps is sufficient apart from this. No one can be truly discerning apart from mastery of the Word of God. All the desire in the world cannot make you discerning if you don't study Scripture. Prayer for discernment is not enough.

Obedience alone will not suffice. Good role models won't do it either. Even the Holy Spirit will not give you discernment apart from His Word. If you really want to be discerning, you must diligently study the Word of God.

God's Word is where you will learn the principles for discernment. It is there you will learn the truth. Only there can you follow the path of maturity.

Discernment flourishes only in an environment of faithful Bible study and teaching. Note that in Acts 20, when Paul was leaving the Ephesian elders, he warned them about the deadly influences that would threaten them in his absence (vv. 28-31). He urged them to be on guard, on the alert (vv. 28, 31). How? What safeguard could he leave to help protect them from Satan's onslaughts? Only the Word of God: "And now I commend you to God and to the word of His grace, which is able to build you up and to give you the inheritance among all those who are sanctified" (v. 32).

Let's look once more, closely, at 2 Timothy 2:15: "Be diligent to present yourself approved to God as a workman who does not need to be ashamed, handling accurately the word of truth." Notice what this mandate to Timothy implies. First, it suggests that the discerning person must be able to distinguish between the Word of Truth and the "worldly and empty chatter" mentioned in verse sixteen. That may seem rather obvious. But it cannot be taken for granted. The task of separating God's Word from human foolishness actually poses a formidable challenge for many today. One look at some of the nonsense that proliferates in churches and Christian media will confirm that this is so. Or note the burgeoning stacks of "Christian" books touting weird views. We must shun such folly and devote ourselves to the Word of God. We have to be able to distinguish between the truth and error.

How? "Be diligent." Being diligent pictures a worker giving maximum effort in his or her work. It describes someone driven by a commitment to excellence. "Be diligent to present yourself approved to God." The Greek phrase literally speaks of standing alongside God as a co-laborer worthy of identifying with Him.

Furthermore, Paul says this approved workman "does not need to be ashamed." The word "ashamed" is very important to Paul's whole point. Any sloppy workman *should* be ashamed of low-quality work. But a servant of the Lord, handling the Word of Truth carelessly, has infinitely more to be ashamed of.

What Paul suggests in this passage is that we will be ashamed before God Himself if we fail to handle the Word of Truth with discernment. If we can't distinguish the truth from worldly and empty chatter, if we can't identify and refute false teachers, or if we can't handle God's truth with skill and understanding, we *ought* to be ashamed.

And if we are to divide the Word of Truth rightly, then we must be very diligent about studying it. There is no short cut. Only as we master the Word of God are we made "adequate, equipped for every good work" (3:17). That is the essence of discernment.

Keep Growing

As we have noted, spiritual maturity is the process of learning to discern. We suggested in chapter 2 that the path to real discernment is the path to spiritual growth—and vice versa. Growth in grace is a continuous process throughout this earthly life. No Christian ever reaches complete maturity this side of heaven. "Now we see in a mirror dimly, but then face to face; now I know in part, but then I shall know fully just as I also have been fully known" (1 Cor. 13:12). We must continually "grow in the grace and knowledge of our Lord and Savior Jesus Christ" (2 Peter 3:18). We should hunger "for the pure milk of the word, that by it [we] may grow" (1 Peter 2:2).

As we mature, our senses are exercised to discern good and evil (Heb. 5:14). As we cease to be children, we gain stability (Eph. 4:14-15). Mature people *are* discerning people.

We know this from the natural world. The bulk of every parent's responsibility is training children to be discerning. We continually do it, even when our kids become teenagers. We help them think through issues, understand what is wise and unwise, and prompt them to make the right choices. We help them discern. In fact, the goal of parenting is to raise a discerning child. It doesn't happen automatically, and it doesn't occur without diligent, lifelong instruction.

The same is true spiritually. You don't pray for discernment and suddenly wake up with all wisdom. It is a process of growth.

Stay on the path of maturity. Sometimes it involves suffering and trials (James 1:2-4; 1 Peter 5:10). Often it necessitates divine chastening (Heb. 12:11). Always it requires personal discipline (1 Tim. 4:7-8). But the rewards are rich:

> How blessed is the man who finds wisdom, and the man who gains understanding. For its profit is better than the profit of silver, and its gain than fine gold. She is more precious than jewels; and nothing you desire compares with her. Long life is in her right hand; in her left hand are riches and honor. Her ways are pleasant ways, and all her paths are peace. She is a tree of life to those who take hold of her, and happy are all who hold her fast. . . . My son, let them not depart from your sight; keep sound wisdom and discretion, so they will be life to your soul, and adornment to your neck. Then you will walk in your way securely, and your foot will not stumble (Prov. 3:13-18, 21-23).

The alternative is reckless faith, with all its bitter fruits.

> Whoever is wise, let him understand these things; whoever is discerning, let him know them. For the ways of the Lord are right, and the righteous will walk in them, but transgressors will stumble in them (Hos. 14:9).

4

What Are the Fundamentals of Christianity?

A WOMAN ONCE WROTE ME to say she thought Christianity was fine but, personally, she was "into Zen." She liked to listen to Christian radio while she was driving because the music "smoothed out her karma." Occasionally, however, she would tune in one of the Bible-teaching ministries. In her opinion, all the preachers she heard were too narrow-minded toward other religions, so she was writing several radio ministers to encourage them to be more broad-minded.

"God doesn't care *what* you believe, as long as you're sincere," she wrote, echoing an opinion I have heard many times. "All religions lead ultimately to the same reality. It doesn't matter which road you take to get there, as long as you follow your chosen road faithfully. Don't be critical of the alternative roads other people choose."

To those who accept the Bible as God's Word, the folly of that thinking should be immediately evident. What does the Bible say about following your chosen road faithfully? "There is a way which seemeth right unto a man, but the end thereof are the ways of death" (Prov. 14:12; 16:25, KJV). Jesus said, "The gate is wide, and the way is broad that leads to destruction, and many are those who enter by it" (Matt. 7:13). He urged people to change directions, to enter the small gate that leads to the narrow way that few find.

Actually it is *Satan* who doesn't care what we believe—or how sincerely we believe it—as long as what we believe is error. To portray God as tolerant of all forms of worship is to deny the God of Scripture. After all, this was His first commandment: "I am the Lord your God. . . . You shall have no other gods before Me" (Ex. 20:2-3).

If we believe the Bible, we cannot concede that other religions might be true as well. If we believe that Christ is Lord of all, and if we truly love Him, we cannot countenance the doctrines of those who deny Him (1 Cor. 16:22). *Christianity, if true at all, is exclusively true.* Inherent in the claims of Christ is the assertion that He alone offers truth—and all religious systems that deviate from His truth are false. Jesus said, "I am the way, and the truth, and the life; no one comes to the Father, but through Me" (John 14:6). Peter proclaimed, "there is salvation in no one else; for there is no other name under heaven that has been given among men, by which we must be saved" (Acts 4:12). If this is true, every other religion is a lie (see Rom. 3:4).

The content of our faith is highly crucial. Sincerity is not sufficient.

Of course, such a view contradicts the relativistic values of modern culture. Pluralism and diversity have been enshrined as higher virtues than truth itself. We're not supposed to say our beliefs are right and all others are wrong. That is regarded as backward, outmoded, discourteous. In other words, we're not really supposed to *believe* our religious beliefs; we're only allowed to hold them as personal preferences.

Evangelicalism is beginning to absorb that latitudinarianism. Not that most evangelicals would accept Islam, Hinduism, or other overtly non-Christian religions. But many seem to think it doesn't really matter what you believe, as long as you label it Christianity. With the exception of a few cults that blatantly renounce the Trinity, almost everything taught in the name of Christ is accepted by evangelicals—from Roman Catholicism (which denies that sinners are justified solely by faith) to the extreme charismatic Word Faith movement (which both corrupts the doctrine of Christ and makes temporal health and wealth the focus of salvation).

In the name of unity, such matters of doctrine are expressly *not* supposed to be contested. We are being encouraged to insist on nothing more than a simple affirmation of faith in Jesus. Beyond that, the specific *content* of faith is supposed to be a matter of individual preference.

THE RISE AND FALL OF FUNDAMENTALISM

These are not new issues; the church has waged an ongoing struggle over these very matters at least since the turn of the century. This very same appeal for broad-mindedness in religious standards and beliefs has always been at the heart of the agenda of theological liberalism; indeed, it is precisely what the term *liberal* originally meant. What is new about today's appeals for tolerance is that they come from within the evangelical camp.

Liberalism first began to dominate the major Protestant denominations nearly a hundred years ago. Schools formerly committed to biblical truth began to attack the very doctrines they had been founded to uphold. Even Princeton Theological Seminary, long a bastion of Reformed orthodoxy, ultimately succumbed to the spirit of the age. For a time it seemed that evangelicalism would be completely overwhelmed and overthrown by liberalism.

Liberals characterized evangelicalism as outmoded, unenlightened, and hopelessly intolerant. They argued that Christianity should be broad enough to embrace all kinds of beliefs. In their opinion the narrowness and intolerance of historic evangelicalism did not appropriately represent Christ; tolerance and liberality were more fitting for modern Christianity. That argument evidently fell on receptive ears. Sound doctrine began to give way to compromise, liberalism, and even rank unbelief within the church.

Then a remarkable movement began. Evangelicals from both sides of the Atlantic united in writing and publishing a series of articles titled *The Fundamentals.*[1] Originally published in twelve volumes, those articles laid the basis for a movement that became known as fundamentalism. With men like J. Gresham Machen, James Orr, and R. A. Torrey leading the way, fundamentalism employed sound doctrine to combat liberalism, higher criticism, evolutionary theory, and modernism.

The doctrinal basis for fundamentalism was broad enough to involve evangelical Anglicans, Lutherans, Presbyterians, Methodists, Baptists, Mennonites, Independents, and others—including theologians from both Reformed and dispensationalist backgrounds. The issues they identified as "fundamentals" were doctrines they collectively viewed as essential, primary, non-negotiable truths. These were, of course, the very articles of faith that distinguished evangelicalism from liberalism. The fundamentalists believed they were also the doctrines that separated the true church from false Christianity. What were the fundamental articles they identified?

The most basic were the authority, inspiration, and infallibility of Scripture. Against the higher critics, fundamentalists argued that the Bible is the literal Word of God, that it is historically and factually accurate, and that it is the complete and only binding rule of faith for believers. These precepts, of course, determine a host of other issues. If we agree that Scripture is the authoritative and inerrant Word of God, we have no legitimate reason to dispute its historical assertions, such as the creation account, the virgin birth of Christ, His bodily resurrection, and the miracles. If we believe Scripture is the *only* authority in matters of faith and practice, we cannot set religious speculation or church tradition alongside it.

All those issues were enumerated as "fundamentals," along with the deity of Christ, the doctrine of the Trinity, Christ's substitutionary atonement on the cross, the resurrection, justification by faith alone, salvation by grace through faith, the necessity of sanctification, and the rejection of every cult that distorts or contradicts any of the other fundamental doctrines.

In short, the early fundamentalists used *sound doctrine* to define true Christianity—against the liberals, who insisted that the only issues that really mattered were practical, not theoretical. A well-worn liberal slogan was "Christianity is a life, not a doctrine." The fundamentalists correctly argued that true Christianity is a doctrine that affects all of life.

So in contrast to those who were willing to enlarge the designation "Christian" to embrace the broadest possible spectrum of beliefs, the fundamentalists sought to identify the core of objective truth that was absolute and non-negotiable. That body of sound doctrine, they claimed, is the very foundation of all genuine Christianity. Every brand of religion that rejected the fundamentals was regarded as pseudo-Christian or non-Christian.

Fundamentalists were not able to recover most of the mainline denominations from encroaching liberalism. But they did manage to establish new schools, new denominations, and new churches faithful to historic biblical truth. Those institutions have enjoyed a century of vigorous growth and spiritual influence while mainline denominational churches have suffered severe decline.

Sadly, however, the fundamentalist movement began to unravel almost as soon as it had experienced its initial successes. One wing of fundamentalism, desperate for academic respectability, could not resist the pluralism of the modern age. Schools that had been founded to counter theological liberalism were overexposed to liberal theology and began to compromise on the issue of biblical inerrancy, capitulating at the very point where early fundamentalism had taken its strongest stand. Incredibly, some fundamentalist schools and churches abandoned their commitment to biblical inerrancy within *one generation* of their founding![2] Most of these institutions and the people associated with them quickly repudiated the designation *fundamentalist*.

Another wing of fundamentalism moved the opposite direction. They were keenly aware that an obsession with academic respectability had led their brethren to abandon the fundamentals. For that reason they distrusted scholarship or spurned it altogether. This right wing of the fundamentalist movement was relentlessly fragmented by militant separatism. Legalism led to an extreme emphasis on external issues. Petty concerns often replaced serious doctrine as the matter for discussion and debate. This branch of the movement quickly reached the point where some of its adherents spent more time arguing about men's hair length and women's clothing than they spent defending the real fundamentals of the faith.

All the squabbling and extreme legalism eventually sullied the term *fundamentalism*. Intellectually and temperamentally, these fundamentalists utterly abandoned the high ground that the fathers of the movement had held so tenaciously. As a consequence the movement succumbed to a subtle depreciation of doctrine. The published material from this side of fundamentalism is notable for its total lack of any significant works with real doctrinal or biblical depth. The term *fundamentalist* became exclusively linked with this militant group.

In recent years, the term *fundamentalist* has been hijacked by the secular media, who apply it to every conceivable kind of religious fanatic.

SACKING THE FUNDAMENTALS

The polemical, theological spirit of early fundamentalism is all but dead. Modern evangelicals are too willing to downplay doctrine. Unlike our fundamentalist forebears, many today are perfectly agreeable to the suggestion that true Christianity ought to be broad enough to accommodate widely differing—even contradictory—belief systems. Many evangelicals are seeking to forge spiritual alliances with Catholicism, Eastern Orthodoxy, charismatic extremists, and even rank liberals—without regard to the fundamental doctrinal differences.

Historically, evangelicals and fundamentalists almost universally have rejected the ecumenical movement. The primary force in ecumenism has been the World Council of Churches, an organization that never really cared for biblical Christianity, preferring to recruit its membership primarily from among ultra-liberal denominations. Consequently, ecumenism has had little or no influence among evangelicals.

Even during the ecumenical movement's most prosperous era,

during the 1960s, evangelical churches experienced dramatic growth while ecumenical churches quickly waned. A decade ago the World Council of Churches appeared to be a monument to a lost cause.

But now the picture is changing. Incredibly, today's most powerful ecumenical forces are all under the banner of a foundering evangelicalism: the charismatic movement, Catholic-evangelical accords, cooperative mass evangelism, and a host of voices in the Christian media.

An aggressive effort is being made to divest "the fundamentals" of key evangelical distinctives. Influential voices within evangelicalism are urging us to pare back the essentials to the barest possible statement of faith, and these voices can be heard across the spectrum of evangelicalism. Appeals for broader tolerance and more inclusivism have come from charismatics, dispensationalists, Calvinists and Arminians, Reformed and Lutheran leaders—so-called evangelicals of almost every stripe.

Paul Crouch, for example, president of the Trinity Broadcasting Network, writes, "As I have said so often, one theologian's heresy is another theologian's orthodoxy."[3] Crouch nevertheless acknowledges that Jude chapter 3 commands us to contend earnestly for the faith once delivered to the saints. "So what is 'the faith'?" he asks rhetorically, then writes,

> The answer is simple; read it in the Apostle's [sic] Creed or any number of other confessions such as the Heidelberg Confession: Jesus Christ, born of a virgin, crucified, risen again, ascended to heaven, by whose blood our sins are forgiven, who will return in power and glory to judge the living and the dead. Beyond these absolute essentials of "FAITH," there is infinite room for honest men and women to disagree and debate the limitless issues of "doctrinal purity."[4]

In other words, Crouch suggests that all who profess faith in those few essentials that he lists should be permitted to teach whatever else they feel is right, and no one should publicly subject those teachings to any further theological scrutiny. It is all right for us to disagree, he concedes, but Christians should "NEVER judge a brother or sister by name" in any sort of critical doctrinal appraisal. To do so, he believes, is unbecoming to the cause of Christ. He labels the practice "heretic hunting."

The Apostles' Creed is one of the earliest and simplest statements of faith in the history of creeds. We will examine it more closely later in this chapter, but for now we simply note that the Creed was probably not written by the apostles, although it does summarize some of the major points of apostolic doctrine. It is not an exhaustive statement of faith, nor was it ever intended to be. It was a brief, rudimentary confession designed to distinguish Christianity from Judaism or pagan religions. It does not even address the issue of Jesus' deity.

Crouch's reference to "the Heidelberg Confession" is difficult to decipher. Perhaps he refers to the Heidelberg *Catechism* (1562). The principal author of this catechism was Ursinus, a student of Philip Melanchthon. The document is far more detailed in its teachings than the Apostles' Creed. In fact, this catechism was written to address a controversy that arose when a fight broke out over the communion cup during a church service. The dispute had to do with whether the real presence of Christ was in the communion elements.[5] Of course, this was one of the issues that was hotly debated in the Reformation. Ursinus rejected the Roman Catholic view that the elements literally *become* the body and blood of Christ (transubstantiation). He also rejected Martin Luther's view that the elements *contain* the real presence of Christ (consubstantiation). He embraced instead the view of Ulrich Zwingli and most of the Reformers; namely, that the communion elements are *only symbolic*. The Heidelberg Catechism therefore includes several questions about the Lord's Supper designed to clarify these issues, such as: "Do, then, the bread and wine become the real body and blood of Christ?" and "What difference is there between the Lord's Supper and the Popish Mass?" Far from being an elementary list of basic beliefs, the Heidelberg Catechism was a rather intensive theology lesson, a polemic designed to draw a clear line between even Lutheranism and Reformed theology. It is actually a far more meticulous form of theo-

logical hairsplitting than has been practiced by the critics Paul
Crouch wishes to silence.

The Heidelberg Catechism *does* contain a lengthy commentary
on the Apostles' Creed. But even that section of the catechism is
designed to take the meager statements of the Apostles' Creed and
explain them in terms of the Reformed faith. The catechism explicitly interprets the Creed in a way that refutes Roman Catholic
doctrine.

The truth is that virtually all the historic creeds of the church
serve a purpose that is diametrically opposed to the benign broad-
mindedness Crouch is appealing for. The creeds were written to confront error. They present truth dogmatically, in specific and
well-delineated terms. All of them are polemic, controversial, argumentative. They aim at separation, not unity. The Nicene Creed
(325) defended the doctrine of the Trinity. The Athanasian Creed (c.
428) spells out the doctrine of Christ's two natures. Then there are
Roman Catholic creeds, Greek and Russian creeds, and Protestant
creeds. Virtually every creed after the Apostles' Creed addressed matters of doctrinal controversy.

So despite Paul Crouch's assertion that "any number of other
confessions" might be adduced to make his point, it is very unlikely
that he could point to *any* creed ever adopted by a church council or
denominational body that fits his parameters. He is almost certainly
attempting to define "the faith" in terms of the Apostles' Creed only.
In fact, his list of essentials is actually an abbreviated paraphrase of
the Apostles' Creed.

Paul Crouch is not alone in suggesting that the test of orthodoxy
ought to be nothing more than the Apostles' Creed. That view evidently is shared by increasing numbers of evangelical leaders.

Perhaps the most popular and persuasive defender of this view is
Charles Colson, former counsel to the Nixon White House and
founder of Prison Fellowship. Colson is an influential and highly
respected leader within evangelicalism, known for his well-honed
writing and speaking ministries. I have deeply appreciated much of
what he has written over the years. Often his insights are extremely
perceptive. I find myself on the same side of the fence with him on

most important issues. It is evident that he has a warm heart for the things of the Lord.

That is why it is so hard to understand the way Colson defines Christian orthodoxy. His frequent appeals for Christian unity are surely noble, but he fails to identify which doctrines are truly essential to real Christianity. Colson is by no means the only evangelical leader to make this error. But because he is one of the most outspoken and aggressive proponents of the new ecumenism, we need to examine some of the ideas he has proposed and their implications.

Appeals for broader Christian unity have been a running theme in Colson's writings over the years, but the subject is especially prominent in his 1992 book, *The Body*.[6] Again, there is much in this book with which we can wholeheartedly agree. For example, Colson writes,

> We must begin with a renewed commitment to the truth. . . . We must stand boldly in the tradition of those who have gone before us, many of whom have shed blood in their defense of the historic, orthodox confession of our faith. In theology, as in other areas of life, fads come and go, but truth is validated as it survives the assaults that come its way. Tested through the centuries, the tenets of Christian orthodoxy have been passed on and entrusted to us. And here we must stand—without equivocation—even when the world hangs labels on us that represent everything considered ugly and backward.[7]

Colson acknowledges that the kind of ecumenism that means "reducing all elements of faith to the lowest common denominator" is not true unity.[8] It is obvious that Colson desires to avoid the trap of doctrinal minimalism that led the World Council of Churches into destructive radical politics. He says he is *not* in favor of that brand of ecumenism. True unity, he correctly observes, is achieved by finding a "common ground of orthodoxy on which [Christians] can stand together."[9]

Colson mounts a brilliant attack against moral relativism. He laments the fact that "relativism is firmly established as the reigning orthodoxy of American life."[10] And he notes a Gallup poll that revealed 69 percent of Americans question the existence of any moral absolutes, comparing the rise of such existentialism in society to a "moral lobotomy." "As a result, the only stable virtue left in this relativistic world is unbridled tolerance," he writes. "There are no absolutes except the absolute that there can be no absolute."[11]

Colson also declares that he is a fundamentalist. He defends the term *fundamentalism*, recounting briefly how *The Fundamentals* came into being after the turn of the century. He rehearses, much as I have in this chapter, how the fundamentalist movement took a stand against early liberalism.[12] Fundamentalism, he writes, "means adherence to the fundamental facts—in this case, the fundamental facts of Christianity. It is a term that was once a badge of honor, and we should reclaim it."[13] To all of that I heartily say Amen.

But then Colson lists his idea of the fundamentals: the infallibility of Scripture, the deity of Christ, the Virgin Birth and miracles of Christ, Christ's substitutionary death, and Christ's physical resurrection and eventual return. (Note, by the way, that his list includes two items missing from the Apostles' Creed and from Paul Crouch's list: the infallibility of Scripture and the deity of Christ.)

Those five doctrines, Colson says, are "the backbone of orthodox Christianity."

> If a fundamentalist is a person who affirms these truths, then there are fundamentalists in every denomination—Catholic, Presbyterian, Baptist, Brethren, Methodist, Episcopal. . . . Everyone who believes in the orthodox truths about Jesus Christ—in short, every Christian—is a fundamentalist.[14]

Colson's thesis in *The Body* is that all who adhere to those basic doctrines ought to view one another as members of the same body, refuse to allow any other doctrinal differences to divide them, and put up a united front against what Colson believes are the church's two great enemies—secularism and Islam.[15] The church universal desperately needs to get back to "mere Christianity," he suggests. "Articulated in the classic confessions and creeds, [mere Christianity] embraces such fundamentals as the Virgin Birth, the deity of Christ, the Atonement, the Resurrection, the authority of Scripture, and the Second Coming."[16]

Is Colson's list of fundamental doctrines really comprehensive enough? Although he seems to be affirming *The Fundamentals*, his appeal for solidarity with Rome is seriously out of sync with the design of those articles.[17] Moreover, his five- or six-point creed lacks any reference to the way of salvation. He excludes justification by faith. He says nothing about the *sufficiency* of Scripture as our sole rule of faith. What in his brief list of doctrines would exclude Mormonism? Do these few doctrines really provide an adequate creed to exclude false Christianity?

IS THE APOSTLES' CREED A FULL ENOUGH STATEMENT OF FAITH?

Note that Colson, like Paul Crouch, suggests that "the classic confessions and creeds" all support his bare-bones platform of fundamentals. Yet as we noted earlier, virtually all the historic creeds served purposes that were controversial, not conciliatory. Not one of the major creeds was written to try to bring together widely differing religious bodies. On the contrary, those who drafted the creeds had exactly the opposite design in mind. The Roman Catholic Council of Trent wrote a creed that assails the work of the Reformers (see the fifth chapter). And all the Reformed creeds are outspokenly anti-Catholic. Which of those opposing creeds would Colson select as an acceptable standard for the whole church? He must either reject them all or abandon his efforts to blend the Catholic-evangelical-Orthodox traditions. Ecumenical interests cannot be supported by an appeal to the church's creedal heritage, because the creeds themselves are in conflict with the goals of ecumenism.

Colson also implies that the true nonnegotiables of Christianity were all settled by the Apostles' Creed.[18] He suggests that all evangelical Christians should be willing to embrace as brothers and sisters in Christ everyone who can give assent to this ancient creed.

What is the Apostles' Creed? Is it a full enough statement of faith so that *all* who give assent to it can be embraced as Christians? Does it contain sufficient safeguards against false doctrine to serve as a test of fellowship?

The Apostles' Creed cannot be traced to any specific author or date. The earliest known text comes to us from the middle of the fourth century, but it is assumed to have existed before then. This is the most common form of the creed as it is recited today:

> I believe in God the Father Almighty; Maker of heaven and earth.
>
> And in Jesus Christ His only Son our Lord; who was conceived by the Holy Ghost, born of the Virgin Mary; suffered under Pontius Pilate, was crucified, dead, and buried; He descended into hell; the third day He rose from the dead; He ascended into heaven; and sitteth at the right hand of God the Father Almighty; from thence He shall come to judge the quick and the dead.
>
> I believe in the Holy Ghost; the holy catholic church; the communion of saints; the forgiveness of sins; the resurrection of the body; and the life everlasting. Amen.

Roman Catholic tradition says the apostles themselves wrote the Creed, each contributing one article of faith. But the historical evidence does not support that.[19] The phrase "he descended into hell," for example, was not part of the Creed until the late fourth century; it is borrowed from another creed of that era. The word "catholic," the phrase "the communion of saints," and the final phrase ("life everlasting") are all later additions to the creed.[20] The full Creed as it is known today did not come into general use until the seventh or eighth century.[21]

Is This a Full Statement of All the Essentials?

The Creed is by no means a complete statement of all the doctrines essential to genuine Christianity. For example, since there is no statement about the deity of Christ, a Jehovah's Witness, who denies Christ's deity, could give full assent to the Creed as it stands. In fact, the ancient forerunners of Jehovah's Witnesses, the followers of a heretic named Arius, defended themselves by appealing to the Creed. William Cunningham wrote, "Nay, it is well known that

Arians, who deny the divinity of the Son and the Holy Ghost, have no hesitation in expressing their concurrence in the creed."[22]

In 1681, a godly Dutch Reformed theologian named Herman Witsius published in Latin a series of dissertations on the Apostles' Creed. The two-volume English translation of this work has recently been republished. Witsius wrote,

> If you consider only the truths expressly mentioned in the Creed, *all the necessary articles of our Religion are not contained in this summary.* For it contains *nothing about the Word of God,* which is the immediate object, the rule, and the source of our faith. . . . [It contains] *nothing respecting our sin and misery,* the knowledge of which is inculcated in Scripture as particularly necessary [Jer. 3:13]:—*Nothing relative to justification by faith without the works of the law,* the knowledge of which article, however, the Apostle valued so highly, that in comparison of it he accounted all other things but loss and dung [Phil. 3:8-9]—so highly, that he declares that whosoever desire to be justified by the law, have no part in Christ, and are fallen from grace [Gal. 5:4]:—*Nothing even regarding the worship and service of God,* and the leading of a holy life; which cannot be rightly performed, unless they are both known, and believed to be necessary.[23]

Moreover, Witsius points out, there are issues in the Creed that are clearly *not* essential. Is salvation prerequisite on knowing that it was Pontius Pilate who condemned Christ to death? Must a person understand in what sense Christ "descended into hell" in order for that person to be saved? Must every truly regenerate person be able to define the holy catholic church, or the communion of saints? William Cunningham wrote in the 1800s, "If men appeal to the Creed as a proof of their orthodoxy, they are of course bound to explain its meaning, and to show that they hold its statements in a reasonable sense."[24]

Whose Interpretation of the Creed is Valid?

The truth is, many of the statements in the Apostles' Creed are open to widely varying, or even contradictory, interpretations. There is no general agreement on how those statements should be interpreted.

"Therefore although heretics may say that they receive the [Creed], yet they do not because they reject its true and genuine sense."[25] It is not merely the *words* of the Creed that must be affirmed, but their true meaning. Unfortunately, there is little agreement between the major Christian traditions about what the words mean.

Christ's descent into hell, for example, is interpreted by some to mean that He actually went into the infernal flames—although Scripture teaches nothing like that. Others, appealing to the Latin terminology, believe the Creed simply means that He descended into *hades*, the realm of the dead. In other words, the phrase "he descended into hell" simply means that he actually died. The Roman Catholic Church teaches that Christ descended into hades, gathered up the souls of all the righteous who had died before Him, and carried them to heaven. Still other interpreters suggest that the phrase means only that Christ experienced all the torments of hell in His sufferings on the cross.

Which of those interpretations conveys the actual truth that the Creed intends to teach?

Or what about "the holy catholic church"? Those who follow the Pope dogmatically interpret that as a reference to the *Roman* Catholic Church. Protestants interpret "catholic" in accord with its literal meaning, "universal." Thus, according to most Protestants, the phrase refers to the whole worldwide body of true believers regardless of their denomination.

"The communion of saints" has been interpreted by various commentators as a reference to the fraternity of saints already in heaven, actual communion between earthly and heavenly saints, or simply fellowship among believers here on earth.[26]

William Cunningham cited an essay written by a Lutheran writer named Ittigius, who "exhibited in parallel columns the Lutheran, the Calvinistic, and the Popish interpretations of all the different articles in the Creed. . . . Another writer afterward added a fourth column, containing the Arminian or Pelagian interpretation of all the articles."[27] According to Cunningham, it could not be proved that any one of these systems was inconsistent with the intent of the Creed—though at points they clearly contradict each other. The words of the

Creed are simply not specific enough to determine which of these views it intends to affirm.

But the differences between these various interpretations reveal the difference between true Christianity and false Christianity. As Cunningham wrote,

> The Apostles' Creed, as it is called . . . is not fitted to be of much use, as a summary of the leading doctrines of Christianity. A document which may honestly be assented to by Papists and Arians, by the adherents of the great apostasy and by the opposers of the divinity of our Saviour, can be of no real utility as a directory, or as an element or bond of union among the churches of Christ.[28]

All of this comes back to the problem raised by Charles Colson in his book, *The Body*. Having argued so convincingly against moral relativism, how can he defend a position that is essentially spiritual and doctrinal relativism? If, as Colson points out, "ideas do have consequences,"[29] how can he declare these doctrinal differences inconsequential—especially since they involve matters as significant as the way of salvation and the source of spiritual authority? Having lamented the "moral lobotomy" secular society has been subjected to, should we now plead for the visible church to undergo a spiritual lobotomy?

Again, I deeply appreciate much that Charles Colson has to say, but it seems this matter produces a considerable amount of confusion— and it is contributing to the rise of reckless faith in the evangelical church. *The Body* has been widely hailed as a landmark statement of true unity. At least in part because of the widespread influence Colson has had, the movement to embrace Roman Catholicism and Eastern Orthodoxy is fast gaining momentum. It is essential that evangelicals think these matters through more carefully.

HOW SERIOUS ARE DIFFERENCES OVER THE CENTRAL DOCTRINES OF CHRISTIANITY?

All who call themselves Christian should agree that there is a body of doctrine that is non-negotiable. The articles of faith that make up this constitutional body of truth are the very essence of "the faith which was once for all delivered to the saints" (Jude 3). These are the real fundamentals of the faith. They are doctrines so indispensable to true Christianity that we ought to break fellowship with those who profess Christianity but who deny them (2 Cor. 6:14-17).

Nothing is more clear from Scripture than the teaching that such a boundary exists between true and false doctrine. Paul wrote, "Even though we, or an angel from heaven, should preach to you a gospel contrary to that which we have preached to you, let him be accursed. As we have said before, so I say again now, if any man is preaching to you a gospel contrary to that which you received, let him be accursed" (Gal. 1:8-9). In a similar vein, the apostle John wrote, "Beloved, do not believe every spirit, but test the spirits to see whether they are from God; because many false prophets have gone out into the world" (1 John 4:1). And, "Anyone who goes too far and does not abide in the teaching of Christ, does not have God. . . . If anyone comes to you and does not bring this teaching, do not receive him into your house, and do not give him a greeting; for the one who gives him a greeting participates in his evil deeds" (2 John 9-11).

Those are just a few of the passages in the New Testament that command us to draw a clear line of distinction between sound doctrine and pseudo-Christianity. These verses *command* us to keep spiritually separate from those who corrupt the essential truths of the Gospel. Not only that, they attach the guilt of the false teacher's evil deeds to the one who fails to distinguish clearly between truth and error. We who love Christ should be very conscientious about interpreting and applying those commandments with the utmost care.

Without question, the biblical call to separation is sometimes abused by people who improperly apply it. Some Christians read such commands as if they were a prescription for abusive, spiteful, or venomous behavior toward others. That is not at all the attitude these verses call for. Nor are these passages guidelines for dealing with mere differences of opinion among true believers. They instruct us how to deal with false teachers who have gone astray with regard to the fundamental doctrines of Christianity.

Note the sternness of the language. The apostle, writing under divine inspiration, pronounces a severe curse on those who preach a corrupt gospel. In doing so he condemns both the false teachers and the bogus religious systems they devise. He thus places false Christianity in a category with the most heinous sins imaginable.

Surely, therefore, we ought to be extremely cautious about whom we receive into fellowship. Above all, we cannot possibly justify any sort of spiritual union with anyone whose teaching corrupts the New Testament Gospel.

No one who really believes the Bible should dispute those things. But it is precisely at this point that the real difficulty begins. What *are* the doctrines that are truly fundamental, and how do we decide what they are? Can we take them from a creed that was given to us by tradition, not by inspiration? Shouldn't we turn instead to God's Word for instruction about what is really essential to our faith?

HOW DO WE DECIDE WHICH DOCTRINES ARE TRULY FUNDAMENTAL?

Does the Bible itself identify specific doctrines as fundamental? Indeed it does. We have already noted that the strongest words of condemnation in all the New Testament are aimed at false teachers who corrupt the Gospel. Therefore the Gospel message itself must be acknowledged as a primary point of fundamental doctrine.

It would seem obvious, then, that two religious groups with contradictory evangelistic messages could not unite together for evangelism. Yet that is precisely what many today are appealing for. Charles Colson appeals for ecumenical unity for precisely this reason: "for it means we can cooperate for common witness."[30]

But what message will determine the content of our testimony? The biblical message of instantaneous justification through faith alone—or a system of rituals and sacraments that are supposed to convey grace to the participants with no guarantee of ultimate salvation? What authority will we point people to? The Scriptures alone—or a papal hierarchy and church tradition? Those two gospels are flatly contradictory and mutually exclusive.

All these considerations determine what message we proclaim and whether that message is the authentic Gospel of true

Christianity. Therefore we are dealing with matters that go to the very heart of the doctrines Scripture identifies as fundamental.

Can we get more specific? Let's turn to Scripture itself and attempt to lay out some biblical principles for determining which articles of faith are truly essential to authentic Christianity.[31]

All Fundamental Articles of Faith Must Be Drawn from the Scriptures

First, if a doctrine is truly fundamental, it must have its origin in Scripture, not tradition, papal decrees, or some other source of authority. Paul reminded Timothy that the Scriptures are "able to make thee wise unto salvation" (2 Tim. 3:15, KJV). In other words, if a doctrine is essential for salvation, we can learn it from the Bible. The written Word of God therefore must contain all doctrine that is truly fundamental. It is able to make us "adequate, equipped for every good work" (2 Tim. 3:17). If there were necessary doctrines not revealed in Scripture, those promises would ring empty.

The psalmist wrote, "The law of the Lord is perfect, restoring the soul" (Ps. 19:7). That means Scripture is *sufficient*. Apart from the truths revealed to us in Scripture, there is no essential spiritual truth, no fundamental doctrine, nothing essential to soul-restoration. We do not need to look beyond the written Word of God for any essential doctrines. There is nothing necessary beyond what is recorded in God's Word.

This, of course, is the Reformation principle of *sola Scriptura*—Scripture alone. It contrasts starkly with the practice of the Roman Catholic Church, which commonly threatens eternal damnation for anyone who questions the decrees of the Pope or the dogma of Church Councils. For example, Canon 1 of the seventh session of the Council of Trent pronounces anathema on anyone who says that there are more or less than the seven Sacraments established by the Council. That means if any Catholic questions the sacraments of Confirmation, Penance, or Extreme Unction—mentioned nowhere in Scripture—that person is subject to excommunication and in the Church's eyes is worthy of eternal damnation. The Canons and Decrees of the Council of Trent are larded with similar anathemas—

in effect making all the Council's dictums fundamental doctrines. In Francis Turretin's words, they "are impudent enough often to declare as fundamental their own hay and stubble and whatever the Romish church teaches."[32]

But according to the Bible itself, no supposed spiritual authority outside "the sacred writings" of Scripture can give us wisdom that leads to salvation. No papal decrees, no oral tradition, no latter-day prophecy can contain truth apart from Scripture that is genuinely fundamental.

The Fundamentals Are *Clear* in Scripture

Second, if an article of faith is to be regarded as fundamental, it must be clearly set forth in Scripture. No "secret knowledge" or hidden truth-formula could ever qualify as a fundamental article of faith. No key is necessary to unlock the teaching of the Bible.

The truth of God is not aimed at learned intellectuals; it is simple enough for a child. "Thou didst hide these things from the wise and intelligent and didst reveal them to babes" (Matt. 11:25). The Word of God is not a puzzle. It does not speak in riddles. It is not cryptic or mysterious. It is plain and obvious to those who have spiritual ears to hear. "The testimony of the Lord is sure, making wise the simple" (Ps. 19:7).

The point is not that every fundamental article of faith must be supported with an explicit proof text. The doctrine of the Trinity, for example, is certainly essential to true Christianity—and it is very clear in Scripture—but you will find no comprehensive statement of the Trinity from any single passage of Scripture.

Witsius wrote,

Among articles clearly contained in the Scriptures . . . we must include not only those which they teach in express words, but also those which, to all who apply their minds to the subject, are obviously deducible from them by necessary consequence. Our Lord and his Apostles very frequently confirmed even fundamental articles of faith by consequences deduced from Scripture [cf. Luke 20:37-38]. . . . The knowledge of a fundamental article consists not in understanding this or the other passage of the Bible;

but in an acquaintance with the truth, which in one passage, perhaps, is more obscurely traced, but is exhibited in other places in a clear, nay, in the clearest possible light.[33]

Nor does this mean that a doctrine must be non-controversial in order to be considered a fundamental article. Some would argue that the only test of whether something is essential to true Christianity is whether it is affirmed by all the major Christian traditions. Perhaps this is the very idea behind Charles Colson's appeals for ecumenical unity. But as Witsius points out, according to that rule, hardly anything of any substance would remain to distinguish the Christian Gospel from the "salvation" offered by pagan morality or Islamic theology. "There is much truth in the remark of *Clement of Alexandria;* 'No Scripture, I apprehend, is so favourably treated, as to be contradicted by no one.'"[34]

Everything Essential to Saving Faith Is Fundamental

Third, a doctrine *must* be regarded as fundamental if eternal life depends on it. Scripture is full of statements that identify the terms of salvation and the marks of genuine faith. "Without faith it is impossible to please Him, for he who comes to God must believe that He is, and that He is a rewarder of those who seek Him" (Heb. 11:6). That verse makes faith itself essential to a right relationship with God. It also expressly identifies both the existence and the veracity of God as fundamental articles of the Christian faith.

Elsewhere we are told that eternal life is obtained through the knowledge of the true God and Jesus Christ (John 17:3; 14:6; Acts 4:12). Since Jesus Himself *is* the true God incarnate (1 John 5:20; John 8:58; 10:30), the fact of His deity (and by implication the whole doctrine of the Trinity) is a fundamental article of faith (see 1 John 2:23). Our Lord Himself confirmed this when He said all must honor Him as they honor the Father (John 5:23).

The truths of Jesus' divine Sonship and Messiahship are also fundamental articles of faith (John 20:31).

Of course, the bodily resurrection of Christ is a fundamental doctrine, because 1 Corinthians 15:14 tells us, "If Christ has not been raised, then our preaching is vain, your faith also is vain."

Romans 10:9 confirms that the resurrection is a fundamental doctrine, and adds another: the lordship of Christ. "If you confess with your mouth Jesus as Lord, and believe in your heart that God raised Him from the dead, you shall be saved."

And according to Romans 4:4-5, justification by faith is a fundamental doctrine as well: "Now to the one who works, his wage is not reckoned as a favor, but as what is due. But to the one who does not work, *but believes in Him who justifies the ungodly,* his faith is reckoned as righteousness" (emphasis added). In other words, those who seek acceptance before God on the ground of their own righteousness will find they fall short (Rom. 3:27-28; Gal. 2:16–3:29). Only those who trust God to impute Christ's perfect righteousness to them are accounted truly righteous. This is precisely the difference between Roman Catholic doctrine and the Gospel set forth in Scripture. It is at the heart of all doctrine that is truly fundamental.

In fact, an error in understanding justification is the very thing that was responsible for the apostasy of the Jewish nation: "For not knowing about God's righteousness, and seeking to establish their own, they did not subject themselves to the righteousness of God" (Rom. 10:3). Is that not the precise failure of Roman Catholicism? But "Christ is the end of the law for righteousness to everyone who believes" (v. 4). In chapter 5 we will return for a closer look at the doctrine of justification by faith.

Every Doctrine We Are Forbidden to Deny Is Fundamental

Certain teachings of Scripture carry threats of damnation to those who deny them. Other ideas are expressly stated to be affirmed only by unbelievers. Such doctrines, obviously, involve fundamental articles of genuine Christianity.

The apostle John began his first epistle with a series of statements that establish key points of the doctrine of sin (hamartiology) as fundamental articles of faith. "If we say that we have fellowship with Him and yet walk in the darkness, we lie and do not practice the truth" (1:6). That condemns wanton antinomianism (the idea that Christians are under no law whatsoever) and makes some degree of doctrinal and moral enlightenment essential to true Christianity. A second statement rules out the humanistic notion that people are basically good: "If we say that we have no sin, we are deceiving ourselves, and the truth is not in us" (v. 8). And a third suggests that no true Christian would deny his or her own sinfulness: "If we say that we have not sinned, we make Him a liar, and His word is not in us" (v. 10).

First Corinthians 16:22 makes love for Christ a fundamental issue: "If anyone does not love the Lord, let him be accursed." And a similar verse, 1 Corinthians 12:3, says that no one speaking by the Spirit of God can call Jesus accursed.

The truth of Jesus' incarnation is also clearly designated a fundamental doctrine: "Every spirit that confesses that Jesus Christ has come in the flesh is from God; and every spirit that does not confess Jesus is not from God; and this is the spirit of the antichrist" (1 John 4:2-3). "For many deceivers have gone out into the world, those who do not acknowledge Jesus Christ as coming in the flesh. This is the deceiver and the antichrist" (2 John 7). Those verses by implication also condemn those who deny the Virgin Birth of our Lord, for if He was not virgin-born, He would be merely human, not eternal God come in the flesh.

And since those who twist and distort the Word of God are threatened with destruction (2 Peter 3:16), it is evident that both a lofty view of Scripture and a sound method of Bible interpretation (*hermeneutics*) are fundamental tenets of true Christianity.

The Fundamental Doctrines Are All Summed up in the Person and Work of Christ

Paul wrote, "No man can lay a foundation other than the one which is laid, which is Jesus Christ" (1 Cor. 3:11). Christ Himself embodied or established every doctrine that is essential to genuine Christianity. Those who reject any of the cardinal doctrines of the faith worship a christ who is not the Christ of Scripture.

How are the fundamentals of the faith personified in Christ?

With regard to *the inspiration and authority of Scripture*, He is the incarnate Word (John 1:1, 14). He upheld the written Word's absolute authority (Matt. 5:18). Christ Himself established *sola Scriptura* as a fundamental doctrine when He upbraided the Pharisees for nullifying Scripture with their own traditions: "Rightly did Isaiah prophesy of you hypocrites, as it is written, 'This people honors Me with their lips, but their heart is far away from Me. But in vain do they worship Me, teaching as doctrines the precepts of men.' Neglecting the commandment of God, you hold to the tradition of men. . . . You nicely set aside the commandment of God in order to keep your tradition" (Mark 7:6-9). Our Lord had much to say about the authority and infallibility of the Word of God.

In the doctrine of *justification by faith*, it is Christ's own perfect righteousness, imputed to the believer, that makes the pivotal difference between true biblical justification and the corrupted doctrine of Roman Catholicism and the cults. That is what Paul meant when he wrote, "Christ is the end of the law for righteousness to everyone who believes" (Rom. 10:4). It is also why Paul wrote that Christ is become to us righteousness (1 Cor. 1:30), and it is why Jeremiah called Him "The Lord our righteousness" (Jer. 23:6). The Lord Himself, Jesus Christ, is our righteousness (Jer. 33:16). That is the very essence of justification by faith alone, *sola fide*.

Of course, all the fundamental doctrines related to the incarnation—the Virgin Birth of Christ, His deity, His humanity, and His sinlessness—are part and parcel of who He is. To deny any of those doctrines is to attack Christ Himself.

The essential doctrines related to His work—His atoning death, His resurrection, and the reality of His miracles—are the very basis of the Gospel (cf. 1 Cor. 15:1-4; Heb. 2:3-4). Reject them and you nullify the heart of the Christian message.

The fundamentals of the faith are so closely identified with Christ that the apostle John used the expression "the teaching of Christ" as a kind of shorthand for the set of doctrines he regarded as fundamental. To him, these doctrines represented the difference between true Christianity and false religion.

That is why he wrote, "Anyone who goes too far and does not

abide in the teaching of Christ, does not have God; the one who abides in the teaching, he has both the Father and the Son" (2 John 9). Far from encouraging union with those who denied the fundamental truths of the faith, John forbade any form of spiritual fellowship with or encouragement of such false religion (vv. 10-11).

RECOVERING THE SPIRIT OF EARLY FUNDAMENTALISM

It is not my purpose here to attempt to give an exhaustive list of fundamental doctrines. To do so would be beyond the scope of this book, and certainly beyond my own abilities as a theologian. As Witsius has written:

> To point out the articles necessary to salvation, and precisely determine their number, is a task, if not utterly impossible, at least extremely difficult. There are, doubtless, more articles fundamental, than those to which the Scriptures have appended an express threatening of destruction. . . .
>
> Nor is it absolutely necessary that we should possess an exact list of the number of fundamental articles. It is incumbent on each of us to labour with the utmost of diligence to obtain an enlargement of saving knowledge, lest, perhaps we should be found ignorant of truths that are necessary. . . . [But] to ascertain precisely the number of necessary articles, is not requisite to our spiritual comfort. . . .
>
> It is of no great importance, besides, to the church at large, to know quite correctly the precise number of fundamental articles.[35]

In a similar vein, Turretin wrote,

> The question concerning the number of fundamental articles . . . besides being rash (since Scripture says nothing definitely about it) is also useless and unnecessary because there is no need of our knowing particularly the number of such articles, if we can prove that [our adversaries] err fundamentally in one or more. . . . Nor does it follow from this that the perfection of Scripture in neces-

sary things is detracted from. . . . For the Scriptures [still] contain most fully all things necessary to salvation, although their actual number is not accurately set forth.[36]

Certainly any list of fundamentals would have to begin with these doctrines Scripture explicitly identifies as non-negotiable: the absolute authority of Scripture over tradition (*sola Scriptura*), justification by faith alone (*sola fide*), the deity of Christ, and the Trinity. Since the Apostles' Creed omits *all* those doctrines, it clearly cannot be regarded as a doctrinal basis for building ecumenical bridges.

At the same time, we must acknowledge that some people are tempted to wield fundamental doctrines like a judge's gavel and consign multitudes to eternal doom. It is not our prerogative to exercise such judgment. As Witsius sagely observed, "It does not become us to ascend into the tribunal of God, and to pronounce concerning our neighbour, for how small a defect of knowledge, or for how inconsiderable an error, he must be excluded from heaven. It is much safer to leave that to God."[37]

This is wise advice. We dare not set ourselves up as judges of other people's eternal fate.

Nevertheless, we must recognize that those who have turned away from sound doctrine in matters essential to salvation are condemning themselves. "He who does not believe has been judged already" (John 3:18). Our passion ought to be to proclaim the fundamentals with clarity and precision, in order to turn people away from the darkness of error. We must confront head-on the blindness and unbelief that will be the reason multitudes will one day hear the Lord say, "I never knew you; depart from Me" (Matt. 7:23). Again, it must be stressed that those who act as if crucial doctrines were of no consequence only heap the false teacher's guilt on themselves (2 John 11).

We have no right to pronounce a sentence of eternal doom against anyone (John 5:22). But by the same token, we have no business receiving just anyone into the communion and fellowship of the church. We should no more forge spiritual bonds with people whose religion is fundamentally in error than we would seek fellowship with those guilty of heinous sin. To do so is tantamount to the arrogance shown by the Corinthians, who refused to dismiss from their fellowship a man living in the grossest kind of sin (1 Cor. 5:1-3).

We must also remember that serious error can be extremely subtle. False teachers don't wear a sign proclaiming who they are. They disguise themselves as apostles of Christ (2 Cor. 11:13). "And no wonder, for even Satan disguises himself as an angel of light. Therefore it is not surprising if his servants also disguise themselves as servants of righteousness" (vv. 14-15). And it should not be surprising even to hear false teachers and heretics recite the Apostles' Creed. Again, hear Witsius:

> Our faith consists not in words, but in sense; not in the surface, but in the substance; not in the leaves of a profession, but in the root of reason. All the heretics of the present day, that claim the name of Christians, are willing enough to subscribe to the words of the [Apostles'] Creed; each however affixing to them whatever sense he pleases, though diametrically opposed to sound doctrine.[38]

Witsius concludes his chapter by pointing out that people who plead for all creeds to be as brief and general as possible—as well as people who reject all doctrinal expressions not confined to the precise words of Scripture—usually do so because they "are secretly entertaining some mischievous design."[39]

Nothing is more desperately needed in the church right now than a new movement to reemphasize the fundamental articles of the faith. Without such a movement to restore true biblical discernment, the true church is in serious trouble. In the chapter that follows we will examine a controversial document that reveals precisely how ecumenism is already beginning to undermine the foundations of evangelical Christianity. It is an object lesson about the dangers of reckless faith. It may also represent one of the most serious threats to evangelicalism in our day.

If the current hunger for ecumenical compromise gains a foothold within evangelicalism, it will result in an unmitigated spiritual disaster. Reckless faith will virtually have free reign in the church. And far from strengthening the church's witness to an unbelieving world, it will spell the end of any clarion voice of truth.

5

Evangelicals and Catholics Together

MARCH 29, 1994, SAW a development that some have touted as the most significant event in Protestant-Catholic relations since the dawn of the Reformation. A document titled "Evangelicals and Catholics Together: The Christian Mission in the Third Millennium" was published with a list of more than thirty signatories—including well-known evangelicals Pat Robertson, J. I. Packer, Os Guinness, and Bill Bright. They were joined by leading Catholics such as John Cardinal O'Connor, Bishop Carlos A. Sevilla, and Catholic scholar Peter Kreeft.

The twenty-five-page document was drafted by a team of fifteen participants led by Richard John Neuhaus and Charles Colson. Neuhaus is a former Lutheran minister who converted to Catholicism in 1990, and has since been ordained to the priesthood. Like Colson, he is an influential author and speaker.

Colson explained that "Evangelicals and Catholics Together" resulted from a series of meetings sponsored by Neuhaus a few years ago in New York. The original purpose of the meetings was to discuss tensions in Latin America between Protestant missionaries and Catholic officials. "In some countries the Catholic Church was using political power to suppress Protestant evangelistic efforts; Protestant missionaries were being persecuted for their faith," Colson said. "On the other side, some evangelicals were promoting the gospel by calling the Catholic Church the 'whore of Babylon,' the Pope, the 'antichrist,' and the like."[1]

Colson says he and others at the meetings "were moved by the words of our Lord, calling us to be one with one another as He is one with us and with the Father, in order that the world might know, as Jesus prayed, that 'Thou didst send me.'" Colson added, "We were agreed that the scripture makes the unity of true Christians an essential—a prerequisite for Christian evangelism."[2]

The lengthy statement of accord that resulted has been praised in both the secular and Christian press as a landmark ecumenical agreement. Especially notable is the fact that the Catholics who signed are not from the liberal wing of Catholicism. Signatories on both sides are conservatives, many of whom are active in the pro-life movement and other conservative political causes. Historically, evangelicals and conservative Catholics have opposed ecumenical efforts.

An editorial in *Christianity Today* praised the accord for bringing conservatives into the ecumenical movement: "For too long, ecumenism has been left to Left-leaning Catholics and mainline Protestants. For that reason alone, evangelicals should applaud this effort and rejoice in the progress it represents."[3]

But does this new accord really represent progress, or are the essentials of the Gospel being relegated to secondary status? Asked another way, is the spirit of the Reformation quite dead? Should we now rejoice to see conservative evangelicals pursuing ecumenical union with Roman Catholicism?

The list of Protestant signatories to the document is certainly impressive. Some of these are men who have given their lives to proclaiming and defending Reformation theology. J. I. Packer's work is well-known through his many valuable books. His book *Evangelism and the Sovereignty of God*, in print for several decades, has introduced multiplied thousands to the Reformed emphasis on divine sovereignty. He has capably defended the key Reformation doctrine of justification by faith in several of his books. His book *Fundamentalism and the Word of God* is an able defense of the authority of Scripture. Few in our generation have been more effective advocates of Reformation theology than Dr. Packer.

As we noted in the previous chapter, Charles Colson is one of evangelicalism's most capable writers. Many of the recurring motifs in his writings over the years sound very much like echoes of Reformation themes—the sovereignty of God, the lordship of Christ, and the authority of Scripture. In fact, several of the teachers whom Colson himself names as his mentors are men whose ministries are closely aligned with the ideals and objectives of the Protestant Reformation.

Both of these men surely understand the gulf that divides Roman Catholicism from the evangelical faith. It is not a philosophical or political difference, but a theological one. And it is not a matter of trivia. The key difference between evangelicalism and Roman Catholicism is a difference over the *Gospel*. The issues that separated the Reformers from the Roman Catholic Church go to the heart of what we believe about salvation.

Many people assume that with signatures from men of this stature on it, "Evangelicals and Catholics Together" must be a trustworthy document, not a compromise of Reformation distinctives. But is that a safe assumption to make?

"Evangelicals and Catholics Together" is an object lesson on the importance of biblical discernment. But it is much, much more than that. Surely it is also a harbinger of things to come. As the pressure mounts for evangelicals to succeed in the political realm and fight for cultural morality, they often capitulate to the new ecumenism. This may become one of the most hotly contested issues of the decade. The future of evangelicalism may hang in the balance.

WHAT DOES THE DOCUMENT SAY?

"Evangelicals and Catholics Together" is a lengthy document. Unfortunately, it is impossible to reproduce the entire text here. But here are some of the highlights:

A Declaration of Unity

The document begins with this: "We are Evangelical Protestants and Roman Catholics who have been led through prayer, study, and discussion to common convictions about Christian faith and mission. This statement cannot speak officially for our communities. It does intend to speak responsibly from our communities and to our communities."[4]

Later in the Introduction, the document states, "As Christ is one, so the Christian mission is one. That one mission can and should be advanced in diverse ways. Legitimate diversity, however, should not be confused with existing divisions between Christians that obscure the one Christ and hinder the one mission" (2).

"Visible unity" is the stated goal (2) of the document, which quotes John 17:21, where the Lord Jesus prayed "that they may all be one; even as Thou, Father, art in Me, and I in Thee, that they also may be in Us; that the world may believe that Thou didst send Me." Then this follows: "We together, Evangelicals and Catholics, confess our sins against the unity that Christ intends for all his disciples" (2).

At this point the document's drafters are very explicit about who they believe is included in Christ's prayer for unity: "The one Christ and one mission includes many other Christians, notably the Eastern Orthodox and those Protestants not commonly identified as Evangelical. All Christians are encompassed in the prayer, 'May they all be one'" (2).

The section that follows has the heading "We Affirm Together." It includes this:

> All who accept Christ as Lord and Savior are brothers and sisters in Christ. Evangelicals and Catholics are brothers and sisters in Christ. We have not chosen one another, just as we have not chosen Christ. He has chosen us, and he has chosen us to be his together (John 15). However imperfect our communion with one another, we recognize that there is but one church of Christ. There is one church because there is one Christ and the Church is his body. However difficult the way, we recognize that we are

called by God to a fuller realization of our unity in the body of Christ (5).

Similar declarations of unity—and appeals for more visible manifestations of unity—are included in every section of the document.

A Statement of Common Faith

The document highlights areas of common faith between Catholics and evangelicals. It affirms the lordship of Christ as "the first and final affirmation that Christians make about all of reality" (5). It identifies Christ as "the One sent by God to be Lord and Savior of all" (5). It declares that the Scriptures are divinely inspired and infallible (6). And it affirms the Apostles' Creed "as an accurate statement of Scriptural truth" (6). The Apostles' Creed is reproduced in its entirety as a part of the document.

The pact also includes this statement about salvation:

> We affirm together that we are justified by grace through faith because of Christ. Living faith is active in love that is nothing less than the love of Christ, for we together say with Paul: "I have been crucified with Christ; it is no longer I who live, but Christ who lives in me; and the life I now live in the flesh I live by faith in the Son of God, who loved me and gave Himself for me" (Galatians 2) (5).

Although that statement has been celebrated as a remarkable concession on the Catholic participants' part, as we shall see, it actually says nothing that has not been affirmed by the Catholic Church since the time of the Reformation. The real issue under debate between Roman Catholicism and historic evangelicalism—justification by faith *alone*—is carefully avoided throughout "Evangelicals and Catholics Together."

A Statement of Doctrinal Differences

Those who drafted the accord did acknowledge other important areas of doctrinal difference between Roman Catholicism and evangelicalism. And they correctly observed that real unity cannot be achieved merely by glossing over Catholic-evangelical differences. In fact, near the end of the Introduction, they state, "we reject any appearance of harmony that is purchased at the price of truth" (4).

In a section titled "We Search Together," they said, "we do not presume to suggest that we can resolve the deep and long-standing differences between Evangelicals and Catholics. Indeed these differences may never be resolved short of the Kingdom Come" (9).

How are differences to be addressed? They "must be tested in disciplined and sustained conversation. In this connection we warmly commend and encourage the formal theological dialogues of recent years between Roman Catholics and Evangelicals" (9).

The document continues,

We note some of the differences and disagreements that must be addressed more fully and candidly in order to strengthen between us a relationship of trust in obedience to truth. Among points of difference in doctrine, worship, practice, and piety that are frequently thought to divide us are these:

- The church as an integral part of the Gospel, or the church as a communal consequence of the Gospel.
- The church as visible communion or invisible fellowship of true believers.
- The sole authority of Scripture (*sola Scriptura*) or Scripture as authoritatively interpreted in the church.
- The "soul freedom" of the individual Christian or the Magisterium (teaching authority) of the community.
- The church as local congregation or universal communion.
- Ministry ordered in apostolic succession or the priesthood of all believers.
- The Lord's Supper as eucharistic sacrifice or memorial meal.
- Remembrance of Mary and the saints or devotion to Mary and the saints.
- Baptism as sacrament of regeneration or testimony to regeneration.

This account of differences is by no means complete (9-10).

The document even acknowledges the solemn importance of many Catholic-evangelical differences. The signers expressly confess that some of the differences are so profound that they impinge on the Gospel itself:

> On these questions, and other questions implied by them, Evangelicals hold that the Catholic Church has gone beyond Scripture, adding teachings and practices that detract from or compromise the Gospel of God's saving grace in Christ. Catholics, in turn, hold that such teachings and practices are grounded in Scripture and belong to the fullness of God's revelation. Their rejection, Catholics say, results in a truncated and reduced understanding of the Christian reality (10-11).

A Mandate for Common Mission

But the theme that runs like a thread through "Evangelicals and Catholics Together" is identified by the document's subtitle: "The Christian Mission in the Third Millennium." The primary motivation behind the accord is the desire to eradicate differences that supposedly "obscure the one Christ and hinder the one mission" (2). How this can be done without *resolving* doctrinal matters that affect the Gospel is not explained.

But the Gospel is clearly *not* the driving concern of "Evangelicals and Catholics Together." The "one mission" envisioned by the accord places temporal goals alongside—and in effect, ahead of—eternal ones. Much of the document focuses on "the right ordering of society" (12). The longest section, "We Contend Together," states that "politics, law, and culture must be secured by moral truth" (12). The mandate they assume is cultural and temporal, not spiritual and eternal.

Therefore the catalog of issues that the document's signers "contend together" for is made up of religious freedom, right-to-life issues, moral education, parental choice in education, anti-obscenity laws, human equality, a free-market economy, esteem for Western culture, pro-family legislation, and a responsible foreign policy.

Another section, "We Witness Together," deals with evangelism.

No attempt is made to outline the *content* of the Gospel message. Indeed, since the document already lists key elements of the Gospel as points of disagreement, consensus on this would seem utterly impossible. Nevertheless, as if oblivious to the insurmountable difficulty this poses, the document unequivocally calls for evangelicals and Catholics to demonstrate "the evidence of love" toward one another that "is an integral part of [our] Christian witness" (20).

Beyond that, no positive guidelines are given for *how* Catholics and evangelicals can "witness together." Instead, the primary concern of this entire section on evangelism is to "condemn the practice of recruiting people from another community for the purposes of denominational or institutional aggrandizement" (22).

The document states unequivocally that our witness is *not* to be directed at people already in the "Christian community." That is, evangelicals are not supposed to proselytize active Roman Catholics (22-23). This is labeled "sheep stealing" (22). Signers of the document believe that such "attempt[s] to win 'converts' from one another's folds . . . undermine the Christian Mission" (20). Besides, proselytizing one another is deemed utterly unnecessary, because "we as Evangelicals and Catholics affirm that opportunity and means for growth in Christian discipleship are available in our several communities" (22).

Much of the controversy regarding "Evangelicals and Catholics Together" stems from this statement: "In view of the large number of non-Christians in the world and the enormous challenge of our common evangelistic task, it is neither theologically legitimate nor a prudent use of resources for one Christian community to proselytize among active adherents of another Christian community" (22-23).

THE FATAL FLAW

But it is another statement in the section "We Witness Together" that betrays the document's fundamental weakness:

> There are, then, differences between us that cannot be resolved here. But on this we are resolved: All authentic witness must be aimed at conversion to God in Christ by the power of the Spirit.

Those converted—whether understood as having received the new birth for the first time or as *having experienced the reawakening of the new birth originally bestowed in the sacrament of baptism*—must be given full freedom and respect as they discern and decide the community in which they will live their new life in Christ (24, emphasis added).

The document acknowledges "a major difference in our understanding of the relationship between baptism and the new birth in Christ. For Catholics, all who are validly baptized are born again and are truly, however imperfectly, in communion with Christ" (23). But how "major" is this difference? Signers of the accord evidently didn't feel it was anything fundamental. "*There are*," after all, "*different ways of being Christian*" (22, emphasis added). The temporal, cultural, political issues are so compelling that the Gospel must be ameliorated to whatever degree necessary to achieve a superficial "Christian" morality.

So people who believe they are "born again" because they were baptized Catholic "must be given full freedom and respect" to remain Catholic. That is, they should not be approached by evangelicals and told that no amount of sacraments or good works can make them acceptable to God.

Having declined to address the profound difference between the evangelical message of justification by faith *alone* and the Roman Catholic Gospel of faith plus works, the document here simply treats that difference as an optional matter of preference.

It is not. Catholicism places undue stress on human works. Catholic doctrine denies that God "justifies the ungodly" (Rom. 4:5) without first *making* them godly. Good works therefore become the ground of justification. And Scripture says that relegates people to an eternal reward that is reckoned not of grace, but of debt (v. 4). As thousands of former Catholics will testify, Roman Catholic doctrine and liturgy obscure the essential truth that we are saved by grace through faith and not by our own works (Eph. 2:8-9). It has trapped millions of Catholics in a system of superstition and religious ritual that insulates them from the glorious liberty of the true Gospel of Christ.

Adding works to faith as the grounds of justification is precisely the teaching Paul condemned as "a different gospel" (see 2 Cor. 11:4; Gal. 1:6). It nullifies the grace of God. If meritorious righteousness can be earned through the sacraments, "then Christ died needlessly" (Gal. 2:21). "For we maintain that a man is justified by faith apart from works of the Law" (Rom. 3:28).

Furthermore, justification by faith *plus* works was exactly the error that condemned Israel: "Pursuing a law of righteousness, [they] did not arrive at that law. Why? Because they did not pursue it by faith, but as though it were by works" (Rom. 9:31-32). "For not knowing about God's righteousness, and seeking to establish their own, they did not subject themselves to the righteousness of God" (Rom. 10:3). Throughout Scripture we are taught that "a man is not justified by the works of the Law but through faith in Christ Jesus . . . since by the works of the Law shall no flesh be justified" (Gal. 2:16).

Yet ignoring the gravity of this defect in the Roman Catholic system, evangelical signers of the document in effect pledge that none of their evangelistic work will ever be aimed at guiding Catholic converts out of Roman Catholicism—with its daily sacrifices, meritorious sacraments, confessional booths, rosary beads, fear of purgatory, and prayers to Mary and the saints. The document insists that "opportunity and means for growth in Christian discipleship are available" in the Catholic Church (22). Therefore winning a Catholic to the evangelical faith is nothing but "sheep stealing"—a sin against the body of Christ.

Having declared all active Catholics "brothers and sisters in Christ," and having given *de facto* approval to baptismal regeneration and justification by faith plus works, the accord has no choice but to pronounce Catholic Church members off-limits for evangelism.

A STEP IN THE RIGHT DIRECTION?

Signers of the document nonetheless hailed what they had done "as historic." Some applauded it as a major step toward healing the breach caused by the Reformation. Catholic signatories said the document had even circulated inside the Vatican, where it was received with great enthusiasm. *Christianity Today* ran an editorial welcoming the new ecumenism as a reflection of the changing pattern of American church life. Two major agency heads from the Southern Baptist Convention were signatories to the document. One of them wrote me to say this accord fulfills the whole intent of the Reformation.

But not all evangelicals responded so warmly. Many see the document as confusing, misleading. Some have said it sells out the Gospel. Evangelicals who are former Catholics have called the accord a betrayal. Missionaries taking the Gospel to predominantly Roman Catholic nations read it as an attack on their ministries. Evangelicals in Latin America fear that the pact will be used as a weapon against them.

Even some Catholics have taken exception. Christians United for Reformation (CURE) featured on their weekly radio broadcast a dialogue with a leading Catholic apologist who agreed with CURE's assessment: the document muddles and simply sweeps aside the important doctrinal differences that prompted the Reformation. CURE scrambled to produce an alternative document that would affirm Catholic-evangelical cobelligerence on moral and political issues without validating Roman Catholicism as authentic Christianity.

I am convinced that "Evangelicals and Catholics Together" is a step in exactly the *wrong* direction. It contradicts the very truths it professes to stand for. It expresses a wish for unity but threatens to split the evangelical community. It claims to reject the appearance of harmony purchased at the price of truth, but it treats precious truths thousands have died for as if they were of negligible importance. It calls for the removal of tensions that supposedly hinder the testimony of the Gospel, then renders the Gospel moot by suggesting that perhaps "the sacrament of baptism" is efficacious for spiritual regeneration. It condemns moral relativism and nihilism, yet it attacks the very foundation of absolute truth by implying that all forms of "Christianity" are equally valid. It calls for a clearer witness, but it denigrates evangelism among active Catholics as "sheep stealing"—while unduly elevating the importance of social and political issues. It is, frankly, an assault *against* evangelism. It suggests that "the right ordering of society" takes precedence over discerning between true Christianity and "a different gospel." It sets aside personal salvation in favor of national morality. It is nothing but the old ecumenism with moral conservatism rather than radical politics as its real agenda.

In an age already prone to reckless faith and lacking in biblical discernment, this accord seems fraught with potential mischief. It blurs doctrinal distinctives and therefore inflames the very worst tendencies of modern religion. It falls lock-step into line with our culture's minimalist approach to truth issues. Far from signaling "progress," it may mark the low point of post-Reformation evangelicalism.

That may seem like a harsh judgment of a document endorsed by so many stellar evangelicals. But quite honestly, one of the most distressing aspects of "Evangelicals and Catholics Together" is that men of such caliber would lend their support to an effort that camouflages the lethal errors of the Roman Catholic system. Having studied both the document and the different rationales for signing given by various signatories, I am convinced that "Evangelicals and Catholics Together" is a grave mistake, and it poses profound dangers for the future of evangelicalism.

WHY WOULD KNOWLEDGEABLE EVANGELICALS SIGN THIS ACCORD?

I wrote to the men I know personally who signed the accord and asked them to explain their position. Most responded with very gracious letters. Virtually all who replied explained that their signatures on the document do not necessarily indicate *unqualified* support, and they admitted they have concerns about the document. Most said they signed anyway because they wanted to express support for evangelical-Catholic alliances against social and moral ills. Some said they hoped the document would open the door for more dialogue on the pivotal doctrinal issues.

I must confess that I find all such explanations unsatisfying, because both the public perception of the accord and the language of the document itself send the signal that evangelicals now accept Roman Catholicism as authentic Christianity. That grants an undeserved legitimacy to Roman Catholic doctrine.

Moreover, the document confuses Christendom with the true church. It makes the unwarranted and unbiblical assumption that every breach of unity between professing Christians wounds the body of Christ and violates the unity Christ prayed for. The reality is that the true body of Christ is far less inclusive than the document implies. The document wants to include "many other Christians, notably the Eastern Orthodox and those Protestants not commonly identified as Evangelical." Who could this latter group include besides theological liberals? Yet Eastern Orthodoxy and most Protestant liberals would side with Rome in rejecting the biblical doctrine of justification by faith alone. Having abandoned the true faith for "another gospel," these groups are not entitled to be embraced as members of Christ's body (Gal. 1:9).[5]

The evangelical signers of the document—particularly those who have studied Reformation theology—surely are aware that official Roman Catholic doctrine is antithetical to the simple Gospel of grace. So why would theologically-informed evangelical leaders sign a document like this? Here is what some of them say:

One writes,

> This document is not about theology or doctrine. From the outset we admit that there are doctrinal differences that are irreconcilable and we specifically identify many of these. This document is about religious liberty (i.e., the right of all Christians to share their faith without interference from church or state), evangelism and missions (e.g., not only the right but the responsibility under the Great Commission of all Christians to share Christ with all nations and all people), and the need all Christians have to cooperate, without compromise, in addressing critical moral and social issues, such as abortion, pornography, violence, racism, and other such issues.
>
> In our battle for that which is good and godly, we must stand with those who will stand at all.[6]

Another signer wrote, "Why did I sign the recent statement 'Evangelicals and Catholics Together: The Christian Mission in the Third Millennium'? I did so because the document—though by no means perfect—presents an unusually strong combination of basic Christian truth and timely Christian response to the modern world."

Another suggested, "To non-Christians and the non-believing world who know nothing about Christianity and who may think Protestants and Catholics worship a different God, this affirmation should be a great testimony to the Lordship of Christ and the truth of His Word."

And one well-respected evangelical leader wrote,

> It was and is in harmony with the two-pronged approach to Rome that I have pursued for three decades: maximizing fellowship, cooperation, and cobelligerence with Roman Catholics on the ground, at grass roots level, while maintaining the familiar polemic against the Roman church and system as such. The document is not official, it is ad hoc and informal, and is designed to lead to honest cobelligerence against sin and evil in evangelism and community concerns.

Here are some other reasons evangelical signers give to justify their support for the document. All of these are taken verbatim either from letters these men wrote or papers they have circulated:

- I think the document is correct in saying that the scandal of conflict between Christians often has overwhelmed the scandal of the cross.

- I also thought the document's stand for life (especially in protest against abortion) and against the "relativism, anti-intellectualism, and nihilism" that are rampant today are exactly the stands that all Christians should be taking.

- The document is clear about what it is *not* trying to do. It is not put forth as an anticipation of church union, does not hide the fact that real differences continue to divide Catholics and evangelicals, and does not hide the fact that conditions outside North America are often different from those here.

- We have differences, but on the ancient creeds and the core beliefs of Christianity we stand together. Christianity is besieged on all sides—by a militant nation of Islam, by pantheists who have invaded many areas of life through the New Age Movement, and by aggressive secularism of Western life.

- If we are to reverse the surging tides of apostasy in Western culture and resist the advancing forces of secularism, then it is absolutely vital that those of us who share conservative, biblically-based views stand together, that we make common cause. Regardless of one's Christian tradition or even past prejudices, should we not affirm John Paul II and Mother Teresa for their uncompromising and stirring defense of the sanctity of human life?

- [The document states,] "All who accept Christ as Lord and Savior are brothers and sisters in Christ." Isn't "accepting Christ as Lord and Savior" what it means to be saved?

- The issue addressed is not theology. The primary issues addressed are missions, evangelism, societal concerns, and religious liberty.

- I believe the document represents the ultimate victory of the Reformation!

There, in the words of the evangelical signers themselves, is as complete a list of their arguments as I can assemble. To those must be added, of course, the arguments contained in the document itself.

But all those reasons ring hollow in view of everything the agreement surrenders.

WHAT IS COMPROMISED BY THE AGREEMENT?

Notice that a common theme running through the signers' arguments is the protest that "this document is not about theology or doctrine." After all, "Evangelicals and Catholics Together" explicitly disavows any intent to seek resolution of any doctrinal differences (24). All those who signed point to the document's long list of doctrinal differences as proof that no crucial doctrine was compromised.

But the incredible naivete of that perspective is unworthy of any of the men who attached their signatures to this document. Far from safeguarding evangelical distinctives, the document relegated them all to the status of non-essentials. By expressly stating, "Evangelicals and Catholics are brothers and sisters in Christ," the document suggests that none of the differences between Catholics and evangelicals involve any doctrines of eternal significance.

Yet that was the whole point of the Reformation. Rome viewed the Reformers as apostates and excommunicated them. The Reformers became convinced that Rome's deviation from biblical doctrine was so serious that the Papal system represented false Christianity. Both sides understood that the doctrines at stake were fundamental. "Evangelicals and Catholics Together," while acknowledging that *all* those doctrinal differences still exist, simply assumes without discussion that none of them represents the difference between authentic Christianity and "a different gospel." That assumption itself is a monumental doctrinal shift—abandoning more than four hundred years of evangelical consensus. So it is disingenuous to suggest that the document "is not about theology or doctrine."

In fact, one might argue that the document is *against* doctrine. By downplaying or denying the importance of crucial doctrinal distinctions, "Evangelicals and Catholics Together" amounts to a virtual assault against discernment. The sort of Christianity it proposes— broad fellowship based on the barest possible confession of faith— will provide a hothouse environment for reckless faith.

The *Christianity Today* editorial I mentioned earlier includes this welcome caveat: "Lest anyone be carried away by the ecumenical euphoria of the moment, it needs to be stated clearly that the Reformation was not a mistake." But quite unaccountably, the editorial also assures readers that the accord as it stands sufficiently safeguards the essential doctrines of the Reformation: "Both the formal and material principles of the Reformation—that is, the infallibility of Holy Scripture and justification by faith—are duly affirmed in this statement."[7]

That language may be unfamiliar to some readers, but "the formal principle" and "the material principle" are terms most students of Reformation doctrine will immediately recognize. One excellent textbook on Reformation doctrine says this: "Historians have frequently referred to the doctrine of *sola scriptura* as the *formal* principle of the Reformation, as compared to the *material* principle of *sola fide*."[8] The *formal* principle has to do with the form, or the essence, of the theological debate between Rome and the Reformers: the sufficiency of the Scriptures alone (*sola Scriptura*). The *material* principle defined the matter in question: whether sinners are justified by faith alone (*sola fide*), or by faith plus works.

The truth is, *Christianity Today*'s endorsement notwithstanding, "Evangelicals and Catholics Together" utterly compromises both the formal and the material principles of the Reformation.

Sola Scriptura—The Formal Principle

Notice that the *Christianity Today* editorial identifies the formal principle of the Reformation as "the infallibility of Holy Scripture." But the actual issue under debate in the Reformation was the *sufficiency*, not the *infallibility*, of Scripture. From the beginning of the Reformation, Catholics and Protestants have agreed on the questions of biblical inspiration and infallibility. Even in Luther's day, church officials "were in perfect agreement with him" on biblical infallibility.[9] What the papists objected to was Luther's doctrine of *sola Scriptura*. In Luther's own words, *sola Scriptura* means that "what is asserted without the Scriptures or proven revelation may be held as an opinion, but need not be believed."[10]

Catholicism flatly rejects that principle, adding a host of traditions and Church teachings and declaring them binding on all true believers—with the threat of eternal damnation to those who hold contradictory opinions. In Roman Catholicism, "the Word of God" encompasses not only the Bible, but also the Apocrypha, the Magisterium (the Church's authority to teach and interpret divine truth), the Pope's *ex cathedra* pronouncements, and an indefinite body of church tradition, some formalized in canon law and some not yet committed to writing. Whereas evangelical Protestants believe the Bible is the ultimate test of all truth, Roman Catholics believe *the Church* determines what is true and what is not. In effect, this makes the Church a higher authority than Scripture.

The documents of the Second Vatican Council affirm that "it is not from sacred Scripture alone that the [Catholic] Church draws her certainty about everything which has been revealed," but "sacred tradition [transmits] in its full purity God's word which was entrusted to the apostles."[11] *"Therefore both sacred tradition and sacred Scripture are to be accepted and venerated with the same sense of devotion and reverence."*[12]

How does "Evangelicals and Catholics Together" address the issue of biblical authority? As *Christianity Today* pointed out, the document expressly affirms "that Christians are to teach and live in obedience to the divinely inspired Scriptures, which are the infallible Word of God" (6). But the document also lists the question of the Bible's *sufficiency* as one of the disputed issues: "The sole authority of Scripture (*sola Scriptura*) or Scripture as authoritatively interpreted in the church" (10).

The way that statement is framed in the document implies that the difference between evangelicals and Catholics has to do with the question of who is authorized to interpret Scripture. It implies that evangelicals allow for individuals to interpret the Bible according to their personal preferences, while Catholics insist on following the hierarchy of Church authority. But that is a gross misstatement of the issue.

Evangelicals certainly believe Scripture must be correctly interpreted. That is why they have creeds and doctrinal statements. But evangelicals believe that creeds, decisions of church councils, all doctrine, and even the church itself *must be judged by Scripture*—not vice versa. Scripture is to be accurately interpreted in its context by comparing it to Scripture (1 Cor. 2:13; Isa. 28:9-13)—certainly not according to anyone's personal whims. Scripture itself is thus *the sole binding rule of faith and practice* for all Christians. Protestant creeds and doctrinal statements simply express the churches' collective understanding of the proper interpretation of Scripture. In no sense could the creeds or pronouncements of the churches ever constitute an authority equal to or higher than Scripture. Scripture always takes priority over the church in the rank of authority.

Catholics, on the other hand, believe the infallible touchstone of truth is the Church itself. The Church not only infallibly determines the proper interpretation of Scripture, but also *supplements* Scripture with additional traditions and teachings. That combination of Church tradition plus the Church's interpretation of Scripture is what constitute the binding rule of faith and practice for Catholics. *De facto*, the Church sets herself *above* Holy Scripture in rank of authority.

Therefore the real point of disagreement between evangelicals and Catholics regarding *sola Scriptura* is not the question of *who* should interpret Scripture but whether Scripture alone is a sufficient rule of faith and practice.

"Evangelicals and Catholics Together" not only misrepresents *sola Scriptura*, but it also consigns the whole issue to the status of a secondary, non-essential point of disagreement. In that regard, it represents a major victory for Rome and a sorry defeat for the Reformation.

Sola fide—the Material Principle

The other great plank in the Reformers' platform—the material principle—was justification by faith alone. *Christianity Today's* contention that *sola fide* was "duly affirmed in this statement" is mystifying. In the entire twenty-five-page document, not one reference to *sola fide* can be found anywhere! Yet this is what Martin Luther called "the article of the standing or falling church." In other words, Luther believed—and the rest of the Reformers were of one accord on this— that the test of authentic Christianity is the doctrine of justification by faith alone. Rome disagreed, declared the doctrine a damnable heresy, and pronounced a series of anathemas against anyone who dared to side with the Reformers.

It is surely significant that in "Evangelicals and Catholics Together" the issue of justification—the doctrine that launched the Reformation—is not even mentioned in the list of points of disagreement! Are the drafters of the document satisfied that evangelicals and Catholics now agree on this issue? Indeed, where justification is mentioned, it is given as a point of *agreement*: "We affirm together that we are justified by grace through faith because of Christ" (5).

What's wrong with that? many evangelicals will ask. So what if it leaves out the disputed word *alone*? After all, the phrase "justification by grace through faith" is certainly biblical as far as it goes. It may not be a full discourse on the doctrine of justification, but isn't it really adequate? Doesn't it seem like theological nitpicking to insist on technical precision in an informal statement like this?

But it is *not* nitpicking to fault this statement. For five hundred years the question of whether people are justified by faith *alone* has been the main point of theological dispute between Catholics and evangelicals. Both sides have taken rather clearly defined positions on the issue. Any document that purports to bring Catholicism and evangelicalism into harmony *must* address this fundamental disagreement. The difference is so crucial that it cannot and should not merely be glossed over with ambiguous language.

In fact, it does not overstate the case to say that on the matter of justification the difference between the Roman Catholic view and that of Protestant evangelicalism is so profound as to constitute *two wholly different religions*. Error at this point is damning heresy. If one view represents authentic Christianity, the other certainly cannot. They are antithetical. There is no common ground here.

The doctrine of justification by faith has been something of a focus in my personal study for the past few years. It rose to prominence as a major point in the so-called "lordship controversy"—a debate mostly among evangelicals about the role of good works in the Christian life. That debate was sparked by several prominent evangelicals who insisted that people can be saved by accepting Jesus as Savior—even if they choose to defer obedience to His lordship indefinitely. Justification by faith was the issue on which they staked their claim. If we are truly justified by faith *alone*, they reasoned, all good works must remain optional for Christians. I rejected that position, known as *antinomianism*, on biblical grounds.

But the lordship controversy launched me on a very profitable study of justification by faith from both the biblical and the historical perspectives. As I read what the Reformers had to say about justification, I gained a new appreciation for their biblical thoroughness. I also began to see in a clearer light than ever before how vitally important it is to be absolutely sound on the doctrine of justification by faith. Luther did not overstate the case when he called justification the article by which the church stands or falls. A right understanding of justification is the only safe course between the Scylla of works-righteousness and the Charybdis of radical antinomianism.

The Reformers' Firm Stance on Justification

The Roman Catholic Church defined its views on justification at the Council of Trent. That Council began its work in 1545 and continued for nearly twenty years. The doctrine of justification was high on the Council's list of priorities. The canons and decrees on justification were written in 1547 at the Council's sixth session.

Trent was the Catholic Church's answer to the Protestant Reformation. In 1517, when Martin Luther nailed his Ninety-Five Theses to the door of the castle church at Wittenberg, attacking the sale of indulgences, he "cut a vein of mediæval Catholicism."[13] The bleeding continued for at least three decades. The Council of Trent was a desperate attempt to stanch the flow.

Philip Schaff described the work of Trent:

> The decisions of the Council relate partly to doctrine, partly to discipline. The former are divided again into Decrees (*decreta*), which contain the positive statement of Roman dogma, and into short Canons (*canones*), which condemn the dissenting views with the concluding "*anathema sit*" ["let him be damned"]. The Protestant doctrines, however, are almost always stated in exaggerated form, in which they could hardly be recognized by a discriminating Protestant divine, or they are mixed up with real heresies, which Protestants condemn as emphatically as the Church of Rome.[14]

So rather than replying to the Reformers' teaching, Trent often attacked straw men of its own making. Bear that in mind as we look at some of the Council's pronouncements about justification. Sometimes the view they condemn is merely a caricature of Reformation teaching.

On the other hand, many of Trent's decrees sound quite evangelical. For example, the Council of Trent explicitly denied that anyone can be justified by good works apart from grace: "If anyone says that man may be justified before God by his own works . . . without the grace of God through Jesus Christ—let him be anathema" (*Trent*, sess. 6, canon 1).[15]

The council also affirmed that "God justifies sinners by his grace, through the redemption that is in Christ Jesus" (*Trent*, sess. 6, chap. 6) and that "we are said to be justified by faith because faith is the beginning of human salvation" (*Trent*, sess. 6, chap. 8). It also stated that the *meritorious* cause of justification is "our Lord Jesus Christ, who . . . merited justification for us by His most holy passion on the wood of the cross, and made satisfaction for us unto God the Father" (*Trent*, sess. 6, chap. 7).

So when the recent "Evangelicals and Catholics Together" document stated that "we are justified by grace through faith because of Christ," *it was saying nothing that the Roman Catholic Church has not consistently affirmed for the past 450 years.*

If that is true, why did the Reformers object so strenuously to the Roman Catholic Church's doctrine of justification?

The dispute had to do with the very nature of justification. The Reformers said justification is an act of God whereby the believing sinner is *declared* righteous. The Council of Trent argued that justification is a process that actually *makes* the sinner righteous. Here is Trent's definition: "[Justification is] not remission of sins merely, but *also the sanctification and renewal of the inward man*, through the voluntary reception of the grace and gifts by which an unrighteous man *becomes righteous*" (*Trent*, sess. 6, chap. 7, emphasis added).

Certainly all true evangelicals believe that the believer's "inward man" is renewed and sanctified in the salvation process. But, as we shall see momentarily, evangelicals are careful to distinguish between *justification* and *sanctification*. The distinction must be drawn in order to make clear that it is Christ's righteousness imputed to us—not something in the "inward man"—not even an infusion of divine grace—that makes us acceptable to God. *This is the essential theological difference that underlies every other point of disagreement between Catholicism and evangelicalism.* Only if this issue is settled can there ever be any real spiritual unity between Rome and evangelicals.

According to Trent, justification is a lifelong process (*Trent*, sess. 6, chap. 10). Perseverance is not guaranteed (*Trent*, sess. 6, chap. 13); but "those who, by sin, have fallen from the received grace of justification may be again justified . . . through the sacrament of penance" (*Trent*, sess. 6, chap. 14). The council also stated that justification must be preserved through good works, which are energized by the grace of God infused into the believer (*Trent*, sess. 6, chap. 16).

What consistently comes through in Trent's pronouncements is a clear and definite repudiation of the doctrine of justification by faith *alone*. According to the Council, "unless hope and love are *added to faith*, it neither unites a man perfectly with Christ nor makes him a living member of His body" (*Trent*, sess. 6, chap. 7, emphasis added). In the Catholic scheme, justification means that God's grace is poured forth into the sinner's heart, making the person progressively more righteous. It then becomes the sinner's responsibility to preserve and increase that grace by various good works. The system mixes works with grace, so that justification is not *sola fide*, by faith alone. And it makes justification an ongoing process rather than an accomplished fact.

Here are the Council of Trent's own words:

- If anyone says that *by faith alone* the sinner is justified, so as to mean that nothing else is required to cooperate in order to obtain the grace of justification . . . let him be anathema (*Trent*, sess. 6, canon 9).

- If anyone says that men are justified either by the imputation of the righteousness of Christ alone, or by the remission of sins alone, to the exclusion of the grace and love that is poured forth in their hearts by the Holy Spirit and is inherent in them; or even that the grace by which we are justified is only the favor of God—let him be anathema (*Trent*, sess. 6, canon 11).

- If anyone says that the righteousness received is not preserved and also not increased before God *by good works*, but that those works are merely the fruits and signs of justification obtained, but not a *cause* of its increase, let him be anathema (*Trent*, sess. 6, canon 24).

- If anyone says that the guilt is remitted to every penitent sinner after the grace of justification has been received, and that the debt of eternal punishment is so blotted out that there remains no debt of temporal punishment to be discharged either in this world or in the next in Purgatory, before the entrance to the kingdom of heaven can be opened—let him be anathema (*Trent*, sess. 6, canon 30).

- If anyone says that the Catholic doctrine of justification set forth in this decree by this holy Synod derogates in any way the glory of God or the merits of our Lord Jesus Christ, and not rather that the truth of our faith and the glory of God and of Jesus Christ are rendered more illustrious—let him be anathema (*Trent*, sess. 6, canon 33).

Trent also declared that the *instrumental* cause of justification (the means by which it is obtained) is not faith, but "the sacrament of baptism" (*Trent*, sess. 6, chap. 7). The Council also said justification is forfeited whenever the believer commits a mortal sin (*Trent*, sess. 6, chap. 15)—clearly making justification contingent on human works. So according to Trent, justification is neither procured nor maintained through faith; works are necessary both to begin and to continue the process.

The Reformers objected to Trent's pronouncements solely on biblical grounds. They filled many thick volumes with scriptural proofs against Rome's position. But since the Council of Trent's rulings were deemed infallible and those who questioned them threatened by the Church with eternal damnation, the breach between Rome and the Reformers was in effect made irreparable.

The Biblical Doctrine of Justification

The Reformers' objections to the Catholic Church's stance on justification may be summed up in four biblical arguments.

First, Scripture presents justification as *instantaneous, not gradual.* Contrasting the proud Pharisee with the broken, repentant tax-gatherer who smote his breast and prayed humbly for divine mercy, Jesus Himself said that the tax-gatherer "went down to his house justified" (Luke 18:14). His justification was instantaneous, complete before he performed any work, based solely on his repentant faith. Jesus also said, "Truly, truly, I say to you, he who hears My word, and believes Him who sent Me, has eternal life, and does not come into judgment, but has passed out of death into life" (John 5:24). Eternal life is the present possession of all who *believe*—and by definition eternal life cannot be lost. The one who believes immediately passes from spiritual death to eternal life, because that person is instantaneously justified. "Therefore having been justified by faith, we have peace with God through our Lord Jesus Christ" (Rom. 5:1). A few verses later we read, "*Having now been justified* by His blood, we shall be saved from the wrath of God through Him" (v. 9, emphasis added). Those verses put justification for the believer in the past tense, not the present or the future. Justification occurs in an instant. At the first moment of faith it is already an accomplished fact: "There is therefore now no condemnation for those who are in Christ Jesus" (Rom. 8:1).

Second, justification means the sinner is *declared righteous, not actually made righteous.* This goes hand in hand with the fact that justification is instantaneous. There is no process to be performed. Justification is a purely forensic reality, a declaration God makes about the sinner. Justification takes place in the court of God, not in the sinner's soul. It is an objective fact, not a subjective phenomenon. It changes the sinner's status, not his nature. Certainly at the moment of conversion the sinner's nature is changed miraculously; old things pass away and all things are made new (2 Cor. 5:17). But the actual changes that occur in the believer have to do with *regener-*

ation and *sanctification*, not justification. Again, it is absolutely vital to keep these ideas separate. Regeneration is a spiritual quickening in which the sinner is born again with a new heart (Ezek. 36:26; John 3:3); sanctification is a lifelong process whereby the believer is conformed to the image of Christ (2 Cor. 3:18). But *justification* is an immediate decree, a divine "not guilty" verdict on behalf of the sinner. This is inherent in the meaning of the word *justify*. The word itself (*dikaioō* in the Greek) means "to declare righteous"; the sense it conveys is the exact opposite of the word *condemn*.

Third, the Bible teaches that justification means righteousness is *imputed, not infused*. Righteousness is "reckoned," or credited to the account of those who believe (Rom. 4:3-25). They stand justified before God not because of their own righteousness, but because of a perfect righteousness outside themselves that is reckoned to them by faith (Phil. 3:9). Where does that perfect righteousness come from? It is God's own righteousness (Rom. 10:3), and it is ours in the person of Jesus Christ (1 Cor. 1:30; cf. Jer. 23:6; 33:16). We are united to Christ by faith—we are "in Christ"—and therefore accepted by God in His beloved Son (Eph. 1:6-7). Christ's own perfect righteousness is credited to our personal account (Rom. 5:17, 19), just as the full guilt of our sin was imputed to Him. "He made Him who knew no sin to be sin on our behalf, that we might become the righteousness of God in Him" (2 Cor. 5:21). So once again we see that the ground on which we stand before God is the perfect righteousness of Christ imputed to us by faith, and not (as the Catholic Church teaches) the imperfect righteousness that is wrought by God's grace infused into us. The point is that the only merit God accepts for salvation is that of Jesus Christ; nothing we can ever do could earn God's favor or add anything to the merit of Christ.

Fourth and finally, Scripture clearly teaches that we are justified *by faith alone, not by faith plus works*. "If it is by grace, it is no longer on the basis of works, otherwise grace is no longer grace" (Rom. 11:6). Contrast that with Trent's ruling:

If anyone says that by the said sacraments of the New Law[16] grace is not conferred through the act performed [*ex opere operato*, lit., "the work worked"] but [says] that faith alone in the divine promises is sufficient for the obtaining of grace, let him be anathema (*Trent*, sess. 7, canon 8).

In other words, grace is received not by faith but through works—specifically, through the Roman Catholic sacraments.

But again, the Bible says, "By grace you have been saved *through faith*; and that not of yourselves, it is the gift of God; *not as a result of works*, that no one should boast" (Eph. 2:8-9, emphasis added). The only correct answer to the question "What must I do to be saved?" is the one the Bible gives: "*Believe* in the Lord Jesus, and you shall be saved" (Acts 16:31).

> For what does the Scripture say? "And Abraham believed God, and it was reckoned to him as righteousness." Now to the one who works, his wage is not reckoned as a favor, but as what is due. *But to the one who does not work, but believes in Him who justifies the ungodly, his faith is reckoned as righteousness*, just as David also speaks of the blessing upon the man to whom *God reckons righteousness apart from works* (Rom. 4:3-6, emphasis added).

None of this renders good works, obedience, or sanctification optional in Christian living, as I have argued at length in two other books.[17] But it does mean emphatically that works play no role in justification. Works of righteousness and religious ritual can never make anyone acceptable to God. For that, we must depend wholly by faith on the merit of the Lord Jesus. Any system that mingles works with grace is "a different gospel" (Gal. 1:6), a distorted message that is anathematized (v. 9)—not by a council of medieval bishops, but by the very Word of God that cannot be broken.

Other Essentials of the Faith

"Evangelicals and Catholics Together" compromises and obfuscates several other essential evangelical truths. Notice, for example, that fourth from the end in the document's list of "differences and disagreements" is this: "The Lord's Supper as eucharistic sacrifice or memorial meal" (10). Here another fundamental doctrine is treated as if it were a peripheral matter.

Roman Catholicism teaches that the communion wafer is transformed through a miracle into the literal body of Christ, and the communion wine is transformed into the literal blood of Christ. Trent stated, "The whole Christ is contained under each form" of the communion elements (*Trent*, sess. 13, canon 3). Therefore, whoever participates in the Mass actually eats the flesh of Jesus Christ, and the priests who partake of the wine actually drink His blood. This is the doctrine known as *transubstantiation*.

Its corollary is the teaching that every time Mass is said, the sacrifice of Christ is offered over again. "A true and real sacrifice" is offered to God in the Mass and "Christ is given to us to eat" (*Trent*, sess. 22, canon 1). Rome believes that the "Savior instituted the Eucharistic Sacrifice of His Body and Blood. He did this in order to perpetuate the sacrifice of the Cross throughout the centuries until He should come again."[18]

That teaching nullifies the crucial biblical truth that "we have been sanctified through the offering of the body of Jesus Christ *once for all*. And every priest stands daily ministering and offering time after time the same sacrifices, which can never take away sins; but He, having offered *one sacrifice for sins for all time*, sat down at the right hand of God" (Heb. 10:10-12, emphasis added). There is no more need for daily sacrifices or an intercessory priesthood.

In fact, those things have encumbered the Roman Catholic system with pure idolatry. Each Mass features a moment where the consecrated wafer ("the host") is held up, and all present are supposed to bow and worship the communion elements. The Council of Trent ruled,

> If anyone says that in the holy sacrament of the Eucharist, Christ the only begotten Son of God [in the form of the wafer], is not to be adored with the worship of *latria* [worship due God alone], also outwardly manifested; and is consequently neither to be venerated with a special festive solemnity, nor to be solemnly borne about in procession according to the laudable and universal rite

> and custom of Holy Church; or is not to be proposed publicly to
> the people to be adored and that the adorers of it are idolaters—
> let him be anathema (*Trent*, sess. 13, canon 6).

In other words, the host—the transubstantiated wafer—is deemed
worthy of the kind of worship reserved only for God.

On the other hand, Mary, the saints, and relics are objects for *veneration*, which is supposed to be something less than *worship*—but
practically it is difficult to see any meaningful difference. Indeed, the
word *venerate* originally meant "worship"—from a Latin, rather than
Anglo-Saxon, root.

Mary is practically vested with attributes of deity. The Church
teaches—with no biblical warrant whatsoever—that she is sinless,
that she "was taken up body and soul into heavenly glory," and that
"she was exalted by the Lord as Queen of all."[19] The current Pope is
well known for his devotion to Mary. He and millions of other
Catholics pray to Mary daily—as if she were omniscient. She is said
to have a "saving role" because of her heavenly intercession and is
deemed "Advocate, Auxiliatrix, Adjutrix [words meaning "Helper,"
"Benefactor"], and Mediatrix"[20]—all roles mirroring those ascribed in
Scripture to both Christ and the Holy Spirit. Vatican II specifically
ordered "that the cult, especially the liturgical cult, of the Blessed
Virgin, be generously fostered" and that "exercises of devotion
toward her . . . [as well as] decrees issued in earlier times regarding
the veneration of images of Christ, the Blessed Virgin, and the saints,
be religiously observed."[21]

The Second Vatican Council stated at least one thing accurately:
"When Christians separated from us [Protestants] affirm the divine
authority of the sacred Books, *they think differently from us.* . . . According
to Catholic belief, an authentic teaching office plays a special role in
the explanation and proclamation of the written word of God."[22]

In other words, in Catholicism, the plain sense of Scripture apart
from the authoritative interpretation of the Church has no relevance
whatever. So Catholics can quote and affirm 1 Timothy 2:5: "There
is one God, and one mediator also between God and men, the man
Christ Jesus." But "they think differently from us" about whether

God speaks directly to us through the plain sense of His Word. According to Roman Catholicism, 1 Timothy 2:5—and every other verse of Scripture—is subject to the Church's infallible interpretation. The Scriptures do not speak for themselves as the Word of God. *The Church* determines what the Bible means, and *that authoritative interpretation* becomes the infallible Word of God.

Thus—ironically—the section of the Vatican II document that asserts Mary's "saving role" as intercessory Mediatrix *begins* by quoting 1 Timothy 2:5![23] In a popular edition of the Vatican II documents, a footnote after the word *Mediatrix* explains, "The Council applies to the Blessed Virgin the title of Mediatrix, but carefully explains this so as to remove any impression that it could detract from the uniqueness and sufficiency of Christ's position as Mediator (cf. 1 Tim. 2:5)."[24]

Of course, simply *denying* that 1 Timothy 2:5 is violated does not resolve the obvious contradiction between ascribing to Mary an ongoing "saving role" as intercessory "Mediatrix" and Scripture's plain meaning. But that does not matter in Catholicism, since authoritative truth is not determined by the plain sense of Scripture, but by the church's teaching authority. If the Church says Mary's "saving, mediatorial role" does not encroach on Christ's uniqueness as sole Mediator between God and men, Catholics are supposed to believe it with unquestioning faith.

That is reckless faith. Evangelicals must continue to oppose it.

IS UNION WITH ROME A WORTHY GOAL?

Should evangelicals wish to see the Protestant Reformation undone? Certainly not. The Reformation was not a tragedy but a glorious victory for Christianity. The result of the Reformation was not a breach in the true body of Christ but the recovery of the Gospel of grace from the near obscurity it had fallen into under Catholic abuses. Protestants who doubt that ought to study church history.

Some claim the Second Vatican Council in the 1960s brought Rome and evangelicals closer together doctrinally. They say Rome further reformed herself and opened the door for ecumenical rapprochement. But as Appendix 1 shows, Vatican II only solidified the stance Rome took against the Reformation. Rome declared herself "irreformable."[25]

It would certainly be wonderful for the Roman Catholic Church to repudiate her opposition to justification by faith and abandon her extrabiblical doctrines. But there is nothing to suggest that might happen. All the dialogue between evangelicals and Roman Catholics has not brought Rome one hair's breadth closer to a biblical position on any pivotal doctrinal issue. Nor is there any sensible reason to think that *more* dialogue might accomplish this. On the contrary, changes in Rome's doctrinal position have never been a matter for discussion.

The fact is that the Colson-Neuhaus accord was made possible not because Roman Catholicism moved closer to the evangelical position, but because the evangelical drafters of the document either downplayed, compromised, or relinquished all the key evangelical distinctives. The document "Evangelicals and Catholics Together" capitulated precisely where the Reformers stood firm. Far from being an incentive for Rome to reconsider her position, this document grants an unwarranted stamp of legitimacy on the Roman Catholic system. It makes it harder than ever for doctrinally-minded evangelicals to mount an effective polemic against Rome's "different gospel."

Now is the time when evangelicals must carefully reexamine how dearly they hold their doctrinal convictions. We ought to pause and ask ourselves if we really are willing to consider all who recite the Apostles' Creed as true members of the body of Christ. Either the Protestant Reformation was all a big mistake, or we must be willing to stand with the Reformers. Are we ready to concede that the thousands of martyrs who gave their lives to oppose the tyranny and false doctrine of Rome all died for an unworthy cause?

These are not minor issues. Nor will they go away if evangelical leaders merely keep silent. "Evangelicals and Catholics Together" will be followed by other treaties and more doctrinal compromise. Those who hold biblical convictions will find themselves forced either to make peace with enemies of the Gospel, or to take a clear and vigorous stand against Rome's "different gospel" and against ecumenical homogeneity.

"Don't you want to see Christian unity?" someone asked who had heard of my stand against "Evangelicals and Catholics Together." I certainly do want to see *true* Christian unity. But remember that the unity our Lord prayed for goes hand in hand with His request that we be sanctified in the *truth* (John 17:17-21). And the familiar principle in 2 Corinthians 6:14-17—while it certainly pertains to marriage—is actually far broader, encompassing all forms of spiritual union:

> Do not be bound together with unbelievers; for what partnership have righteousness and lawlessness, or what fellowship has light with darkness? Or what harmony has Christ with Belial, or what has a believer in common with an unbeliever? Or what agreement has the temple of God with idols? For we are the temple of the living God; just as God said, "I will dwell in them and walk among them; and I will be their God, and they shall be My people. Therefore, come out from their midst and be separate," says the Lord. "And do not touch what is unclean; and I will welcome you."

Unity is never to be sought at the expense of truth. "Evangelicals and Catholics Together" gave lip service to that principle—but failed to follow through.

To those who ask "Don't you want to see unity?" I ask in return, "Are you willing to allow souls to be led into darkness by false religion and error?"

"Evangelicals and Catholics Together" practically demands that evangelicals regard all active Catholics as true Christians and refrain from "proselytizing" them. To accede to that request is to capitulate to reckless faith.

I have heard testimonies from literally hundreds of former Roman Catholics who affirm unequivocally that while they were in the Catholic Church they did not know Christ at all. They were blindly following the religious system, attempting to earn grace and work their way into divine favor. They actively partook in the sacraments and ceremonies and rituals, but they had unregenerate hearts. Hardly a Sunday evening passes without at least one or two former Roman Catholics giving a testimony to that effect from our church baptistery. None of these people passed from death to life until they abandoned their blind faith in the Roman Catholic system and embraced the message of God's free grace.

For evangelicals to sign a pact labeling such conversions "sheep stealing" is to my mind unconscionable. And for the document to declare that "it is neither theologically legitimate nor a prudent use of resources for one Christian community to proselytize among active adherents of another Christian community" (23) is simply incredible. By the document's own definitions, that puts all churchgoers who are Catholic, Eastern Orthodox, or liberal Protestant off-limits for evangelism.

But *most* "active adherents" of those communities simply do not know Christ as Lord and Savior. The christ they worship is not the One who offers full salvation freely to those who trust Him. Most of them are hoping to earn enough divine favor for themselves through good works and religious ritual—as if Christ had never said, "It is finished!" (John 19:30). Those people desperately need to hear the liberating message of the Gospel of grace. For evangelicals to sign a document agreeing to place them off-limits for evangelism is a gross act of betrayal.

Ecumenical unity with Roman Catholicism is not essential to the furtherance of the kingdom of God. Evangelism of Roman Catholics is. To waive the latter goal in pursuit of the former is a serious mistake. One wonders what the evangelical leaders who signed "Evangelicals and Catholics Together" were thinking when they approved such strictures against evangelizing Catholics.

Do the evangelical signers of the document really intend to follow the path it lays out? Let us fervently pray that they will not. Those who pursue that course will find that they have traded away their evangelical birthright for a mess of ecumenical pottage. Rather than honoring our Lord, they will dishonor Him. Rather than clarifying the Gospel for a watching world, they will be substituting a muddled message. And rather than steering people to the small gate and the narrow way, they will be pointing multitudes to the wide gate and broad way that lead to destruction.

6

Laughing Till It Hurts

W

E HAVE IDENTIFIED two extremes of reckless faith: mysticism and rote tradition. Roman Catholicism is virtually built on rote tradition. Rome has historically encouraged the faithful to believe *without* understanding. That is why in the previous chapter we focused on the movement toward Rome as a threat of reckless faith.

But now we turn our attention to the other extreme, mysticism. Mysticism, as we noted early in the book, draws truth from personal experiences, inner promptings, feelings, and other subjective criteria. As one authority on mysticism has written, "a mystical experience is primarily an emotive event, rather than a cognitive one."[1] The emotive event apart from any cognitive functioning (an emotional high while the intellect is passive) has become for many Christians the ultimate spiritual experience. Multitudes have concluded that God's most powerful work in our lives is not in the realm of truth but in the realm of emotion. This idea is rapidly changing the face of evangelicalism.

Evangelicals have historically waged their most important battles in defense of truth and sound doctrine—and against an undue emphasis on emotion and experience. As we noted in chapter 4, the early fundamentalist movement was a broad-based coalition of evangelicals who understood that sound doctrine is the litmus test of authentic faith. They defined true Christianity in terms of its essential doctrines. The doctrines they labeled fundamental were nothing new; these were truths all Christians had held in common since before the Protestant Reformation. But the fundamentalists were responding to the threat of liberalism, which had attacked doctrines at the very core of the historic Christian faith.

Liberals argued that Christianity is supposed to be an experience, not a doctrine. They wanted to discard the core of Christian doctrine but call themselves Christians on the basis of their lifestyle. The original fundamentalists rescued evangelicalism from the liberal threat by unashamedly declaring that Christianity must be doctrine before it can be legitimate experience. Christianity is grounded in *truth*, they maintained, and no experience can be authentic Christianity if it does not spring from essential Christian truth. That is why they put such an emphasis on doctrine.

Today's evangelicals are losing the will to hold that line. Voices within the camp are now suggesting that experience may be more important than doctrine after all. The evangelical consensus has shifted decidedly in the past two decades. Our collective message is now short on doctrine and long on experience. *Thinking* is deemed less important than *feeling*. Ironically, we have succumbed to the very ideas the early fundamentalists argued so convincingly against. We have absorbed the same existential influences they fought so hard to overthrow.

Modern evangelicals can no longer define their identity in terms of doctrines they hold in common because the movement has become fragmented doctrinally. The obvious solution would be a return to our common doctrinal roots. Unfortunately, the panacea that is usually offered instead is an appeal to soften our doctrinal stance and unite on the basis of common *experiences*. This may be the most serious assault on truth evangelicalism has ever faced, because it comes from within the movement and has met with little resistance.

Lest anyone misunderstand, I am by no means appealing for doctrine divorced from experience, or truth apart from love. That would be worthless. The apostle James said it this way: "Just as the body without the spirit is dead, so also faith without works is dead" (2:26). Truth genuinely believed is truth acted upon. Real faith *always* results in lively experience, and this frequently involves deep emotion. I am wholly in favor of those things. But genuine experience and legitimate emotions always come *in response to truth*; truth must never become the slave of sheer emotion or unintelligible experiences.

At least that is the position evangelicalism has always taken. Are we prepared to abandon that conviction? Shall we now exalt experience at the expense of sound doctrine? Will we allow emotion to run roughshod over truth? Will evangelicalism be swept away with unbridled passion?

Unfortunately, those things are already happening by default. Sound doctrine and biblical truth are practically missing from evangelical pulpits. They have been replaced by show business, pop psychology, partisan politics, motivational talks, and even comedy. Many pastors and church leaders are woefully ill-equipped to teach doctrine and Scripture. The love of sound doctrine that has always been a distinguishing characteristic of evangelicalism has all but disappeared.

Add a dose of mysticism to this mix and you have the recipe for unmitigated spiritual disaster. People begin seeking spiritual experiences in everything *except* the objective truth of Scripture. Sheer emotion begins to replace any sensible understanding of truth. Anyone who dares voice doctrinal concerns is likely to be labeled legalistic (or worse). More and more people are therefore encouraged to seek God through emotional experiences practically divorced from truth. They eventually get caught in an endless cycle where in order to maintain the emotional high, each experience must be more spectacular than the previous one.

FEELING GOOD, THINKING NOTHING

A classic example of this trend is the much-publicized "laughing revival" that broke out in early 1994 and has been the subject of widespread attention in both the secular and Christian press. *Time* magazine described the scene in a formerly staid Anglican church:

> The youthful throng buzzes with anticipation more common at a rock concert or rugby match. After the usual Scripture readings, prayers and singing, the chairs are cleared away. [The curate] prays that the Holy Spirit will come upon the congregation. Soon a woman begins laughing. Others gradually join her with hearty belly laughs. A young worshiper falls to the floor, hands twitching. Another falls, then another and another. Within half an hour there are bodies everywhere as supplicants sob, shake, roar like lions and, strangest of all, laugh uncontrollably.[2]

This is pure mysticism, rooted in feeling but devoid of any cognitive element. The worshiper sees the mystical "emotive event" divorced from any objective truth as an encounter with God.

The "laughing revival" began in January of 1994 at the Airport Vineyard in Toronto. That church has become a Mecca for seekers of mystical experiences, with thousands making pilgrimages to witness the phenomenon firsthand. Crowds in excess of a thousand people gather nightly for meetings where paroxysms of laughter constitute the order of service. An article in *Charisma* reports, "On a typical evening, dozens of people can be found lying or rolling around on the floor, many of them laughing uncontrollably."[3] One pastor associated with the movement "described it as a 'party with the Lord' because he often has to preach to people who are rolling on the floor and laughing hysterically. The meetings often extend until 3 A.M."[4]

From Toronto the "holy laughter" has been carried around the world.

The *Charisma* article includes an account that perfectly illustrates reckless faith at work. It describes the spiritual journey of Randy Clark, a Vineyard pastor from St. Louis, who was one of the men instrumental in starting the movement:

> Clark, a former Baptist minister, was a candidate for renewal six months ago because he was so discouraged. "I felt empty, power-less and so little anointed," he told *Charisma*. "Emotionally, spiritually and physically I knew I was burning out."
>
> Last summer, however, hope was rekindled after he talked with an associate who had just returned from a conference led by

South African evangelist Rodney Howard-Browne. Clark's friend talked to him for hours about how he had been spiritually revived during the meeting.

"What my friend was describing—people shaking, falling, laughing—was what I'd seen many years earlier in the Vineyard revivals," Clark said. "I knew this was what I needed."

To Clark's disappointment, he learned that Howard-Browne's next meetings were to be held at Kenneth Hagin, Jr.'s Rhema Bible Church in Tulsa, Okla.—a church Clark opposed because of theological differences. Then Clark sensed the Lord was reproving him for his smug attitude.

Said Clark: "The Lord spoke to me immediately, and said, 'You have a denominational spirit. How badly do you want to be touched afresh?'"

Clark attended the meetings at Rhema Church and received prayer for a fresh infilling of the Holy Spirit. When he returned to St. Louis, unusual things began to happen in his church services.

One person, he said, fell on the floor after being overwhelmed by the presence of the Holy Spirit. "That had never happened in my church," he noted.

As similar manifestations continued, Clark began to desire reconciliation with Rhema Church leaders and leaders of other churches he had opposed. "I still didn't agree with some of what they taught, but I saw how sacrificially they worked at their college, and I saw their love for Jesus," he said. "The Lord said to me, 'Look how much they love me.'"[5]

It is important to understand that Rhema Bible Church in Tulsa is the flagship church of the Word Faith movement, and Kenneth Hagin, Sr. is its spiritual father. The errors of this movement are far more serious than denominational preferences; they are fallacies that corrupt the very heart of the Gospel and mangle the doctrine of Christ. These errors are well documented—and even many charismatic leaders regard them as serious heresy.[6] So the "theological differences" Randy Clark was willing to overlook for the sake of the experience he was seeking are no mere trifles.

Note that it was not a rational understanding of any truth, but the *phenomena*—"people shaking, falling, laughing"—that convinced Clark "this was what [he] needed." Clark's own testimony indicates that he purposefully closed his mind to rational truth in order to receive the "blessing" he sought. So hungry was he for the mystical experience that he became willing to lay aside legitimate, fundamental, theological concerns. In fact, he was actually convinced that the Lord was requiring him to close his mind to these doctrinal objections before He would touch him afresh.

Clark even states that he still does not agree with Word Faith doctrine, but he has evidently now concluded that such doctrinal differences are unimportant. Shared experiences, good feelings, and spectacular phenomena have become more important to him than unity in truth. He rationalizes his new perspective by noting that Word Faith teachers labor sacrificially and seem to love Jesus. Of course, many cults whose doctrine is far worse than the Word Faith movement also work sacrificially and profess to love Christ. "Loving Jesus" means nothing if one's Christology is seriously perverted—and that is precisely the issue with Word Faith doctrine.

But the laughing revival is simply not concerned with doctrinal issues. It has already crossed all denominational boundaries from the most formal high-church Anglicanism to the most outlandish charismatic sects. And it has done so precisely because it has nothing whatever to do with objective truth. It is all about sensation, emotion, and feeling good. Thousands have concluded that something that feels so good cannot possibly be wrong.

Hysterical laughter totally divorced from any rational thinking may in fact be the most profound religious experience pure mysticism can produce.

It would seem fair to question the validity of a movement whose most visible fruits are meetings marked by hysterical laughter, and a tendency to downplay sound doctrine. But advocates of the laughing revival usually condemn any such attempts at discernment as censorious and pharisaical.

A Christian newspaper in New Zealand recently ran a front-page news item on the "holy laughter," and a couple of readers wrote the paper to suggest that the phenomena sounded suspicious. In the next issue, at least two-thirds of the letters to the editor were about the laughing revival. *Every one of them* chided readers who dared question whether the laughter was a work of God. Here are some excerpts:

- Christians who have written . . . expressing adverse comments about the record of the happenings in Toronto and England need to take warning as they may be grieving the Holy Spirit.

- In New Zealand we have not known revival on any great scale; therefore [critics] need to take warning unless we stop what God wishes to do.

- Be careful please of judging. It's dangerous ground to walk on. Is it honestly possible to use our carnal minds to try and understand things of the Spirit of God?

- Too many judge from the written word rather than from personal witnessing. . . . May God soften the readers' hearts to respond to His reviving in whatever form it comes.[7]

Presumably the reader who complained that too many people "judge from the written word" was referring to people who evaluate things on the basis of newspaper accounts instead of what they have personally witnessed. We can only hope she was not suggesting that people rely too much on Scripture rather than personal experience.

But notice the thrust of all those letters. They appeal to readers *not* to be discerning. "Be careful . . . of judging. It's dangerous ground to walk on"? As we saw in chapter 3, when Paul commanded the Thessalonians to "examine everything carefully; hold fast to that which is good" (1 Thess. 5:21), this is precisely the kind of judgment he was ordering them to exercise. Far from being "dangerous ground," such discernment is the only *safe* ground for true Christians.

Is there really a risk that being overly discerning might grieve the Holy Spirit? Scripture never indicates that the Holy Spirit wants us to close our minds to objective truth and blindly accept sensational phenomena as proof that He is at work. Quite the opposite is true. We're commanded to examine such things with extreme care. To fail to do so is the essence of reckless faith.

QUENCHING THE SPIRIT?

Defenders of phenomena such as "holy laughter" frequently admonish critics that they are in danger of grieving, quenching, or worst of all, blaspheming the Holy Spirit. Often this is nothing more than a form of spiritual intimidation. But it usually proves quite effective, silencing the voice of reason and absolving the promoters of mystical phenomena from any responsibility to give a sound biblical basis for what they are doing.

Notice, however, that all the stern warnings against quenching the Spirit constitute a very obvious circular argument. They assume from the outset the very point they wish to establish—that these phenomena are the work of the Holy Spirit. This is the essence of the argument: if things happen we cannot explain or find a basis for in Scripture, we dare not question or challenge them. Such phenomena are *de facto* proof that the Holy Spirit is working. Thus sheer mysticism is equated with the moving of the Holy Spirit. Any discerning souls who attempt to "examine everything carefully" in accord with 1 Thessalonians 5:21 are warned that they are sinning against the Holy Spirit.

One of the fullest efforts to defend this perspective is a book by William DeArteaga titled *Quenching the Spirit*.[8] The blurb on the book's cover reads, "Examining Centuries of Opposition to the Moving of the Holy Spirit." DeArteaga is convinced that all who oppose modern charismatic phenomena are simply latter-day Pharisees—and he implies that some may have already committed the unpardonable sin.[9]

Pharisaism becomes the metaphor for all that DeArteaga opposes. His appraisal of the Pharisees is revealing:

The Pharisees' real problem came from two sources. First, they drastically overvalued the role of theology in spiritual life and made theological correctness the chief religious virtue. Somewhere in the process the primary command to love God and mankind was subordinated to correct theology. Second, they had a man-given confidence in their theological traditions as being the perfect interpretation of Scripture. They falsely placed their theology, referred to as the traditions of the elders, on the same level as Scripture.[10]

Notice that DeArteaga's portrayal of pharisaism amounts to a not-so-subtle attack on theology—especially "theological correctness." He implies that love for God is somehow in conflict with a concern for correct theology. He even pits sound theology against Scripture, suggesting that those concerned with "theological correctness" are guilty of placing their theology on the same level as Scripture.

But those are false dichotomies. Real love for God is inseparable from love of the truth. The heart that genuinely loves God will be inclined to truth (see 2 Thess. 2:10; 2 John 6). And true theological correctness is found only in an accurate understanding of Scripture (1 Tim. 6:3-4; Titus 1:9). Those determined to cast sound theology aside must also abandon Scripture (2 Tim. 4:2-3). Scripture and sound theology are not antithetical; they are indissolubly bound together. One simply cannot esteem Scripture highly yet scorn sound doctrine. One cannot love God and remain indifferent to His truth. Scripture is how He makes Himself known. So a sound understanding of Scripture is essential to a true knowledge of God.

Moreover, DeArteaga completely misunderstands the Pharisees. As we saw in chapter 2, the Pharisees were in no sense guilty of an undue emphasis on theological orthodoxy. If anything, their problem was the opposite. They weren't careful *enough* in seeking to understand the Scriptures. In fact, they set Scripture aside in favor of their own rote traditions. *Tradition*, not *theology*, was their downfall. If they had stuck to Scripture and built their theology on that alone, they would not have fallen into error. Jesus confronted the Pharisees for their pride, their spiritual blindness, their legalism, their want of compassion, their love of power and recognition, and their lack of knowledge about the Word of God. At no time did He rebuke them for overemphasizing "theological correctness."

DeArteaga's book is a freewheeling romp through revisionist history. For example, he uses the Great Awakening as a model to show how "theological correctness" poses a threat to the working of the Holy Spirit. This argument is worth examining more closely, because the Great Awakening is becoming a favorite paradigm for modern-day mystics.[11]

A LOOK AT THE GREAT AWAKENING

The Great Awakening was a dramatic revival that began in New England in the mid-eighteenth century and swept the colonies before it finally subsided. Multitudes were converted in the Awakening, and the spiritual climate of colonial America was transformed. Even in secular history books, the Great Awakening is treated as one of the most significant events in early American history.

Signs of revival first appeared in New Jersey among Dutch Reformed congregations as early as 1726. A few years later a young but already well-known Massachusetts pastor named Jonathan Edwards began to see a remarkable increase in the number of conversions among his flock. In 1736 Edwards published his first work on the revival, *A Narrative of Surprising Conversions*.[12] He could not have known then that the conversions he was witnessing in his own parish were the first stirrings of the greatest revival in American history. Moreover, Edwards himself, along with English evangelist and open-air preacher George Whitefield, would be the chief human instruments God used to bring the movement to full fruition in the 1740s. By the time it was over, virtually every community in the colonies had been touched by the revival. Everywhere the Awakening went, it was marked by strong preaching, a resurgence of sound doctrine, a distinct emphasis on justification by faith, powerful conviction of sin, immediate conversions, and dramatically changed lives.

But another significant mark of the revival was the potent emotional response it generated. Some people responded to the preaching with intense physical reactions—fainting, trembling, crying out, and shock. Those phenomena occasionally gave way to even more extraordinary manifestations—jumping, twitching, dancing, ecstasies, trances, visions, and even uncontrolled laughter.

Obviously there are some rather remarkable parallels between the phenomena that occurred in the Great Awakening and what is happening today. This fact has not escaped advocates of the laughing revival. Gerald Coates, a British charismatic leader, writes,

> Those who have studied Whitefield and Wesley, Jonathan Edwards and other revivalists will know that it is precisely this phenomena ["laughter and tears and people's strength failing them" as seen in the Toronto movement] which took place [during the Great Awakening] in worship, through testimonies and the preaching of the gospel. These things are not new and marked very many (though not every) [sic] revivals.[13]

Since Jonathan Edwards was the most outspoken defender of the Great Awakening, many modern charismatics hope to enlist Edwards as an apologist for their cause. William DeArteaga, for example, is convinced that "Edwards would have relished [the faith-cure] movement," and that "Edwards would rejoice in the way Jesus is unabashedly praised and worshiped within the charismatic community."[14]

Edwards, who is arguably the greatest theologian and most profound thinker America has ever produced, would certainly serve as a formidable ally for the movement.

But would Edwards defend today's laughing revival as a true work of God? He left several volumes that make his opinions on these matters quite clear. The historical facts actually suggest he would be appalled by the movement. He would almost certainly label it fanaticism. Why do so many promoters of mystical phenomena believe he would be sympathetic to their cause?

First of all, Edwards wrote to defend the Great Awakening as a true revival. And he wrote in response to a wave of severe attacks that focused largely on the movement's emotional excesses. Edwards's nemesis in the days of the Great Awakening was Charles Chauncy, pastor of Boston's First Church. Chauncy became the most outspoken opponent of the Awakening, while Edwards was its most articulate defender.

DeArteaga's thesis is that opposition killed the Great Awakening. He claims that "consensus orthodoxy"—the prevailing doctrinal opinions in New England—grieved the Holy Spirit because men like

Chauncy could not tolerate the displays of emotion that went with the revival.

And, oddly, the chief theological villain of DeArteaga's account is *Calvinism*—the belief that God is sovereign in the salvation of sinners. *Arminianism*—the teaching that the human will ultimately determines whether a person is saved or lost—is portrayed by DeArteaga as a benign but often misunderstood refinement of evangelical theology. In DeArteaga's assessment, "pure Calvinist theology could not interpret the spiritual experiences that were to accompany the Great Awakening."[15] And so, DeArteaga summarizes, "using the assumptions of Calvinist theology," Charles Chauncy "ensured the defeat of the Awakening."[16]

One or two rather significant historical details render that thesis altogether untenable. The facts are that Chauncy leaned toward Arminianism and ultimately helped found Unitarianism[17]—while Jonathan Edwards remained a staunch Calvinist all his life. Moreover, the other towering figure in the Great Awakening, George Whitefield, was also a committed Calvinist.

The "consensus theology" of that day was, in fact, Arminian. In the thirty years before the Awakening, Calvinism was in serious decline. Edwards and Whitefield were perceived as theological dinosaurs by most of their contemporaries because they held to the old theology.[18] They brilliantly defended Calvinism against attacks from men like Chauncy. Their preaching of the Calvinist doctrines of human depravity and divine sovereignty were the very thing that sparked the Awakening. Edwards recorded this:

In some, even the view of the glory of God's sovereignty, in the exercises of his grace, has surprised the soul with such sweetness, as to produce [weeping, joy, and crying out.] I remember an instance of one, who, reading something concerning God's *sovereign* way of saving sinners, as being self-moved—having no regard to men's *own righteousness* as the motive of his grace, but as magnifying himself and abasing man, or to that purpose—felt such a sudden rapture of joy and delight in the consideration of it.[19]

Far from posing a threat to the Great Awakening, Calvinist doctrine was at the heart of the movement.

None of that matters to DeArteaga. Nowhere in his book does he even acknowledge that Edwards was a Calvinist or that the Awakening was prompted by the preaching of doctrines precious to Calvinists. He simply recounts the Great Awakening with his own revisionist slant. Throughout the book, Calvinist theology remains DeArteaga's favorite bogeyman, the epitome of latter-day pharisaism.[20] But the Calvinism he attacks is a caricature, exaggerated to make an easy target. He suggests, for example, that Calvin's view of God "is closer to the concept of God depicted in the Koran, all sovereign yet ruling the universe capriciously"[21]— an altogether untrue and unfair way to represent the Calvinist conception of God's sovereignty. Citing Catholic historian Haire Belloc as his authority, DeArteaga even blames Calvinism for Europe's spiritual decline[22]—a view impartial historians would roundly reject.

And, of course, according to DeArteaga, Calvinist theology was responsible for the demise of the Great Awakening[23]—an assertion that utterly disregards the facts of history.

No one was in a better position to evaluate the Great Awakening than Jonathan Edwards. He watched it firsthand from beginning to end. He personally witnessed the remarkable emotional and physical responses in congregations where he preached. He defended the Awakening when critics denounced it as pure hysteria. And when it was over, he carefully analyzed the reasons it died out.

Edwards concluded it was, in fact, the friends of the revival, not its enemies, who were responsible for its death. One biographer of Edwards has written,

> He came to believe that there was one principal cause of the reversal, namely, the unwatchfulness of the friends of the Awakening who allowed genuine and pure religion to become so mixed with "wildfire" and carnal "enthusiasm," that the Spirit of God was grieved and advantage given to Satan.[24]

Edwards, even while defending the Awakening against its critics, had long acknowledged that a strain of fanaticism was undermining the true work of God in the revival. In *The Distinguishing Marks of a Work of the Spirit of God*, written in 1741 at the height of the revival, Edwards acknowledged that "imprudences, irregularities, and [a] mixture of delusion" had attached themselves to the movement. He attributed these things to "chiefly young persons . . . who have less steadiness and experience, [who] being in the heat of youth are much more ready to run to extremes."[25] He saw runaway passions as the work of the devil, who tries to keep people apathetic as long as possible, then when he is no longer able to do that, "endeavours to drive them to extremes, and so to dishonour God."[26]

Soon after Edwards wrote those words, in the summer of 1741, the first recorded outbreaks of faintings, shakings, and outcries began.[27] The phenomena grew more pronounced as people began to associate the Spirit's work with the bizarre sensations. Iain Murray writes that some observers

> began to encourage the idea that the greater the outcries and commotion, the more glorious was the evidence of God's power, and once this idea was accepted the door was open to all manner of excess. . . . Far from attempting to restrain themselves, people sometimes willfully gave way to sheer emotion.[28]

At this point division crept into the revival. Many who were swept up in the emotion and excitement of the phenomena began to distrust any voice of caution. Pastors who warned that mere noise and excitement were no proof of the Spirit's working often found themselves the targets of a backlash. Wise words of friendly caution were discarded as if they were hostile criticism. Godly pastors who raised the concerns were even labeled unconverted. A fanatical element began to commandeer the Awakening. One author noted "the rapid progress of a spurious religion, under the guidance of pride, ignorance, and spiritual quackery."[29]

Iain Murray concludes,

Without question, the rise of the fanatical element coincided with the decline of the spiritual power of the Awakening. *Those who spoke most loudly of being led by the Spirit were the very persons responsible for quenching the Spirit's work.* . . . For Edwards the turning point in the revival came when men . . . failed to guard against excesses.[30]

In his biography of David Brainerd, Edwards gave his own assessment of the revival's failure:

> An intemperate imprudent zeal, and a degree of [fleshly] enthusiasm soon crept in, and mingled itself with that revival of religion; and so great and general an awakening being quite a new thing in the land, at least as to all the living inhabitants of it; neither people nor ministers had learned thoroughly to distinguish between solid religion and its delusive counterfeits; even many ministers of the Gospel, of long standing and the best reputation, were for a time overpowered with the glaring appearances of the latter.[31]

Clearly Jonathan Edwards believed the Great Awakening was quenched not by concerns for "theological correctness" but by spiritual extremism that was tolerated and even encouraged by the revival's most enthusiastic supporters. The unbridled emotional excesses, far from being the supreme spiritual achievement of the revival, were the very thing that killed it. It was fanaticism, not pharisaism, that ended the Great Awakening.

William DeArteaga is aware of but refuses to accept Edwards's conclusion. Against all the historical evidence, DeArteaga insists that "doctrinal correctness" led to the demise of the revival:

> In spite of Edwards's own theories, it seems that the Great Awakening was not quenched because of its extremists. It was quenched because of the condemnation of its opponents. This condemnation demoralized the supporters and marred the faith of the public to the point where they no longer welcomed the presence of the Spirit.[32]

Oddly enough, at this point in DeArteaga's book, he speaks of the need for discernment. He concludes that "Edwards was at a tremendous disadvantage [because] he had no readily available theology of discernment." In fact, according to DeArteaga, "the Reformers rejected the need for discernment when they threw out the whole of Catholic mystical theology."[33]

This astonishing interpretation of church history must not be allowed to go unchallenged. In the first place, Edwards *did* have a very clear-cut "theology of discernment." This is evident from the clarity of his work *The Distinguishing Marks of a Work of the Spirit of God* (see Appendix 2). DeArteaga would do well to apply Edwards's prescription for discernment to many of the ideas he defends in his book, including Word Faith theology, visualization techniques, and Catholic mysticism.

In the second place, what DeArteaga means when he speaks of "a theology of discernment" is not altogether clear. Apparently he is suggesting that objective criteria of truth (Scripture and sound theology) should be laid aside in favor of a purely mystical approach to discernment. "Discernment" in DeArteaga's scheme seems to be nothing more than intuition—a sanctified gut reaction.

He writes, "Although discernment is principally a spiritual [DeArteaga equates this with *mystical*] function, it is based on certain biblical principles which must be taught publicly." What principles these are and how they differ from "theological correctness" DeArteaga does not attempt to explain. He continues, "In its most basic form such a theology must accept that the Holy Spirit can operate in the current age and that the Holy Spirit's operations can be discerned from the surrounding noise of psychic and demonic interference."[34]

I certainly believe that the Holy Spirit operates today and that His operations are distinguishable from psychic and demonic noise. Edwards believed that too. But in DeArteaga's assessment, neither Edwards nor I have any "theology of discernment."[35] So what does DeArteaga mean by this statement?

What he actually seems to be saying (indeed, it is the main message of the book) is that objective truth *cannot* be the standard by which we discern between what is true and what is false spiritually. Discernment in DeArteaga's scheme is a mystical ability. It begins when we "accept that the Holy Spirit can operate in the current age"—and by this DeArteaga seems to mean that we must accept mystical phenomena as the work of the Spirit. Then the Spirit-filled individual is supposed to be able to tell instinctively whether unusual phenomena are truly the work of the Holy Spirit. Since "theological correctness" is *a priori* ruled out as a standard for discernment, we must assume that the criteria for discerning are predominately subjective. The front-to-back message of DeArteaga's book affirms that this is in fact what he means.

But that isn't a theology of discernment; it is a sure road to spiritual confusion. As we have seen repeatedly, discernment is related to wisdom. It is a function of the biblically informed and Spirit-taught intellect. It is not a feeling or a "sixth sense." Discernment is utterly dependent on a right understanding of Scripture—"theological correctness" in William DeArteaga's terminology. But having attacked all that as pharisaism, he has ruled out true discernment.

GOD IN THE HANDS OF GIDDY SINNERS

Those who focus on the emotional phenomena of the Great Awakening are likely to miss the real import of that revival. It was a movement based on strong preaching and sound theology. Far from challenging orthodox theology, it reestablished the Puritan heritage of Calvinist orthodoxy and put a halt (at least temporarily) to the serious erosion of doctrinal clarity that was the hallmark of the age. The emotional displays began in *response* to the clear preaching of God's Word.

Edwards, Whitefield, and all the other leading preachers of that era were known for the vividness and directness of their preaching. When they applied their plainness of speech, graphic imagery, and logical precision to the truths of Scripture—all under the Holy Spirit's sovereign power—the impact on audiences was dramatic.

One of the earliest recorded incidents of congregational outcries, swooning, and weeping happened during the Sunday evening worship service at Enfield, Connecticut, July 8, 1741. Jonathan Edwards was the visiting preacher, and the text he preached from was Deuteronomy 32:35: "Vengeance is Mine, and retribution, in due time their foot will slip; for the day of their calamity is near, and the impending things are hastening upon them." Edwards's sermon that night has become the message for which he is most famous: "Sinners in the Hands of an Angry God." Anyone who has ever read the text of that sermon knows it is as far from the don't-worry-be-happy spirit of our age as it is possible to get.

Steven Williams attended the service that night. He recorded the event in his diary:

> We went over to Enfield, where we met dear Mr. Edwards of New Haven, who preached a most awakening sermon from these words—Deut. 32:35. And before the sermon was done, there was a great moaning and crying out through the whole house—"What shall I do to be saved?"; "Oh, I am going to hell!"; "Oh, what shall I do for Christ?" etc. So that the minister was obliged to desist. The shrieks and cries were piercing and amazing. After some time of waiting, the congregation were still, so that a prayer was made by Mr. W. And after that we descended from the pulpit and discoursed with the people, some in one place and some in another. And amazing and astonishing the power of God was seen, and several souls were hopefully wrought upon that night. And oh, the cheerfulness and pleasantness of their countenances that received comfort. Oh that God would strengthen and confirm! We sang a hymn and prayed and dismissed the assembly.[36]

Such emotional outbursts in the Great Awakening invariably happened in response to the messages preached. There were no random or irrational eruptions of raw passion. If there was weeping, it was provoked by genuine sorrow. If there was wailing, it reflected real terror of the Lord. If there was laughter, it was the expression of a joyful heart, not just empty, spontaneous hysterics.

At least that was the case until fanaticism seized the movement.

Clearly, from the Great Awakening to the laughing revival is a quantum leap. The difference between the two movements is so pronounced that it has been noticed even by secular observers. A London newspaper wrote,

> The difference between the present movement and the revivals of the 18th century is that the latter were characterised by powerful preaching, a strong sense of self-loathing and of repentance, none of which is a feature of the Toronto Blessing or the charismatic movement from which it came.[37]

A Christian newspaper in England made a similar observation:

> People are likening these things to those seen in Whitefield's day, but the comparison seems hardly fitting as his followed the preaching of the Word when these seem to follow little more than a very shallow summary of "what we saw in Toronto."[38]

Now contrast Steven Williams's firsthand record of the Enfield incident with this eyewitness account of the laughing revival:

> A lady wearing a dress is lying down on the ground seemingly writhing in agony and screaming. A man with a thick accent in a dark suit is standing over her barking orders while a crowd of people stand all around laughing. The lady appears to be possessed by a demon because her body jumps off the floor in an unnatural way. The man pushes her back down ordering her to "stay down" and "Let it bubble out your belly!" A woman with an armful of airline blankets covers her thighs to hide the view of her undergarments.
>
> The lady continues to flop up and down for several minutes screaming hysterically. She shouts "Dear Jesus" and the man orders her not to pray but to submit to the power. She puts her hands over her face and continues laughing uncontrollably and the man proclaims "There it is! Now you got it." The audience jumps up and down applauding while the man shouts "The bar is open. The bar is open. Drink deeply! Get drunk on the spirit!"[39]

Surely this is a far cry from "Sinners in the Hands of an Angry God."

Now God is in the hands of a giddy mob—or so the mob thinks. It is reminiscent of the scene at the foot of Sinai where the Israelites danced around a god of their own making (Ex. 32).

GOD IS NOT THE AUTHOR OF CONFUSION

A close friend of mine recently attended a service at a large church of international renown where the laughing revival had been going on for several weeks. After a brief, perfunctory sermon with a minimum of references to Scripture and a lot of mangled theology, the worship leader called everyone to the front who wanted to experience the power of God. The scene that followed was utter chaos—dozens of people writhing on the floor, moaning, screaming, and jerking, while "ministry team" members coached them through the stages of the various phenomena. Other people were dancing, jumping, quivering, sobbing, wailing, and running in place.

All the commotion was there, but the laughter had subsided. The revival's chief characteristic is supposedly joy, but my friend noticed that people's faces were virtually devoid of expression. No one was laughing anymore. It was as if they were emotionally exhausted, unable to fan the fervor to the same intensity week after week. Instead of true, abiding joy, they had settled for sheer bedlam—in direct defiance of Paul's instructions in 1 Corinthians 14:40: "Let all things be done properly and in an orderly manner."

The apostle Paul was very clear in pointing out that "God is not a God of confusion" (1 Cor. 14:33). Where pandemonium rules, we can be certain God is not the author of it.

Unfortunately, the truth of Scripture is too often set aside in pursuit of the emotional high of a mystical experience. At this same worship service, the pastor admonished people that they needed to be "more free." He suggested that too much concern about sound doctrine might inhibit what God could do in their lives. He told them they shouldn't be afraid to break out of the constraints of their belief systems and "let God work in His own way, even if it challenges your theology." At one point in the service a woman from the church staff led the congregation in prayer and said, "Holy Spirit, we give You permission to be who You want to be in our midst."[40]

The effrontery of such an attitude is appalling. The Holy Spirit is sovereign God! He certainly doesn't need *our* permission to be who He is. He can do whatever He wills. But He will not deny Himself. He will not mystically reveal Himself to us as someone different from the holy God the Scriptures reveal. Since the Bible tells us He is not the author of confusion—and specifically that He does not approve of disorder in the churches—we can know with absolute certainty that He is not the power behind a movement whose *main features* are hysteria, tumult, and frenzy.

More important, the Scriptures reveal Him as the Spirit of *truth* (John 14:17); who bears witness not of Himself but of Christ (15:26); who speaks not on His own initiative, but guides us into all truth (16:13); and sanctifies us in the truth. Where is this sanctifying truth found? Not through mystical means. God's Word is the truth through which we are sanctified (17:17). This means that one of the Holy Spirit's primary ministries is to convey the truth of Scripture to our understanding. Nothing in Scripture indicates that He works by stirring up our emotions while bypassing our minds.

That is, after all, the whole point of 1 Corinthians 14. It is why Paul valued prophecy more than tongues. "For one who speaks in a tongue does not speak to men, but to God; for no one *understands*. . . . But one who prophesies speaks to men for *edification* and exhortation and consolation" (vv. 2-3, emphasis added). "If I come to you speaking in tongues, what shall I profit you, unless I speak to you either by way of revelation or of knowledge or of prophecy or of teaching?" (v. 6). The point is to communicate *truth*. Ministry that bypasses the understanding is pointless: "If the bugle produces an indistinct sound, who will prepare himself for battle?" (v. 8). All the gifts are meant to *edify*, which is an expression Paul uses to speak of ministering to the *mind* (v. 3). That is why Paul insisted that tongues be interpreted. "So also you, since you are zealous of spiritual gifts, seek to abound for the *edification* of the church" (v. 12, emphasis added).

It is for this very reason that Jonathan Edwards distinguished between the *affections* and the *passions*. He argued that righteous affections engage the faculties of the mind and will; whereas mere passions tend to overpower the mind.[41] *Love to Christ* and *joy in Christ* are biblical examples of godly affections that are no mere passions—because they always involve the mind as well as the emotions.[42] Edwards saw little spiritual value in indulging in raw emotion while the intellect remained neutral. In reference to 1 Peter 1:8, for example, Edwards wrote,

> Their joy was "full of glory": although the joy was unspeakable, and no words sufficient to describe it; yet something might be said of it, and no words more fit to represent its excellency, than these, that it was "full of glory"; or as it is in the original, "glorified joy." In rejoicing with this joy, *their minds were filled*, as it were, with a glorious brightness, and their natures exalted and perfected: *it was a most worthy, noble rejoicing, that did not corrupt and debase the mind*, as many carnal joys do; but did greatly beautify and dignify it: it was a prelibation of the joy of heaven, that *raised their minds* to a degree of heavenly blessedness: *it filled their minds* with the light of God's glory, and made 'em themselves to shine with some communication of that glory.[43]

Edwards continually tied the nobility of true religious affections to the working of the *mind*. Having witnessed so much of people's runaway passions at the end of the Great Awakening, he wanted nothing to do with that sort of thing.

So it should be quite clear what Jonathan Edwards would think of twentieth-century emotionalism. "Holy laughter" epitomizes the fanaticism he blamed for the demise of the Great Awakening. He insisted that the mind must be active in all legitimate religious affections. There is no way he can be enlisted as an apologist for modern mysticism.

When the laughing revival has run its course, what will be next? How can a movement stoked by the heat of raw passion rekindle the flames when people's emotions finally grow cold?

Those who really know Christ and love Him must come back to

His Word with a passion for interpreting it correctly and *understanding* its truths. The tragedy is that thousands swept up in the emotionalism of the movement have never been exposed to enough objective truth and sound doctrine to come to a saving knowledge of the Christ of Scripture. The christ they worship is a figment of their imagination. So inevitably, their imagination is where they will turn when they want to hear Him speak. That tendency has given rise to the flood of private prophecies that we will examine in the next chapter.

7

Looking for Truth in All the Wrong Places

J AMES RYLE SAYS he awoke from a strange dream one night and heard the Lord tell him, "I am about to do a strange, new thing in My church. It will be like a man bringing a hippopotamus into his garden. Think about that."[1]

Ryle did think about it and concluded God was telling him He was going to "[return] the power of His prophetic word by His Holy Spirit into churches that (presumptuously) no longer have any place for it."[2] Ryle adds this: "Not only is the hippo in the garden the unusual thing God will do prophetically *within* His church, but it also heralds His release of a prophetic voice into the world *through* His church, bringing in a great last-days harvest." Ryle quotes Acts 2:17-21 and then says, "A vast prophetic movement inspired by the Holy Spirit within the church in the midst of the world resulting in an evangelistic ingathering—that is the 'hippo in the garden.'"[3]

In other words, Ryle says the spirit of prophecy will come like a lumbering beast upon the whole church, making revelatory prophecy commonplace and ushering in a new wave of revival. When this happens it will seem as unlikely and out of place—and disruptive—as a man taking a hippo for a walk in a neatly manicured garden. Ryle is convinced God gave him this prophecy.

Ryle, pastor of Boulder Valley Vineyard Fellowship in Boulder, Colorado, is no stranger to dreams and visions. A few years ago Ryle said the Lord revealed to him in a dream the secret of the Beatles' success: they received a special anointing from God. According to Ryle, God told him, "they were gifted by My hand; and it was I who anointed them, for I had a purpose, and the purpose was to usher in the Charismatic renewal with musical revival around the world."

Unfortunately, John, Paul, George, and Ringo squandered the sacred anointing on fame and riches. "The four lads . . . went AWOL and did not serve in My army"—Ryle says he heard God say. "They served their own purposes and gave the gift to the other side." According to Ryle, the Lord's plan was thwarted, so He withdrew the anointing in 1970. Ryle says God has told him He is about to release that same anointing again. This time He plans to use *Christian* musicians.[4] Thousands listen breathlessly as Ryle recounts his prophetic message.

Ryle regularly has dreams, sees visions, and hears messages he insists come from God. "I dreamed I was literally inside the Lord," he writes of one such incident. "I had the ability to look through His eyes and to see what He was seeing—without being seen."[5] Ryle recounts these dreams and visions with remarkably detailed interpretations. He is thoroughly convinced they all contain prophetic truth from the Lord.

Ryle does not claim to be unique. He believes all Christians who will listen can hear the voice of God through dreams, visions, and personal prophecies. "God will speak to us as He spoke to Jesus," he declares.[6] "We are not merely to look back and sigh at how wonderful it must have been to hear God's voice and be led by His Spirit. No! God speaks to us today."[7] Elsewhere he writes, "God is a supernatural being and surely speaks through supernatural means. I refer to the audible voice of God, divine manifestations of His presence, angelic encounters and similar phenomena."[8] According to Ryle, all those phenomena are supposed to be happening today—and *will* happen to anyone who is receptive enough.

Ryle believes the Bible is the infallible record of God's *past* speaking, but he doesn't seem to believe the Bible alone is a sufficient word from God for *today*.[9] He suggests that believers who do not listen for fresh words from God daily are missing an important source of spiritual sustenance:

> Jesus taught us to pray that our Father would give us each day our daily bread. Since He declared that man should not live on bread alone but on every word that comes from the mouth of God, doesn't this imply that He wants us to hear His voice every day of our lives? I think so.[10]

Ryle even offers some hermeneutical principles for dream interpretation: "Be committed to researching the symbols and sayings of the revelations given. . . . Don't ever force an interpretation, trying to make it fit a predetermined opinion or desire," and so on.[11] Good advice for people studying Scripture. But are we supposed to exegete our dreams that way?

Ryle says yes. He tells his readers, "There is absolutely no doubt in my mind that God still speaks audibly to His people today. My prayer is that you will hear His voice for yourself; that will be proof enough."[12] Much of his book is filled with instructions for people who want to hear the voice of God.

James Ryle is illustrative of a growing number of pastors and church leaders who claim they receive truth directly from God. Ryle is perceived by many as something of an expert in this type of "revelation." His teaching is peppered with "truths" drawn not from the Scriptures but from his own dreams and visions. The Beatles' anointing, the hippo in the garden, a pig on a billboard, a rhino in a field, visions of Popeye and Olive Oyl, an angel with a vat of acid, dreams about the Colorado Buffalo football team's success—these are the "revelations" about which Ryle writes and preaches. "The Word of God" is much broader to him than Scripture, encompassing his own dreams, visions, words of prophecy, and "personal revelations"—Scripture verses taken out of context and applied like fortune-cookie messages.[13] "The Bible is not an end in itself," he claims; "rather, it is the God-given means to an end."[14]

James Ryle represents a growing movement that is propagating extrabiblical revelations from God as the key to renewal in the church. Thousands of churches worldwide have embraced this new movement. People everywhere are listening for—and believe they can hear—the voice of God.

WHETHER THERE BE PROPHECIES, THEY SHALL FAIL

It is not at all hard to find examples from church history of groups and individuals who believed God was speaking directly to them apart from Scripture. But surely in two thousand years of history the quest for this kind of personal prophecy has never been as widespread and as pervasive as it is today.

Church history also reveals that since the canon of Scripture was closed, virtually every "prophet" who ever spoke a "thus saith the Lord" has been proved wrong, recanted, or gone off track doctrinally. And since the apostolic era, every *movement* that has depended heavily on extrabiblical prophecy has ultimately digressed from the true faith, usually falling into serious corruption or heresy.

This is precisely why the sufficiency of Scripture—*sola Scriptura*—is such a crucial doctrine. If the written Word of God truly is able to give us all the wisdom we need for complete salvation, and if it is able to make us adequate, thoroughly equipped for every good work (2 Tim. 3:15-17)—then is there really any necessity for additional "prophecies" in the life of the believer? Does God need to say more to us than He has already said? This is a question advocates of modern prophetic revelation would do well to ponder carefully.

WHAT MORE CAN HE SAY THAN TO YOU HE HATH SAID?

It seems particularly unfortunate that there would be such an affinity for subjective "revelations" in an era when the average "born-again Christian" is so ignorant of the objective revelation God has given us in the Bible. When knowledge of Scripture is at such an ebb, this is the *worst* possible time for believers to be seeking divine truth in dreams, visions, and subjective impressions.

The quest for additional revelation from God actually denigrates the sufficiency of "the faith which was once for all delivered to the saints" (Jude 3). It implies that God hasn't said enough in the Scriptures. It assumes that we need more truth from God than what we find in His written Word. But as we have repeatedly seen, the Bible itself claims absolute sufficiency to equip us for every good work. If we really embrace that truth, how can we be seeking the voice of God in subjective experiences?

In short, I reject modern revelatory prophecy because the New Testament canon is closed and Scripture is sufficient. Elsewhere I have delved into some of the biblical and theological arguments against continuing revelation.[28] In this context my concerns have to do with reckless faith and the dearth of biblical discernment. Here I am primarily concerned with the extreme subjectivity that is introduced into doctrine and daily life when Christians open the door to private messages from God.

So rather than focusing on theological and biblical reasons for believing that prophecy has ceased, for the remainder of this chapter I want to highlight some of the dangers we face when we treat any kind of subjective impression as if it were a message from God. This is an issue that is vital to the matter of true discernment.

ARE MENTAL IMPRESSIONS DIVINE REVELATION?

Even people who believe prophecy and divine revelation have ceased sometimes fall into the trap of thinking God speaks directly to us through subjective means. You have undoubtedly heard people say things like, "God is calling me to the mission field," or "God led me to attend this college," or "we feel God wants us to get married." (Perhaps you have even said such things yourself.) Christians who use expressions like those often mean they have had an impression or a strong feeling that they interpret as a disclosure of the divine will.

Normally people who make such claims have no intention of

equating their mental impressions with divine revelation. They regard the subjective "leading of the Lord" as something far less than prophetic. Yet they believe God somehow communicates His will personally to individuals through inner promptings, signs, feelings of peace or uneasiness, strong impressions on the mind, or other similar means.

For reasons we shall examine, it is not wise to seek divine guidance through subjective impressions like these. Nowhere does Scripture encourage us to attempt to discern God's will through such means. As we shall see, that sort of decision making can lead to confusion, disappointment, and sometimes spiritual tragedy.

And the truth is that treating subjective impressions as messages from the Holy Spirit is not really much different from claiming to receive divine revelation. Though most Christians who follow subjective impressions would not dream of listening to extrabiblical "prophecies," in effect they are doing the same thing.

In fact, some advocates of modern prophetic revelation want to erase any distinction between subjective impressions and the gift of prophecy mentioned in 1 Corinthians 12–14. Professor Wayne Grudem, for example, who has produced the most thorough teological defense of the modern prophecy movement, believes God is giving revelation today chiefly through mental impressions. He even defines *revelation* as "something God brings to mind."[16] He suggests that when God providentially brings a thought to a believer's mind, that is the New Testament gift of prophecy in operation. Thus he has elevated mental impressions to the level of prophetic revelation.

Grudem's work has had widespread influence. And it is in many respects a fine study. He shows biblically why important distinctions must be made between Old Testament prophecy, apostolic prophecy, and the New Testament gift of prophecy. In places (but not everywhere) his exegesis of the pertinent texts is very helpful. He includes a crucial appendix on the sufficiency of Scripture which, if heeded by his friends in the modern prophecy movement, would provide a remedy against the serious abuses that have so plagued the movement. And he offers another important appendix showing that the canon of Scripture is closed.

But it is at this very point that Grudem's position seems most inconsistent. If the canon of Scripture is really closed; if (as Grudem rightly suggests) "it is in Scripture alone that we are to search for God's words to us";[16] and if, in his words, "the Bible is sufficient to equip us for living the Christian life"[17]—then what point is there in seeking additional "revelations" like the prophetic messages Grudem advocates? It is unfortunate that Grudem relegated his thoughts on the canon of Scripture and the sufficiency of Scripture to the book's final appendixes. If this had been the starting point for his study of prophecy, perhaps he would have reached very different conclusions.

Grudem's defense of prophetic revelation has opened the door to a host of bizarre and misleading "prophecies" that have plagued evangelical Christianity over the past five or six years. Scores of churches worldwide have implemented Grudem's theology and are encouraging people to share mere mental impressions as if they were prophetic messages from God. Ironically, Grudem's work is frequently summoned to defend even the most outlandish aspects of a movement that has utterly ignored his many clear warnings against abuse of the prophetic gifts.

To his credit, Grudem appeals for a view of prophecy that "would still include a strong affirmation of the closing of the New Testament canon (so that no new words of equal authority are given today), of the sufficiency of Scripture, and of the supremacy and unique authority of the Bible in guidance."[18] He writes, "I am asking that charismatics . . . stop calling [prophecy] 'a word from the Lord'—simply because that label makes it sound exactly like the Bible in authority."[19] Elsewhere he writes, "Remember that what is spoken in any prophecy today is not the word of God, but is simply a human being reporting in merely human words something which God has brought to mind."[20] He also warns that modern prophecy

> should not be thought of as "God's very words," nor should the speaker preface his or her remarks with words which would give that impression, such as, "Thus says the Lord," or, "Hear the words of God," etc.—those statements should be reserved for Scripture alone. Something like, "I think the Lord is showing me

that . . ." or, "I think the Lord is indicating that . . ." or, "It seems that the Lord is putting on my heart a concern that . . ." would all be much more appropriate, and far less misleading.[21]

If those warnings were consistently heeded, charismatic "prophets" could save their churches much grief and confusion.

But even in the denomination Grudem himself identifies with—the Association of Vineyard Churches—his words of caution are frequently ignored in the prophets' actual practice.

James Ryle is himself a Vineyard pastor. He does give lip service to Grudem's caution. He writes,

> How often have you heard someone say casually, "The Lord spoke to me," or "The Lord told me" to do this or that?
> . . . Many within the church use these terms to justify their own desires and opinions. Possibly they feel that this puts what they are saying beyond challenge. After all, how does one argue with a "word from the Lord"?
> In light of this problem I have found it a good policy to avoid such expressions and simply say, "It occurred to me" when I am sharing some insight which I've received in prayer or devotions. This removes unnecessary stumbling blocks and allows more people to hear the message without being distracted with the way the word is being presented.[22]

But note the significant difference between Grudem's position and Ryle's. Grudem believes prophecy is merely "something God brought to mind"—not "God's very words." He seems eager to avoid confusion on this point. Ryle's perspective is markedly different. He says he employs terminology like "It occurred to me" to avoid "unnecessary stumbling blocks." But he clearly *does* think of prophecy as *God's very words*. After analyzing the dangers of saying things like "God spoke to me," he states, "Nonetheless, the Lord *does* speak to us today." In practice he cannot avoid placing modern words of prophecy on the same level with the written Word of God.

Ryle does this perhaps without even realizing it. He repeatedly cites Matthew 4:4 in defense of modern prophecy: "Man shall not live by bread alone, but by *every word that proceedeth out of the mouth of God*"[23]—taking a verse that clearly speaks of Scripture and applying it to modern words of prophecy.

Furthermore, despite his stated preference for expressions like, "It occurred to me," Ryle never once uses that expression or any like it in his book. Instead, the book is filled with statements like, "I heard the voice of the Lord," "The voice of the Lord spoke to me," "God was speaking to me again," "The Lord Himself was standing before me . . . speaking directly to me," "Again I heard the voice of the Lord. . . . The Lord continued [speaking]. . . . The Lord seemed to pause. . . . Then He delivered the knockout blow," "The Lord was saying to me," "The Lord spoke to him, telling him to call [me]," "He speaks to me," "I received a word from the Lord," "I sensed the Holy Spirit say to me," "I treasure these words from the Lord, holding them in my heart with the deepest regard," "These were the exact words I was given," "The prophetic word from the heart of the Lord was spoken," "This is what the Holy Spirit showed me," and similar expressions.[24] All Ryle's interpretations of his own dreams and visions are stated with dogmatic conviction.

Ryle continually uses terminology that suggests he has canonized modern prophecy—at least in his own mind. "The Holy Spirit inspires us to speak through any number of means," he says, referring to his prophecies as "inspired utterance."[25] At the end of the book, Ryle suggests that when the hippo of modern prophecy comes into the garden of mainstream evangelicalism, "the church will be found in the midst of the world, speaking forth *the words of God* to a crooked and perverse generation, among whom we will shine as light, holding forth *the word of life*."[26]

So in practice, Ryle finds it impossible not to equate his own prophecies with the words of Scripture, even though he appears to be trying to avoid this error.[27] He is not alone in this failing. Anyone who is truly convinced that God is speaking fresh words of revelation will inevitably view the later prophecies as somehow more relevant and more personal than the message of Scripture, which is more than two thousand years old. Inevitably, wherever personal prophecy has

185

been stressed, Scripture has been deemphasized. Two thousand years of church history confirms that this is true.

WHEN FANCY IS MISTAKEN FOR FAITH

This same issue was hotly debated during the Great Awakening. It was one area where Jonathan Edwards and George Whitefield did not (in the beginning) see eye to eye. Clearly on *this* question Edwards would not have been the least bit sympathetic with modern charismatics. Edwards believed prophecy had ceased along with the rest of the charismatic gifts.[29] Whitefield was far more willing than Edwards to treat subjective impulses as if they could reliably reveal the Holy Spirit's leading. In 1740 Edwards confronted Whitefield on the issue. He later wrote to a friend,

> I indeed have told several persons that I once purposely took an opportunity to talk with Mr. Whitefield alone about [subjective] impulses: and have mentioned many particulars of our conference together on that [matter]: That *I told him some reasons I had to think he gave too great heed to such things*: and have told what manner of replies he made; and what reasons I offered against such things. And I also said that Mr. Whitefield did not seem to be offended with me: but yet did not seem to be inclined to have a great deal of discourse about it: And that in the time of it he did not appear to be convinced by any thing I said.[30]

At the height of the Great Awakening, this issue became, in Iain Murray's words, "the talking-point of the whole country."[31] Edwards clearly warned his congregation not to place much stock in subjective impressions. He saw this as a particular danger in a time of revival, when religious affections are heightened and the imagination more active than usual. Murray writes,

> The "impressions" or "impulses" which [Edwards] criticized were varied in character. Sometimes they involved an element of the visionary. Sometimes they appeared to provide foreknowledge

of future events. And sometimes they were accompanied and supported by random texts of Scripture. . . .

Against this belief Edwards argued that a Christian might indeed have a "holy frame and sense from the Spirit of God" but the "imaginations that attend it are but accidental" and not directly attributable to the Spirit.[32]

Edwards had carefully studied this issue. He was convinced that the tendency to follow subjective impulses was a dangerous path down which to travel: "[An] erroneous principle, than which scarce any has proved more mischievous to the present glorious work of God, is *a notion that it is God's manner in these days to guide His saints . . . by inspiration, or immediate revelation.*"[33] He saw several dangers in the practice, not the least of which was its hardening effect on the person supposedly receiving the revelation. "As long as a person has a notion that he is guided by immediate direction from heaven, it makes him incorrigible and impregnable in all his misconduct."[34]

Edwards also knew from both church history and personal experience that

Many godly persons have undoubtedly in this and other ages, exposed themselves to woeful delusions, by an aptness to lay too much weight on impulses and impressions, as if they were immediate revelations from God, to signify something future, or to direct them where to go, and what to do.[35]

Edwards's advice was straightforward:

I would therefore entreat the people of God to be very cautious how they give heed to such things. I have seen them fail in very many instances, and know by experience that impressions being made with great power, and upon the minds of true, yea eminent, saints . . . are no sure signs of their being revelations from heaven. I have known such impressions fail, in some instances, attended with all these circumstances.[36]

A generation before Edwards, the illustrious Boston pastor

Cotton Mather had experimented with this very tendency, believing that God would grant him "particular faiths" for specific prayers to be answered. Convinced God had promised to grant certain prayer requests, Mather prophesied that his wife would recover from a serious illness, that his father would return to England to serve the Lord, and that his wayward son would return to the Lord. Only after those and several other expectations went unfulfilled did Mather begin to question his doctrine of "particular faiths."[37]

George Whitefield also learned the hard way that subjective impulses can be tragically fallible. When Whitefield's wife was expecting her first child, he prophesied that she would have a son who would become a preacher of the Gospel. The child was indeed a boy, but he died at the age of four months. He was Whitefield's only child. Murray writes,

> Whitefield at once recognized his mistake saying: "I misapplied several texts of Scripture. Upon these grounds, I made no scruple of declaring 'that I should have a son, and that his name was to be John.'" When back in New England, in 1745, he could say feelingly of what had happened there, "Many good souls, both among clergy and laity, for a while, *mistook fancy for faith, and imagination for revelation.*"[38]

SUBJECTIVITY AND THE WILL OF GOD

Many good souls still fall into that same error. As mentioned earlier, many (perhaps *most*) Christians believe God uses subjective promptings to guide believers in making major decisions. A thorough search of church history would undoubtedly confirm that most believers who lean heavily on immediate "revelations" or subjective impressions ostensibly from God end up embarrassed, confused, disappointed, and frustrated.

Nothing in Scripture even suggests that we should seek either the will of God or the Word of God (personal guidance or fresh prophecy) by listening to subjective impressions. So how *are* we supposed to determine the divine will?

Virtually every Christian grapples with the question of how to know God's will in any individual instance. We particularly struggle when faced with the major decisions of adolescence—what occupation or profession we will pursue, whom we will marry, whether and where we will go to college, and so on. Most of us fear that wrong decisions at these points will result in a lifetime of disaster.

Unfortunately, many of the books and pamphlets on discerning God's will are filled with mystical mumbo-jumbo about seeking a sense of peace, listening for a divine "call," putting out a "fleece," and other subjective signposts pointing the way to God's will.

That kind of "discernment" is not at all what Scripture calls for. If we examine everything the Bible has to say about knowing God's will, what we discover is that everywhere Scripture expressly mentions the subject, it sets forth *objective* guidelines. If we put those guidelines together, we get a fairly comprehensive picture of the will of God for every Christian. We can summarize them like this:

- *It is God's will that we be saved.* "The Lord is . . . not wishing for any to perish but for all to come to repentance" (2 Peter 3:9). "God our Savior . . . desires all men to be saved and to come to the knowledge of the truth" (1 Tim. 2:3-4).
- *It is God's will that we be Spirit-filled.* "Do not be foolish, but understand what the will of the Lord is. . . . Be filled with the Spirit" (Eph. 5:17-18).
- *It is God's will that we be sanctified.* "For this is the will of God, your sanctification" (1 Thess. 4:3).
- *It is God's will that we be submissive.* "Submit yourselves for the Lord's sake to every human institution, whether to a king as the one in authority, or to governors as sent by him for the punishment of evildoers and the praise of those who do right. For such is the will of God that by doing right you may silence the ignorance of foolish men" (1 Peter 2:13-15).
- *It is God's will that we suffer.* "Therefore, let those also who suffer according to the will of God entrust their souls to a faithful Creator in doing what is right" (1 Peter 4:19). "For to you it has been granted for Christ's sake, not only to believe in Him, but also to suffer for His sake" (Phil. 1:29). "And indeed, all who desire to live godly in Christ Jesus will be persecuted" (2 Tim. 3:12).

If all those objective aspects of God's will are realities in your life, you needn't fret over the other decisions you must make. As long as the options you face do not involve issues directly forbidden or commanded in Scripture, you are free to do whatever you choose.

Whatever you choose? Yes, within the limits expressly set forth in God's Word. *If* those five objective principles are consistently true in your life—if you are saved, Spirit-filled, sanctified, submissive, and suffering for righteousness' sake—you are completely free to choose whatever you desire.

In fact, God providentially governs your choice by molding your desires. Psalm 37:4 says, "Delight yourself in the Lord; and He will give you the desires of your heart." That doesn't mean merely that He *grants* the desires of your heart; it suggests that He *puts the desires there*. So even when we choose freely, His sovereign providence guides the free choices we make! What confidence that should give us as we live our lives before God!

This is not to suggest that we should attempt to try to decipher God's will through what we can observe of His providence. That would thrust us right back into the realm of determining truth subjectively. But we can be confident as we make choices that God will providentially work all things together in accord with His perfect will (Rom. 8:28; Eph. 1:11). We needn't be paralyzed with fear that a wrong decision might ruin our lives forever.

There are some caveats that need to be stressed here: obviously if your desires are sinful, selfish, or wrongly motivated, then you are not really Spirit-filled, or else you are not pursuing sanctification the way you should. Your first responsibility is to set those areas of your life in order. In other words, if you are pursuing self-will and fleshly desire, you have stepped out of God's will with regard to one or more of the major objective principles. You need to come into line with the objective, revealed will of God before you can make whatever decision you may be contemplating.

And again, our freedom to choose extends only to issues not specifically addressed in Scripture. Obviously, no one who is truly saved, Spirit-filled, sanctified, submissive, and suffering for Christ would willfully disobey the Word of God. No Christian has the freedom, for example, to violate 2 Corinthians 6:14 by marrying an unbeliever.

Above all, we must use *biblical wisdom* in the choices we make. We are to apply wisdom to all our decisions. Look again at the beginning of Ephesians 5:17: "Do not be foolish." To be Spirit-filled is to be *wise*—to be *discerning* (see Ex. 35:31; Deut. 34:9; also see Eph. 5:18 with Col. 3:16). The biblical wisdom that is the hallmark of the Spirit-filled person is the platform on which all right decision making must be based. We are to consider our options in this light and pursue the choices that seem most wise—not merely what *feels* best (Prov. 2:1-6).

This means that if we contemplate God's will biblically, we will remain in the realm of *objective truth*. The Bible never encourages us to try to determine God's will by subjective impressions, "promptings" from the Holy Spirit, the "still, small voice" of God, or miraculous signs like Gideon's fleece (Judg. 6:36-40). If we seek to be led in subjective ways like those—especially if we neglect objective truth and biblical wisdom—we will surely run into trouble. Making decisions based on subjective criteria is a subtle form of reckless faith.

One of the significant contributions of Garry Friesen's landmark book, *Decision Making and the Will of God*, is a chapter that explores the pitfalls of attempting to discern the will of God through subjective impressions. "Impressions Are Impressions" is the title of the chapter.[39] "If the source of one's knowledge is subjective," Friesen writes, "then the knowledge will also be subjective—and hence, uncertain."[40]

At one point Friesen raises the question, "how can I tell whether these impressions are from God or from some other source?" He writes,

This is a critical question. For impressions could be produced by any number of sources: God, Satan, an angel, a demon, human emotions (such as fear or ecstasy), hormonal imbalance, insomnia, medication, or an upset stomach. Sinful impressions (temptations) may be exposed for what they are by the Spirit-sensitized conscience and the Word of God. But beyond that, one encounters a subjective quagmire of uncertainty. For in nonmoral areas, Scripture gives no guidelines for distinguishing the voice of the Spirit from the voice of the self—or any other potential "voice." And experience offers no reliable means of identification either (which is why the question comes up in the first place). . . . Tremendous frustration has been experienced by sincere Christians who have earnestly but fruitlessly sought to decipher the code of the inward witness.[41]

Even more significant than that is the fact that *Scripture never commands us to tune into any inner voice.* We're commanded to study and meditate on Scripture (Josh. 1:8; Ps. 1:1-2). We're instructed to cultivate wisdom and discernment (Prov. 4:5-8). We're told to walk wisely and make the most of our time (Eph. 5:15-16). We're ordered to be obedient to God's commands (Deut. 28:1-2; John 15:14). But we are never encouraged to listen for inner promptings.

On the contrary, we are warned that our hearts are so deceitful and desperately wicked that we cannot understand them (Jer. 17:9). Surely this should make us very reluctant to heed promptings and messages that arise from within ourselves.

This, by the way, is one of the critical deficiencies of Wayne Grudem's position on prophecy. While defining revelation as "something God brings to mind," Grudem never explores the critical issue of how to determine whether an impression in the mind really comes from God. Yet this would seem to be the most pressing question of all for someone who is about to declare a mental impression a prophecy from the Lord.

By contrast, Friesen writes, "Inner impressions are not a form of revelation. So the Bible does not invest inner impressions with authority to function as indicators of divine guidance. . . . Impressions are *not* authoritative. Impressions are impressions."[42] Surely this is the true path of biblical wisdom.

Haddon Robinson goes one step further: "When we lift our inner impressions to the level of divine revelation, we are flirting with divination."[43] In other words, those who treat subjective impressions as revelatory prophecy are actually practicing a form of fortune-telling.

Those willing to heed inner voices and mental impressions may be listening to the lies of a deceitful heart, the fantasies of an overactive imagination, or even the voice of a demon. Once objective criteria are cast aside, there is no way to know the difference between truth and falsehood. Those who follow subjective impressions are by definition undiscerning. Mysticism and discernment simply do not mix.

UPPER ABDOMINAL DISTRESS

It is therefore ironic that advocates of mysticism inevitably treat discernment itself as if it were some kind of subjective, mystical ability. We saw briefly in chapter 6 how one author spoke of discernment as "a spiritual function," by which he evidently meant that discernment does not involve the intellect.[44] In one of my earlier books[45] I quoted Bill Hamon, one of the leading proponents of modern revelatory prophecy. Hamon's recipe for discernment is a classic case of mystical anti-intellectualism. He believes prophecies can be properly evaluated only by people willing to set reason and logic aside:

> I have sometimes heard people say, "I did not witness with that prophecy." But after questioning them, I discovered that what they really meant was that the prophecy did not fit their theology, personal desires or goals, or their emotions reacted negatively to it. They failed to understand that we do not bear witness with the soul—the mind, emotions or will.
>
> Our reasoning is in the mind, not the spirit. So our traditions, beliefs and strong opinions are not true witnesses to prophetic truth. *The spirit reaction originates deep within our being. Many Christians describe the physical location of its corresponding sensation as the upper abdominal area.*
>
> A negative witness—with a message of "no," "be careful" or "something's not right"—usually manifests itself with *a nervous, jumpy or uneasy feeling*. There is a deep, almost unintelligible sensation that something is wrong. This sense can only be trusted when we are more in tune with our spirit than with our thoughts. If our thinking is causing these sensations, then it could be only a soulish reaction.

On the other hand, when God's Spirit is bearing witness with our spirit that a prophetic word is right, is of God and is according to His will and purpose, then our spirit reacts with the fruit of the Holy Spirit. We have *a deep, unexplainable peace and joy, a warm, loving feeling—or even a sense of our spirit jumping up and down with excitement.* This sensation lets us know that the Holy Spirit is bearing witness with our spirit that everything is in order, even though we may not understand everything that is being said, or our soul may not be able to adjust immediately to all the thoughts being presented.[46]

Notice that Hamon's emphasis is entirely on *feeling,* while he derides the intellect, theology, reason, understanding, and by implication, true biblical wisdom. A reaction in the upper abdominal region is supposed to be a more reliable gauge of truth than all those things.

But that is superstition, not discernment. How your upper abdomen feels about a thing is certainly no measure of truth or falsehood. Neither is "a nervous, jumpy, or uneasy feeling" apart from any rational cause. "A deep, unexplainable peace and joy, a warm, loving feeling—or even a sense of [your] spirit jumping up and down with excitement" is no proof that a supposed prophecy is reliable. Those who practice this sort of "discernment" epitomize reckless faith.

And those who seek truth by analyzing inner feelings are likely to wind up with nothing but confusion.

DUELING PROPHETS

My editor once attended a service at the Anaheim Vineyard where two "prophets" gave contradictory prophecies. It happened in a Sunday morning worship service. When the congregational singing was over, John Wimber stepped to the platform. Before he could say anything, a young man in the congregation stood and began loudly to prophesy judgment against the leaders of the church. "Jerusalem! Jerusalem!" he began, echoing Luke 13:34, "you persecute My prophets and stone My messengers. My displeasure burns hot toward the leadership of this church for the way you have scorned My prophets and ignored My prophecies. . . ." and so on. The man evidently was disgruntled at the treatment he had received at the hands of church leaders, and this "prophecy" seemed to be his way of striking back. He prophesied in that manner for five minutes or more, earnestly calling the elders of the church to repentance. His entire message was in first person as if from God.

Immediately when he finished, before John Wimber could respond, another "prophet" from the other side of the congregation popped up and began to prophesy exactly the opposite message. This prophet began with a loose paraphrase of Jeremiah 29:11: "Oh, pastors and leaders of this church, I know My thoughts toward you—thoughts of mercy, and not of judgment. I have loved you with an everlasting love and have laid up for you a crown in heaven, My beloved. You have done according to all My good pleasure, and henceforth all men will rise up and call you blessed. . . ." etcetera, etcetera.

When the second man finished, a woman stood and sang a song, another person spoke in tongues, and one or two others quoted Bible verses or shared something brief. Then the service continued with Wimber making announcements. No reference was made to the two contradictory prophecies. No attempt was made to explain the dilemma or interpret either prophecy. Members of the congregation were simply left to draw their own conclusions about which, if either, of the two prophecies was correct.

That illustrates the impossible situation that arises when people are encouraged to voice their own subjective impressions as if they were divine prophecy. And it also reveals the predicament we are placed in if we must allow a sensation in our upper abdominal area to determine the truth or falsehood of a prophetic message.

Notice that both prophets' messages echoed biblical terminology. Both of them were delivered with great conviction. Both of them employed first-person pronouns, as if God Himself were doing the speaking. Yet they flatly contradicted each other. They might both be false prophecies, but there is no way they could both be true. How were the people in the congregation supposed to determine which, if either, was correct? If they followed the gut-feeling approach, all the disgruntled people in the church undoubtedly opted for the first prophecy, believing they now had a word from the Lord to confirm their displeasure with their leaders.

The obvious fact is that once we stray into the realm of subjectivity, we have no way to determine what is really true.

A MORE SURE WORD OF PROPHECY

Scripture very clearly addresses this issue. The apostle Peter settled the matter by proclaiming the authority and supremacy of Scripture when he wrote,

> We did not follow cleverly devised tales when we made known to you the power and coming of our Lord Jesus Christ, but we were eyewitnesses of His majesty. For when He received honor and glory from God the Father, such an utterance as this was made to Him by the Majestic Glory, "This is My beloved Son with whom I am well-pleased"—and we ourselves heard this utterance made from heaven when we were with Him on the holy mountain (2 Peter 1:16-18).

Peter was describing an event that may have been the most spectacular spiritual experience of his life. This was the transfiguration of Christ, when our Lord appeared in His full glory. Peter heard the voice of God and saw Moses and Elijah face to face. Best of all, he got a preview of Christ in His glory.

This was not a dream or vision. It was not an impression in Peter's mind, or a figment of his imagination. It was real life ("we did not follow cleverly devised tales"). He saw it with his own eyes ("we were eyewitnesses"). He heard the voice of God with his own ears ("we ourselves heard this utterance"). He was there in person with other apostolic eyewitnesses ("we were with Him"). There was nothing subjective about this experience.

Yet Peter goes on to say that even what he heard with his own ears and saw with his own eyes was not as authoritative as the eternal Word of God contained in Scripture:

> We have also a more sure word of prophecy; whereunto ye do well
> that ye take heed, as unto a light that shineth in a dark place, until
> the day dawn, and the day star arise in your hearts: knowing this
> first, that no prophecy of the scripture is of any private interpre-
> tation. For the prophecy came not in old time by the will of man:
> but holy men of God spake as they were moved by the Holy Ghost
> (vv. 19-21, KJV).

Peter is *not* saying that his eyewitness testimony makes the
"prophecy of the Scripture" more sure. He is saying that the written
Word of God by its very nature is *more sure* than his own experience.
This is confirmed by Peter's argument in verses 20-21, where he
establishes the authority and divine origin of every "prophecy of the
scripture."

The Greek word order in verse 19 also supports this as the true
meaning of the text: "We have more sure the prophetic Word." More
sure than what? More sure than experience—even the valid, genuine,
eyewitness experience of the apostles. Peter is saying that the written Word is an even more reliable source of truth than his own experience. To paraphrase Peter's message to his readers, it is this: "James,
John, and I saw Christ's glory firsthand. But if you don't believe us,
there is one authority even more certain than our testimony: the written Word of God."

The "we" at the beginning of verse 19 is generic, not emphatic.
It means "you and I"; not "we who witnessed the Transfiguration."
Peter is saying, in effect, "All of us who are believers have a word of
prophecy that is more sure than any voice from heaven. It is the
'prophecy of Scripture' (v. 20) which is more sure, more reliable, more
authoritative than anyone's experiences."

That surely puts subjective impressions in their proper place.
Remember, Peter's experience was *not* subjective. What he saw and
heard was real. Others experienced it with him. But Peter knew that
the written Word of God is even more authoritative than the shared
experience of three apostles.

Why would anyone seek truth in subjective impressions when we
have such a sure Word? Peter admonishes his readers with the

reminder that they would "do well to pay attention [to Scripture] as to a lamp shining in a dark place" (v. 19). The imagery here speaks of a single source of light, like a night light, shining in an otherwise dark place. Peter's point is that we needn't grope about in the dark in search of truth. Rather we should focus all our vision on the light cast by that single source—the written Word of God.

Moreover, we are to maintain that focus "until the day dawns and the morning star arises in your hearts." This phrase is admittedly difficult to understand, but we discover a clue in the fact that Revelation 22:16 refers to Christ as "the bright morning star." He is the incarnate Word of God, the one who *is* light (John 8:12). The apostle John wrote, "When He appears, we shall be like Him, because we shall see Him just as He is" (1 John 3:2). And Paul wrote of that same day, "Now we see in a mirror dimly, but then face to face; now I know in part, but then I shall know fully just as I also have been fully known" (1 Cor. 13:12).

This is what Peter seems to be saying: "In the midst of the darkness of this age, keep your eyes fixed on the lamp of Scripture—until that day when Christ returns and our knowledge of truth is made perfect—that day when the Morning Star Himself arises in our hearts and we are made like Him, to know as we are known." It is a reference to the Second Coming, the only remaining revelation for which we wait.

Meanwhile, "*Thy word* is a lamp to my feet, and a light to my path" (Ps. 119:105, emphasis added). Those who turn aside from the lamp and grope in the darkness after subjective impressions open themselves up to deception, disappointment, spiritual failure, and all manner of confusion. But those who keep their hearts and minds fixed firmly on the lamplight of Scripture—they are the truly discerning ones. That is Peter's message.

During the Great Awakening Jonathan Edwards wrote,

Why cannot we be contented with the divine oracles, that holy, pure word of God, which we have in such abundance and clearness, now since the canon of Scripture is completed? Why should we desire to have any thing added to them by impulses from above? Why should we not rest in that standing rule that God has given to his church, which the apostle teaches us, is surer than a voice from heaven? And why should we desire to make the Scripture speak more to us than it does?[47]

Why indeed! Elsewhere Edwards penned this warning:

> They who leave the sure word of prophecy—which God has given us as a light shining in a dark place—to follow such impressions and impulses, leave the guidance of the polar star to follow *a Jack with a lantern*. No wonder therefore that sometimes they are led into woeful extravagances.[48]

Surely the best advice of all comes from Scripture itself:

> For if you cry for discernment, lift your voice for understanding; if you seek her as silver, and search for her as for hidden treasures; then you will discern the fear of the Lord, and discover the knowledge of God. For the Lord gives wisdom; *from His mouth* come knowledge and understanding (Prov. 2:3-6, emphasis added).

APPENDIX 1

Is Roman Catholicism Changing?

RECENTLY I WAS GIVEN a centuries-old, leather-bound copy of *Foxe's Book of Martyrs*. It had been years since I last read from that classic work, and I had never seen such an old copy. As I paged through it I was reminded of the cruel price multitudes have paid because they stood for the truth. It occurred to me that most people in our society, so steeped in existential relativism, could never understand why so many would care so much for biblical truth that they would be willing to give their lives rather than adapt their religious convictions.

At one time, while the Puritan movement was at its height, *Foxe's Book of Martyrs* was owned by more people in England and the American colonies than any other book besides the Bible. It is an anthology of accounts about thousands of people who died for their faith in Jesus Christ, and their commitment to the Bible. Almost every page is heart-rending. The book includes several dozen woodcuts depicting godly people being tortured and slain with sadistic brutality. Even in an age inured to graphic violence, these scenes are shocking and deeply troubling.

What is most appalling is that the worst of these unspeakable inhumanities were carried out by Church officials who were acting in the name of Christ—against people who simply wanted to live in obedience to the Word of God.

For the first twelve hundred years of Christianity, the penalty for heresy was excommunication. Then, in the early thirteenth century, the Church began to urge state rulers to treat heresy as a capital crime. In 1231 Pope Gregory IX appointed the first Papal inquisitors for the suppression of heretics. Twenty years later Pope Innocent IV authorized the use of torture against the accused. The penalty for those convicted was death—usually by burning at the stake.

Catholic inquisitors operated with the Popes' blessing for more than six hundred years. Collectively they are responsible for more Christian martyrs than any other tormenter of God's people—including all the emperors of ancient pagan Rome combined.[1]

Of course, the Catholic Church is by no means the only religious body guilty of atrocities. Martin Luther consented to the deaths of thousands in the Peasants' Revolt in sixteenth-century Germany. Many leading Reformers joined with the Catholics in calling for the deaths of Anabaptists. John Calvin sanctioned the burning of Michael Servetus, an arch-heretic who was condemned by both Catholics and Calvinists for his anti-trinitarianism. Oliver Cromwell's Puritan armies treated Irish Catholics with appalling ruthlessness. Cromwell himself signed the death warrant when Charles I was executed. The Puritans in colonial Massachusetts executed four Quakers before laws making heresy a capital offense were repealed.

Yet all those evils pale in comparison to the horrifying waves of tyranny and inhumanity carried out in the name of Roman Catholicism. The Inquisition and all its related pogroms and slaughters eclipse every other Western religious atrocity in both extent and brutality. In one incident alone—the infamous St. Bartholomew's Day Massacre in 1572—thousands of French Protestants (Huguenots) were slaughtered in Paris in a single night. That launched a further bloodbath where thousands more Huguenots were hunted down and killed throughout the nation.[2] "When news of the massacre reached Rome, the pope joyfully announced a day of public celebration; the entire city was illuminated at night, and grand thanksgiving services were held in the cathedral."[3] Gregory XIII was the pope who actually celebrated the butchery with a solemn thanksgiving Mass. He was so pleased about the massacre that he struck a commemorative medal.[4] "He engaged [Renaissance painter Georgio] Vasari to paint, in the Sala Regia of the Vatican, a picture of the massacre, bearing the words *Pontifex Colignii necem probat*— 'The Pope approves of the killing of Coligny.'"[5]

In the hundred years that followed, Protestantism in France was virtually obliterated by Catholic persecution.

The brutality of the Spanish Inquisition is well known. One infamous inquisitor general, Tomás de Torquemada, parlayed his office into a power that rivalled that of the king.[6] Spanish inquisitors made the sentencing and punishment of heretics into a garish, ceremonial "act of faith," the notorious *auto-da-fé*. Unspeakable tortures were devised to induce heretics to confess. This most ruthless of all Inquisitions began in 1479, and the reign of terror finally ended only 160 years ago.

Today, no prominent Catholic leader would seriously argue that heretics should be killed or that the office of the Inquisition should be once again authorized to torture heretics. So why bring up the past? Catholic apologist Karl Keating is convinced most fundamentalists employ the Inquisition only as an unfair argument. "Sooner or later," he writes, "any exchange of views with fundamentalists will come around to the Inquisition. The topic can hardly be avoided. . . . It is a handy stick with which to engage in Catholic-bashing, because most Catholics are at a loss for a sensible reply."[7]

Keating questions the statistics, insisting that "some historians [assert] fewer than three thousand death sentences were handed down during three centuries, others putting the figure higher."[8] He cites the witchcraft executions that occurred in non-Catholic countries and suggests that "severity in punishment was not due to Catholicism as such, but must be attributed to the general character of the times."[9]

In the end, however, Keating acknowledges that there is no use trying to gloss over the incontrovertible historical facts or whitewash the Inquisition. He writes,

> The [Catholic] Church has nothing to fear from the truth or a right appreciation of it. No account of foolishness, misguided zeal, or cruelty by Catholics can undo the divine foundation of the Church. . . . What must be grasped is that the Church contains within itself all sorts of sinners and knaves, and some of them reach high rank. The wheat and chaff coexist in the Kingdom until the end, and that was how the Founder intended it.[10]

He concludes, "The mere existence of the Inquisition does not disprove the church's credentials."[11]

Keating then counsels fellow Catholics how to answer fundamentalists who raise questions about the Inquisition:

> The Catholic should ask the fundamentalist what he thinks the existence of the Inquisition demonstrates. After all, no fundamentalist will bring up the subject unless he thinks it proves something about the Catholic Church. What is that something? That the church contains sinners? Guilty as charged. That at times sinners have reached positions of authority? Ditto. That even otherwise good Catholics, afire with zeal, sometimes lose their balance? True, all true, but such charges could be made and verified even if the Inquisition never existed. . . . [The same argument] can apply equally against Reformation Christianity. If the Inquisition establishes the falsity of Catholicism, the witch trials establish the falsity of Protestantism.[12]

But that evades the point. What the Inquisition demonstrates is how monstrously fallible the popes have been in matters of faith and morals. To say the least, it raises a fair question whether men who behaved so diabolically are entitled to demand veneration as vicars of Christ. It also calls into question the credibility of the Church's claim that it speaks authoritatively on earth for God. And it highlights the error of a doctrine that invests an earthly office with divine authority.[13]

No Protestant churchman—even those who were involved in the persecution of witches—ever claimed that kind of infallibility. In fact, it was the Puritan clergy in Massachusetts who put a stop to the Salem Village witchcraft hysteria.[14] They later proclaimed a day of fasting and repentance for the entire colony. Samuel Sewell, a Puritan layman, was one of the presiding judges at the witch trials. On the day of fasting, he stood in church, "desir[ing] to take the Blame and Shame of it," while his humble confession of sin was read aloud by the pastor.[15] The Puritan leaders themselves confessed that these atrocities were abominable, loathsome, sinful acts.

Roman pontiffs simply do not make such public admissions of guilt. How could they, having assumed the mantle of infallibility? Nor will the Church herself take the blame, for the Church makes a *de facto* claim of infallibility. Its dogma, its tradition, and its very structure are supposed to have apostolic authority. Any admission of official error or wrongdoing on the part of Church or pope would naturally tarnish the claim of divine authority. So while Catholic apologists, like Karl Keating, are quite willing to acknowledge that the Church contains "sinners and knaves," they always refrain from recognizing the guilt of the Church itself.

THE GUILT OF THE CHURCH

About forty years ago Dutch Reformed theologian G. C. Berkouwer wrote a perceptive book titled *The Conflict With Rome*.[16] The book includes a chapter titled "The Guilt of the Church," in which Berkouwer carefully analyzes how Rome consistently shuns any degree of real blame for the atrocities and moral abuses its popes and bishops have perpetrated. Although the evil deeds were done with the Church's official blessing—and often at the behest of the pope himself—the Catholic Church maintains that she is holy and innocent. She will admit no culpability for her own role in the various scandals and schisms she has been party to—especially the Reformation.

Berkouwer cites a few Catholic authors who make noble attempts to come to grips with the sins of the Church. But he notes that inevitably the only guilt they will acknowledge is "something proper to individuals, and outside the sphere of the church."[17] They simply cannot recognize any degree of failure on the part of the Catholic Church herself. To do so would be tantamount to contradicting the Church's claim that she acts infallibly.

When on occasion Catholic spokesmen discuss the abuses and atrocities committed in the name of the Church, they often find it easier to deal with them as "tragedies," as if the church herself were the victim. Referring to one Catholic author's efforts at analyzing the sins of the Church, Berkouwer notes that

> at the beginning of the "confession of guilt" he seizes upon the word "tragedy." For this word obliterates the concrete character essential to any confession of guilt. A mysterious, romantic, mystical and tragic light is shed on the sins of the church, which are almost imperceptibly transformed into a kind of "suffering." . . . In this way the guilt is made superficial and transferred from the clear light of responsibility to an impenetrable twilight.[18]

Moreover, as Berkouwer points out, while individual Catholic writers may occasionally grapple with the issue of guilt, the Church herself, acting officially, simply will not admit any corporate guilt. As an example, Berkouwer pointed to a recent Papal Encyclical that "does not refer to the sins of the church, but to the 'persecutions and tortures and pains'" *suffered by* the church.

All of this is made necessary, Berkouwer believes, by Catholic ecclesiology—the doctrine of the Church. In Catholicism, Christ and the visible Church are virtually seen as one. The Roman Catholic Church claims that it *is* the *corpus Christi*, the body of Christ on earth. But instead of emphasizing the Church's *submission* to Him as Head, Catholicism views the Church as the embodiment of His divine *authority* on earth. The Church therefore *cannot* acknowledge its own sin; that would either taint the sinlessness of the Savior or abdicate the Church's absolute authority. Since neither is a possibility, the Church willfully closes her eyes to her own guilt.

In other words, the Roman Catholic Church has usurped the

place of Christ in His Kingdom. People attach themselves to the *system*, not to the *Savior*, and the Church becomes a surrogate Christ. It is a serious error fraught with all kinds of problems. Jesus Christ is *entitled* to rule with a rod of iron (Rev. 19:15) because He is sinless, spotless, and perfectly just. But when an earthly organization, ruled by sinful men, believes it has been authorized to smite the nations and tread the winepress of the fierce wrath of Almighty God, the worst kinds of disaster will certainly follow. The Middle Ages are a long chronicle of the outworking of that error.

And since the error was rooted in official Roman Catholic doctrine, the guilt belongs to the Church herself, not just to select individuals—"sinners and knaves."

Berkouwer's most important point is this: the Roman Catholic Church is culpable not merely for the atrocities, corruption, and moral abuses that have been perpetrated in her name—but primarily for her *doctrine*. Her chief guilt is that she has spurned the Bible as a test of sound doctrine and in effect set herself up as a higher authority than the Bible.

THE SCANDAL OF THE REFORMATION

The central issues in the Protestant Reformation were all doctrinal. It is a mistake to think that the Reformers were concerned primarily with practical abuses like indulgences, simony (purchasing or selling spiritual things), and other corruptions of practice. Luther insisted he was not calling for a perfect church; his protest had to do with *doctrine*. "The pope boasts that he's the head of the church," Luther said. "I would gladly have conceded this to the pope if he had only taught the gospel."[19]

Luther constantly tried to focus the attention of Rome on the doctrines that were at issue. "One must always look to the doctrine," he said. "The teaching does it! In their books the papists do nothing else than make false accusations about our crimes. They don't attack the chief articles of our faith. False accusations won't do; it's the teaching that matters."[20] As Berkouwer suggests, "the Reformation was really concerned with doctrine, not as a speculative theological construction, but as the simple Biblical doctrine of the truth."[21] Doctrine was the real issue, not worldly corruption in the church.

More precisely, what was at stake was the Gospel.

It is true that the Reformers pointed out and protested many of Rome's *practical* abuses. But their underlying design was to recover the true Gospel. They opposed the selling of indulgences because it corrupted the doctrine of repentance. They denounced the veneration of saints and relics because they abhorred the superstition and idolatry that turned people's minds away from Christ. They abominated the Mass because it purported to repeat daily the once-for-all finished work of Jesus Christ (Heb. 10:11-13)—and thereby obscured the most glorious truth of the Gospel. The Gospel was always the true issue.

If the Reformers had drawn their line in the sand on the issue of the practical abuses in the church, it is very likely no schism would ever have occurred. The morality of the church had sunk so low and public sentiment became so acrimonious that almost everyone agreed *practical* reforms were necessary. One clear call for reform actually came from a new pope, Hadrian VI, elected in 1522, only five years after Luther nailed the Ninety-Five Theses to the church door at Wittenberg. Hadrian, a somewhat naive man, was uncharacteristically frank. He acknowledged

> that for some time many abominations, abuses in ecclesiastical affairs, and violations of rights have taken place in the holy see; and that all things have been perverted into bad. From the head the corruption has passed to the limbs, from the Pope to the prelates: we have all departed; there is none that doeth good, no, not one.[22]

He called on the Church "to purify the court of Rome from which all the evils have perhaps sprung. Then the malady which spread from there will also be cured from there."[23]

As aware as he was of corruption in the Church, Hadrian VI nevertheless defended Catholic *doctrine* as infallible. "He regarded Protestantism as a just punishment for the sins of the prelates."[24] He ordered earlier papal decrees against Luther to be carried out. To him, the Church's problem was "sinners and knaves" in the hierarchy—and the solution was external reforms, not doctrinal correction.

But Hadrian ruled only one year, then died before he could institute any reforms. "Rome rejoiced."[25] Hadrian was replaced by Clement VII, one of the most evil men ever to occupy the papal chair. Clement had no stomach for reforms of any kind.

It was to be more than twenty years before the Council of Trent finally convened to discuss how to reform the Church. The bishops made it clear from the very beginning that doctrinal changes would be no part of their discussion. After all, as Berkouwer points out, "the infallibly guided church . . . is unassailable as to its doctrinal authority."[26] And so the Catholic Church flatly refused to subject its teaching to the test of Scripture.

Many of today's Catholic apologists point to the Council of Trent as evidence that the Church *did* undergo self-reformation. The Protestant Reformation is a scandal, they suggest, because it was unnecessary. If only the Reformers had been more patient, they tell us, the Mother Church would not have been rent asunder, because at Trent the Church herself corralled all the worst abuses.

But that is not true. Rome's worst abuses were *doctrinal*, and the Reformers continually stressed that point. They would not be satisfied with cosmetic changes when they believed the Gospel was being compromised. Yet Rome determined *a priori* that doctrine was in no way subject to reform or review—even in light of sacred Scripture. "Rome did not allow the light of the gospel of grace to shine on the decay of the church."[27] She merely arrogated the claim of infallibility and declared biblical support for her teachings unnecessary. That was the *real* scandal of the Reformation.

At Trent, the Catholic Church summarily condemned Reformation theology and demanded unquestioning obedience to her own doctrinal pronouncements. There was no possibility of doctrinal reform.

What of the positive contributions of the Council of Trent? Weren't there reforms? Certainly some of the practical abuses were curtailed. But far from addressing the doctrinal issues the Reformers had raised, Trent pronounced a very loud and irrevocable anathema against the theology of the Reformation. Berkouwer says, "Trent did not prove that the Reformation had been superfluous. On the contrary, Trent condemned the Reformation and rejected its doctrine."[28]

Bear in mind that the doctrinal position spelled out at Trent, with its strong condemnation of Reformation theology, is the official position of Roman Catholicism even now. All the hard lines drawn by Trent, together with the Council's one hundred anathemas against Protestantism, are steadfastly maintained to this day. The Catholic Church has never changed its stance on the crucial doctrinal questions raised in the Reformation—and even Catholic apologists affirm this.[29]

One other point needs to be made regarding the scandal of the Reformation. The Catholic Church herself must bear much of the blame for the schism that occurred. The Reformers did not initially intend to break with the Church. Splitting the church was the last thing Luther wanted to do. On the contrary, it was Rome that rejected the Reformation—and very early in the process. In 1520, a papal bull, *Exsurge Domine* was issued against Luther, rejecting his ideas as heretical. Twenty-five years later, Trent confirmed that judgment and pronounced its infamous anathemas against anyone who dared question Rome's position.

WHAT ABOUT VATICAN II?

In other words, at Trent, the Roman Catholic Church officially declared the Reformation an act of apostasy. It was the only possible response of a Church determined to promote herself as doctrinally infallible. To this day Roman Catholicism condemns the Protestant doctrine of justification by faith as a damning heresy.[30] As Berkouwer pointed out, "According to Rome there is only one way to reunion, viz., the repudiation of the Reformation and its *doctrine*; and there is no reason to weaken this statement."[31]

To those in his day who believed modern Catholicism was different and that it was time to try to reunite Catholics and Protestants in one Church, Berkouwer replied:

Even at the present moment—many centuries after the breach—
we cannot possibly accept the "evidence" of the superfluity of the
Reformation, but we consider this "evidence" a mere simplicism
ignoring the historical facts. Perhaps we should say: it ignores the
one historical fact that *Rome has rejected the doctrine of the Reformation
and cannot and will not suffer it to be taught in the church.*[32]

Berkouwer wrote that in the 1940s. The English edition of his book
wasn't published in America until 1957. It remains one of the most
perceptive analyses of Catholic-evangelical relations ever published.

In 1959, a new pope, Pope John XXIII—after only ninety days in
office—unexpectedly announced plans for a Second Vatican Council.
His express purpose was to seek worldwide religious unity through
renewal of the Roman Catholic Church and interfaith dialogue. The
Council convened in October 1962 and met in four sessions through
1965.[33]

G. C. Berkouwer attended sessions of Vatican II as a Protestant
observer. Even before the final sessions were complete, Berkouwer
wrote breathlessly, "The [Catholic] Church, holding on to the past,
is listening anew to the gospel according to the Scriptures."[34] But, he
quickly acknowledged, "This bond between current listening for the
gospel and an unbreakable tie with the past unavoidably creates a
great many new problems for the church. These problems are
accepted and put on the agenda for discussion."[35]

When Berkouwer referred to "the agenda for discussion," he was
speaking of the ecumenical dialogue proposed by Vatican II.

Vatican II introduced some of the most sweeping changes in
Roman Catholic practice since the Council of Trent. The Council
made extensive liturgical revisions, allowing the Mass to be said in
the vernacular rather than in Latin. It encouraged lay people to read
the Bible devotionally—something the Catholic Church in earlier
times would have put people to death for. It abolished Friday absti-
nence. In short, it updated and simplified the apparatus of Catholic
worship, issued a plea for dialogue and unity, and made a number of
political and philosophical pronouncements regarding issues such as
war, human dignity, social justice, and religious freedom. The docu-

ments produced by the Council are ponderous, extending to 103,014 words in the Latin text—and that does not count the 992 footnotes, many of which are quite long.[36]

The Council also called for interfaith dialogues with Protestants, Jews, Moslems, Hindus—and all other religions. G. C. Berkouwer saw this and hoped the door was finally open for the Church to discuss Reformation doctrine—and perhaps withdraw the infamous anathemas.

But in spite of Berkouwer's early enthusiasm, doctrinal changes were expressly *not* part of the Vatican II discussion. There was some softening of language (Protestants are referred to throughout as "separated brethren" rather than apostates), but no official dogma was revoked or altered. In fact, Vatican II formally ratified the work of the Council of Trent, declaring itself to be "following in the footsteps of the Councils of Trent and of First Vatican."[37] While urging "all concerned to work hard to prevent or correct any abuses, excesses, or defects which may have crept in here and there,"[38] the Council made clear that it was thinking of *practical* abuses only:

> This most sacred Synod accepts with great devotion the venerable faith of our ancestors regarding this vital fellowship with our brethren who are in heavenly glory or who are still being purified after death. It proposes again the decrees of the Second Council of Nicea, the Council of Florence, and the Council of Trent.[39]

Indeed, in this sense the spirit of Trent was very much alive at Vatican II. Many practical and political reforms were made, but the Church's official stance against the doctrine of the Reformation was clearly reaffirmed. The infallibility of the Church was reasserted. "The dogmatic principles which were laid down by the Council of Trent remain[ed] intact."[40] The Reformation was once again rebuffed. Catholic doctrine was declared "irreformable."[41]

While Vatican II issued no new anathemas, it did ratify all the previous ones. The Council also made clear that Catholics are still forbidden to question official Church doctrine:

In matters of faith and morals, the bishops speak in the name of Christ and *the faithful are to accept their teaching and adhere to it with a religious assent of the soul.* This religious submission of will and of mind must be shown in a special way to the teaching authority of the Roman Pontiff, *even when he is not speaking ex cathedra.* That is, it must be shown in such a way that his supreme magisterium is acknowledged with reverence, the judgments made by him sincerely adhered to, according to his manifest mind and will.[42]

It must be noted that some of the fruits of Vatican II have been quite positive. The effect of the Council's decision on personal Bible reading has been astonishing. Multitudes who were formerly fearful of reading the Bible have now seen the Gospel for themselves in the clear light of God's Word. Quebec and Latin America—once impenetrable bastions of Catholicism—have experienced widespread spiritual revival. Thousands whose religion was formerly laden with Mary-worship and superstition have turned to the Christ of Scripture. Protestant churches now flourish where forty years ago preaching the Gospel was a crime.[43]

Thirty years later, how do we evaluate G. C. Berkouwer's declaration that Rome was "listening anew to the gospel according to the Scriptures"? Was it a case of wishful thinking? Berkouwer himself seemed to recognize the difficulty his expectation posed: "[The Catholic Church's] own unchangeability and continuity is the issue. And for this reason the Roman Catholic Church is faced with tremendously important decisions."[44] While Berkouwer remained hopeful about interfaith dialogue, he ended his book with a warning that common-denominator ecumenism (attempting to eliminate all doctrine except commonly agreed-upon points, such as the Apostles' Creed) is "a fruitless way to seek unity."[45]

It is very clear today that the Catholic Church's appeals for "dialogue" never meant that Rome was "listening anew to the gospel." Nor should the irenic spirit of Vatican II ever have been interpreted as an offer to reassess Catholic doctrine in light of Scripture. All subsequent dialogue has shown that the most Rome will ever settle for is the fruitless unity of common-denominator ecumenism.

Remember that Vatican II also called for dialogue with Jews, Moslems, Buddhists, and Hindus. All religions, according to the Council, represent "a certain perception of that hidden power which hovers over the course of things and over the events of human life."[46] Moreover, the Council declared, "all peoples comprise a single community," and the Church's task is to foster unity and love and promote fellowship among all people of all religions.[47]

> The Church therefore has this exhortation for her sons: prudently and lovingly, through dialogue and collaboration with the followers of other religions, and in witness of Christian faith and life, acknowledge, preserve, and promote the spiritual and moral goods found among these men, as well as the values in their society and culture.[48]

So the *auto-da-fé* is finally replaced with "dialogue and collaboration."

Vatican II represented a dramatic change in methodology for the Catholic Church.[49] The call for dialogue was one of the most profound and far-reaching pronouncements of the whole Synod. Yet in no way did it mean that Rome was prepared to discuss possible doctrinal corrections—or even contemplate the possibility that she might be less than infallible.

How did the Church address the issue of her guilt? In the context of a section on relations with non-Christians, the Council stated that it "repudiates all persecutions against any man."[50] Yet it managed to make that announcement with no mention of the atrocities sanctioned by past popes. Instead, we read, "this most sacred Synod urges all to forget the past and to strive sincerely for mutual understanding."[51]

Not that the Council was wholly silent about the awful past. In the declaration on religious freedom, the Church called for universal tolerance. The obvious contradiction between such an appeal and six hundred years of Catholic Inquisition was addressed in these words:

> The Church therefore is being faithful to the truth of the gospel, and is following the way of Christ and the apostles when

she recognizes, and gives support to, the principle of religious freedom as befitting the dignity of man and as being in accord with divine revelation. Throughout the ages, the Church has kept safe and handed on the doctrine received from the Master and from the apostles. In the life of the People of God as it has made its pilgrim way through the vicissitudes of human history, there have at times appeared ways of acting which were less in accord with the spirit of the gospel and even opposed to it. Nevertheless, *the doctrine of the Church that no one is to be coerced into faith has always stood firm.*[52]

Thus Rome continues to maintain that she is infallible. Incredibly, she claims to have "kept safe and handed on the doctrine" given her by Christ and the apostles, even while violating the very spirit of Christ. Even more incredibly, she now claims she has always believed "that no one is to be coerced into faith."

Thirty years after Vatican II, the "agenda for discussion" still has not come around to fundamental doctrinal issues. Nor is it likely to. Rome is no closer to a biblical position on justification by faith than she was at the Council of Trent.

Clearly the Roman Catholic Church *is* changing—in every way but the crucial one. While the form of Catholicism changes dramatically, the substance remains the same. Catholic doctrine remains unchanged—unchangeable. That is not now and never has been a matter for "dialogue and collaboration."

IS UNITY WITH ROME A LEGITIMATE PURSUIT?

Roman Catholicism put on a new face at Vatican II, but the changes—extensive as they are—are cosmetic only. Rome continues to oppose the doctrine of justification by faith alone. Therefore the gospel according to Roman Catholicism is "a different gospel" from that set forth in the New Testament.

There are undoubtedly many people who identify with the Roman Catholic Church who are authentically born again. In spite of church dogma, they sincerely trust the finished work of Jesus Christ *alone* for salvation. Whether they realize it or not, they have departed from what the Catholic Church teaches. And whether they realize it or not, their Church has anathematized them for it. Still, *Scripture* says they are members of the true body of Christ (Rom. 12:5; 1 Cor. 12:27).

But many more, vast multitudes trapped in Roman Catholicism, are desperately attempting through sacraments, religious cere-monies, and good works to earn God's favor. These people need to hear the unvarnished Gospel preached in a way that confronts the errors of Roman Catholicism. A message that is scaled back to the specifications of the ecumenically-minded is not the whole counsel of God.

The recent "Evangelicals and Catholics Together" accord included a confession of "sins against the unity that Christ intends for all his disciples." Michael Horton's analysis of that document included these insightful comments:

> Confession of sin against unity is a serious business. Schism ranks with heresy itself as a crime against God. Those who willfully per-petuate division on the basis of pride, suspicion, and self-interest are not held guiltless. But this, too, begs the question of whether the historical divisions between evangelicals and Rome are in that category. It assumes that Christ demands unity between Rome and Evangelicals and that an unwillingness to accept this is a sin "against the unity that Christ intends for all his disciples."
>
> We maintain that Christ does intend unity in the truth, but deny that he requires unity with anyone who preaches any other Gospel than the one that was believed by Abraham and delivered by our Lord and His apostles with great clarity.[53]

I would add an even stronger comment: as long as the papal system binds its people to "another gospel," it is the spiritual duty of all true Christians to *oppose* Roman Catholic doctrine with biblical truth and to call all Catholics to true salvation. Appeals for "dialogue" must not be allowed to silence or obscure our clear polemic for the truth and against error. And the focus and goal of all Catholic-evangelical dialogue should always be to seek *truth*—not a superficial peace, not merely common denominators, not even moral and political coalition—but the true answer to the question, "What must I do to be saved?" Meanwhile, evangelicals must not capitulate to the pressures for artificial unity. We cannot allow the Gospel to be obscured. We cannot make friends with false religion, lest we become partakers in their evil deeds (2 John 11).

APPENDIX 2

Jonathan Edwards's Theology of Discernment

(This material is condensed and adapted from
The Distinguishing Marks of a Work of the Spirit of God)

"Beloved, do not believe every spirit, but test the spirits to see whether they are from God; because many false prophets have gone out into the world" (1 John 4:1).

I N THE APOSTOLIC AGE there was the greatest outpouring of the Spirit of God that ever was. But as the influences of the true Spirit abounded, counterfeits also abounded. The devil was abundant in mimicking both the ordinary and extraordinary influences of the Spirit of God. This made it very necessary that the church of Christ should be furnished with some certain rules—distinguishing and clear marks—by which she might proceed safely in judging of the true from the false. The giving of such rules is the plain design of 1 John 4, where this matter is more expressly and fully treated than anywhere else in the Bible. In this extraordinary day, when there is so much talk about the work of the Spirit, we must carefully apply these principles.

Before the apostle proceeds to lay down the signs, first, *he exhorts Christians against an over-credulousness*: "Beloved, do not believe every spirit, but test the spirits to see whether they are from God." And second, *he shows that there are many counterfeits*: "because many false prophets have gone out into the world." These false spirits pretend not only to have the Spirit of God and extraordinary gifts of inspiration, but also to be the great friends and favorites of heaven, to be eminently holy persons, and to have much of the ordinary saving, sanctifying influences of the Spirit of God on their hearts. Therefore we are to examine and try their pretenses.

My design therefore is to show what are the true, certain, and distinguishing evidences of a work of the Spirit of God. And here I would observe *that we are to take the Scriptures as our guide*. This is the great and standing rule which God has given to His church, in order to guide them in things relating to the great concerns of their souls. Scripture is an infallible and sufficient rule. It undoubtedly contains sufficient precepts to guide the church in this great affair of discerning a true work of God. Without such principles, the church would lie open to woeful delusions and would be exposed without remedy to be imposed on and devoured by its enemies.

I shall confine myself to the principles I find in 1 John 4. But before I proceed particularly to speak of these, I will prepare my way first by observing what are *not* reliable evidences whether something is a work of the Spirit of God.

INVALID ARGUMENTS

These things are no evidence that a work is or is not from the Spirit of God:

"We've Never Done It That Way Before"

Nothing can be concluded from the fact that a work is carried on in a very unusual and extraordinary way, provided it does not violate any biblical principles. "What the church is used to" is not a rule by which we are to judge. God often works in extraordinary ways.

The prophecies of Scripture give us reason to think that God has things to accomplish that have not yet been seen. The Holy Spirit is sovereign in His operation. We ought not to limit God where He has not limited Himself.

"People's Reactions Are Too Strong"

A work is not to be condemned merely because of any effects on men such as tears, trembling, groans, loud outcries, agonies of body, or the failing of bodily strength. The Scripture nowhere gives us any such rule. We cannot conclude that persons *are* under the influence of the Holy Spirit just because we see such effects upon their bodies (this is not given as a mark of the true Spirit). Nor on the other hand, should we conclude from such outward appearances that persons *are not* under the influence of the Spirit of God.

It does seem, however, that a proper sense of gospel truth *should* provoke a strong response—failing of strength, bodily agonies, and even loud outcries. Surely the misery of hell is so dreadful and eternity so vast that if a person gains a clear understanding of it, it would be more than his feeble frame could bear—especially if at the same time he saw himself in great danger of being eternally lost. If a person saw himself hanging over a great pit, full of fierce and glowing flames, by a thread that he knew to be very weak and not sufficient to bear his weight; if he knew that multitudes had been in such circumstances before and that most of them had fallen and perished; if he saw nothing within reach that he could take hold of to save him, what distress would he be in! How ready to think that now the thread was breaking—that now, *this minute*, he should be swallowed up in those dreadful flames! Wouldn't he naturally cry out in such circumstances?

No wonder that the wrath of God, even when manifested but a little to the soul, overwhelms human strength! After all, both Saul of Tarsus and the Philippian jailer trembled from real convictions of conscience.

"People Are Talking About It Too Much"

The fact that something provokes a great deal of noise about religion is no argument against its validity. Although true religion is never ostentatious like that of the Pharisees—yet human nature is such that it is morally impossible to experience renewal and revival without causing a commotion in the community.

Surely, there is no reason to dismiss a work of God's Spirit just because people are very much moved. After all, spiritual and eternal things are so great and of such infinite concern, that it would be absurd for people to be only moderately moved and affected by them.

Remember, people said of the apostles that they had turned the world upside down (Acts 17:6).

"People Are Imagining Things"

It is no argument that something is not the work of the Spirit of God because people have great impressions made on their imaginations. Our nature is such that we cannot think of invisible things without a degree of imagination. The more engaged the *mind* and affections are, the more intense will be the imagination.

This is especially true when the truth being contemplated is new to the mind and takes hold of the emotions. When someone is struck with extreme dread, and when at conversion that sense of dread gives way immediately to extreme delight, it is no wonder if such a person cannot easily distinguish between that which is imaginary and that which is intellectual and spiritual. Many people are apt to lay too much weight on the imaginary part, and are most ready to speak of that when they testify of their experiences.

In such cases God seems to condescend to their circumstances and deal with them as babes.

"People Just Do What They See Others Doing"

It is no sign that a work is not from the Spirit of God just because it spreads by means of example. We know that it is God's manner to use various means in carrying on His work. It is no argument against God's involvement in something that a particular means is used to accomplish it.

And certainly it is agreeable to Scripture that persons should be influenced by one another's good example. The Scripture directs us to set good examples to that end (Matt. 5:16; 1 Peter 3:1; 1 Tim. 4:12; Titus 2:7). It also directs us to be influenced by the good examples of others (2 Cor. 8:1-7; Phil. 3:17; 1 Cor. 4:16-17; 2 Thess. 3:9; 1 Thess. 1:7). It appears that example *is* one of God's means. It is both a *scriptural* and a *reasonable* way of carrying on God's work.

"People Are Getting Carried Away"

It is no sign that a work is not from the Spirit of God just because many are guilty of great imprudences and irregularities in their conduct. God pours out His Spirit to make men holy, not to make them politicians. It is no wonder that in a mixed multitude of all sorts—wise and unwise, young and old, people with weak and strong natural abilities, and people under strong impressions of mind—many behave themselves imprudently. There are but few that know how to conduct themselves under vehement affections of any kind. A thousand imprudences will not prove a work to be not of the Spirit of God. Often things occur that are even contrary to the rules of God's holy Word. That it should be this way is due to the exceeding weakness of human nature, together with the remaining darkness and corruption of those who are yet under the saving influences of God's Spirit. The church at Corinth, with all the problems Paul had to correct, is a New Testament example of a true work of the Spirit, accompanied by many human imprudences.

Lukewarmness in religion is abominable. Zeal is an excellent grace. Yet above all other Christian virtues, this needs to be strictly watched and searched, for corruption—and particularly pride and human passion—is exceedingly prone to mix unobserved with zeal.

"People Are Deluded"

Errors in judgment, and even some delusions of Satan might be intermixed with a work; yet that does not mean that the work in general is not wrought by the Spirit of God.

We are not to expect that the Spirit of God should guide us infallibly as He did the apostles. Yet otherwise godly people fail to understand this. Many godly persons have undoubtedly in this and other ages exposed themselves to woeful delusions, by a tendency to lay too much weight on subjective impulses and impressions, as if they were immediate revelations from God to signify something future, or to direct them where to go and what to do.

"People Are Falling into Error"

If some supposed "converts" fall away into gross errors, or scandalous practices, it is no argument that the work in general is not the work of the Spirit of God. Counterfeits are no proof that a thing is untrue: such things are always expected in a time of reformation.

If we look into church history, we shall find that every great revival has been attended with many such things. Instances of this nature in the apostles' days were innumerable; some fell away into gross heresies, others into vile practices—even though they seemed to be the subjects of the Spirit's work and were even accepted for a while as true disciples.

One example of these was Judas, who was intimately conversant with the disciples. Yet he was not discovered or suspected until he discovered himself by his scandalous practice. Jesus Himself treated Judas as if he had truly been a disciple, even investing him with the character of apostle, sending him forth to preach the gospel, and enduing him with miraculous gifts of the Spirit. For although Christ knew him, yet He did not then clothe Himself with the character of omniscient Judge and searcher of hearts, but acted the part of a minister of the visible church and therefore rejected him not.

The devil's sowing of tares is no proof that a true work of the Spirit of God is not gloriously carried on.

"The Preachers Emphasize Judgment Too Much"

It is no argument that a work is not from the Spirit of God that it seems to be promoted by ministers insisting very much on the terrors of God's holy law. If hell's torments are real and multitudes are in great danger of falling into God's eternal condemnation or being lulled into insensitivity about it, then why is it not proper for pastors to take great pains to make people conscious of the awful truth? Why should people not be told as much of the truth as can be?

If I am in danger of going to hell, and if I am prone to neglect due care to avoid it, the greatest kindness anyone can do for me is to tell me the truth in the liveliest manner. We all would go to any extreme necessary to warn people of life-threatening temporal danger; why should we not do even more when it comes to eternal dangers?

Some talk of it as an unreasonable thing to frighten persons to heaven; but I think it is a reasonable thing to endeavor to frighten persons away from hell. They stand on its brink and are just ready to fall into it and are senseless of their danger. Is it not a reasonable thing to frighten a person out of a house on fire?

Not that I think that only the law should be preached. The gospel is to be preached as well as the law. In fact, the law is to be preached only to make way for the gospel. The main work of ministers is to preach the gospel: "Christ is the end of the law for righteousness" (Rom. 10:4). A minister would miss it very much if he were to insist so much on the terrors of the law that he forgot his Lord and neglected to preach the Gospel.

Still, the law is very much to be insisted on, and the preaching of the Gospel is likely to be in vain without it.

BIBLICAL SIGNS OF THE TRUE SPIRIT'S WORK

Having shown what are *not* sufficient evidences to conclude that the Spirit of God is not in a work, I now proceed as was proposed, to show positively what are the distinguishing biblical marks of a work of the Spirit of God. And in this, as I said before, I shall confine myself wholly to the evidences given us by the apostle in 1 John 4. Here this matter is particularly addressed more plainly and fully than anywhere else in the Bible. And in speaking to these marks, I shall take them in the order in which I find them in the chapter.

It Exalts the True Christ

"By this you know the Spirit of God: every spirit that confesses that Jesus Christ has come in the flesh is from God; and every spirit that does not confess Jesus is not from God" (vv. 2-3).

When a ministry raises people's esteem of the one true Jesus Christ, who was born of a virgin and was crucified—if it confirms and establishes their minds in the truth that He is the Son of God and the Savior of men—then it is a sure sign that it is from the Spirit of God.

If the spirit at work among a people convinces them of Christ and leads them to Him; if it confirms their minds in the belief of the history of Christ as He appeared in the flesh; if it teaches them that He is the Son of God, who was sent of God to save sinners; if it reveals that He is the only Savior, and that they stand in great need of Him; and if it begets in them higher and more honorable thoughts of Christ than they used to have; if it inclines their affections more to Him—that is a sure sign that it is the true and right Spirit. This is true even though we are ultimately incapable of determining whether anyone's conviction or affections reflect real saving faith.

The words of the apostle are remarkable. The person to whom the Spirit testifies *must* be that Jesus who appeared in the flesh—not another christ in His stead. It cannot be some mystical, fantastical Christ, such as the "inner light" extolled by the Quakers. This imaginary christ diminishes their esteem of and dependence on Jesus as He came in the flesh. The true Spirit of God gives testimony for that Jesus alone.

The devil has a fierce hatred against Christ, especially in His office as the Savior of men. Satan mortally hates the story and doctrine of redemption; he never would go about to stress these truths. The Spirit that inclines men's hearts to the Seed of the woman is not the spirit of the serpent that has such an irreconcilable enmity against Him.

It Opposes Satan's Interests

"You are from God, little children, and have overcome them; because greater is He who is in you than he who is in the world. They are from the world; therefore they speak as from the world, and the world listens to them" (vv. 4-5).

When the spirit that is at work operates against the interests of Satan's kingdom, against sin, and against worldly lusts—this is a sure sign that it is a true, and not a false spirit.

Here is a plain antithesis. The apostle is comparing those who are influenced by two opposite spirits, the true and the false. The difference is plain: the one is of God, and overcomes the spirit of the world; the other is of the world, and is obsessed with the things of the world. The devil is called "he who is in the world."

What the apostle means by "the world," or "the things that are in the world," we learn by his own words: "Do not love the world, nor the things in the world. If anyone loves the world, the love of the Father is not in him. For all that is in the world, the lust of the flesh and the lust of the eyes and the boastful pride of life, is not from the Father, but is from the world" (2:15-16). So by "the world" the apostle evidently means everything that pertains to the interest of sin. The term also comprehends all the corruptions and lusts of men, as well as all those acts and objects by which they are gratified.

We may also safely determine from what the apostle says that whatever lessens people's esteem of the pleasures, profits, and honors of the world; whatever turns their hearts from an eager pursuit after these things; whatever engages them in a due concern about eternity and causes them earnestly to seek the kingdom of God and His righteousness; whatever convinces them of the dreadfulness of sin, the guilt it brings, and the misery to which it exposes—*must* be the Spirit of God.

It is not to be supposed that Satan would convince men of sin or awaken the conscience. It can no way serve his end to make that candle of the Lord shine the brighter. It is for his interest, whatever he does, to lull conscience asleep and keep it quiet. To have that with its eyes and mouth open in the soul would tend to clog and hinder all his designs of darkness. The awakened conscience would evermore disturb his affairs, cross his interests, and disquiet him. Would the devil, when he is about to establish people in sin, take such a course? Would he make them more careful, inquisitive, and watchful to discern what is sinful, and to avoid future sins, and to be more wary of the devil's temptations?

The man who has an awakened conscience is the least likely to be deceived of any man in the world; it is the drowsy, insensible, stupid conscience that is most easily blinded. The Spirit that operates thus cannot be the spirit of the devil; Satan will not cast out Satan (Matt. 12:25-26). Therefore if we see persons made sensible of the dreadful nature of sin and the displeasure of God against it, we may conclude that whatever effects this concern is from the Spirit of God.

It Points People to the Scriptures

"We are from God; he who knows God listens to us; he who is not from God does not listen to us. By this we know the spirit of truth and the spirit of error" (v. 6).

The spirit that causes people to have a greater regard for the Holy Scriptures and establishes them more in the truth and divinity of God's Word is certainly the Spirit of God.

The devil never would attempt to beget in persons a regard to the divine Word. A spirit of delusion will not incline persons to seek direction at the mouth of God. "To the law and to the testimony!" (Isa. 8:20) is never the cry of evil spirits who have no light in them. On the contrary, it is God's own direction to discover their delusions. Would the spirit of error, in order to deceive men, beget in them a high opinion of the infallible Word? Would the prince of darkness, in order to promote his kingdom of darkness, lead men to the sun? The devil has always shown a mortal spite and hatred towards that holy book, the Bible. He has done all in his power to extinguish that light, or else draw men off from it. He knows it to be that light by which his kingdom of darkness is to be overthrown. He has long experienced its power to defeat his purposes and baffle his designs. It is his constant plague. It is the sword of the Spirit that pierces him and conquers him. It is that sharp sword that we read of in Revelation 19:15, which proceeds out of the mouth of Him that sat on the horse, with which He smites His enemies. Every text is a dart to torment the old serpent. He has felt the stinging smart thousands of times.

Therefore the devil is engaged against the Bible and hates every word in it. We may be sure that he never will attempt to raise anyone's esteem of it.

It Elevates Truth

"We know the spirit of truth and the spirit of error" (v. 6).

Another rule by which to judge spirits is that whatever operates as a spirit of truth, leading people to truth, convincing them of those things that are true—we may safely determine that it is a right and true spirit.

For instance, if the spirit at work makes men more aware than they used to be of the central gospel truths: that there is a God; that He is a great and a sin-hating God; that life is short and very uncertain; that there is another world; that they have immortal souls; that they must give account of themselves to God; that they are exceeding sinful by nature and practice; that they are helpless in themselves—then that spirit operates as a spirit of truth. He represents things as they truly are. He brings men to the light.

On the other hand, the spirit of darkness will not uncover and make manifest the truth. Christ tells us that Satan is a liar, and the father of liars. His kingdom is a kingdom of darkness. It is upheld and promoted only by darkness and error. Satan has all his power and dominion by darkness. Whatever spirit removes our darkness and brings us to the light undeceives us. If I am brought to the truth and am made aware of things as they really are, my duty is immediately to thank God for it without inquiring by what means I have such a benefit.

It Results in Love for God and Others

"The one who does not love does not know God, for God is love" (v. 8).

If the spirit that is at work among a people operates as a spirit of love to God and man, it is a sure sign that it is the Spirit of God. This last mark which the apostle gives of the true Spirit he seems to speak of as the most eminent. He devotes more space to it and so insists much more largely on it than all the rest.

When the spirit that is at work among the people brings many of them to high and exalting thoughts of the Divine Being and His glorious perfections; when it works in them an admiring, delightful sense of the excellency of Jesus Christ, representing Him as the chief among ten thousand and altogether lovely; when it makes Him precious to the soul, winning and drawing the heart with those motives and incitements to free love of God and the wonderful dying love of Christ—it *must* be the Spirit of God.

"We love, because He first loved us," verse 19 says. The spirit that makes the soul long after God and Christ must be the Spirit of God. When we desire the presence and communion of the divine Savior, acquaintance with Him, conformity to Him, a life that pleases and honors Him, we must be under the influence of His Spirit.

Moreover, the spirit that quells contentions among men gives a spirit of peace and good-will, excites to acts of outward kindness, earnestly desires the salvation of souls, and arouses love for all the children of God and followers of Christ. I say that when a spirit operates after this manner, there is the highest kind of evidence that this is the Holy Spirit.

Indeed, there is a counterfeit love that often appears among those who are led by a spirit of delusion. There is commonly in the wildest enthusiasts a kind of union and affection arising from self-love. It is occasioned by their agreeing on issues where they greatly differ from all others and for which they are objects of ridicule from the rest of mankind. That naturally will cause them so much the more to prize those peculiarities that make them the objects of others' contempt. (Thus the ancient Gnostics and the wild fanatics that appeared at the beginning of the Reformation boasted of their great love to one another—one sect of them in particular calling themselves "the family of love.") But this is quite another thing than that Christian love I have just described.

There is enough said in this passage of the nature of a truly Christian love to distinguish it from all such counterfeits. It is love that arises from apprehension of the wonderful riches of the free grace and sovereignty of God's love to us in Jesus Christ. It is attended with a sense of our own utter unworthiness (see vv. 9-11, 19). The surest character of true, divine, supernatural love—distinguishing it from counterfeits that arise from a natural self-love—is that the Christian virtue of humility shines in it. It is a love which above all others renounces, abases, and annihilates what we term *self*. Christian love is a humble love (1 Cor. 13:4-5).

When, therefore, we see a love attended with a sense of one's own littleness, vileness, weakness, and utter insufficiency; when it is united with self-diffidence, self-emptiness, self-renunciation, and poverty of spirit—those are the manifest tokens of the Spirit of God.

He that thus dwells in love dwells in God, and God in him.

CONCLUSION

These marks that the apostle has given us are sufficient to stand alone and support themselves. They plainly show the finger of God and are sufficient to outweigh a thousand such little objections as many make from oddities, irregularities, errors in conduct, and the delusions and scandals of some professors.

But here some may object. After all, the apostle Paul says in 2 Corinthians 11:13-14, "Such men are false apostles, deceitful workers, disguising themselves as apostles of Christ. And no wonder, for even Satan disguises himself as an angel of light."

To which I answer that this can be no objection against the sufficiency of these marks to distinguish the true from the false spirit in those false apostles and prophets—even when the devil is transformed into an angel of light. After all, the very reason the apostle John gave these marks was so that we could test the spirits. Therefore try the spirits by these rules and you will be able to distinguish the true spirit from the false—even under such a crafty disguise.

NOTES

INTRODUCTION

1. Cf. Henry Bettenson, ed., *Documents of the Christian Church* (New York: Oxford, 1963), 201.

CHAPTER ONE: The War Against Reason

1. John W. Kennedy, "Hunting for Heresy," *Christianity Today* (16 May 1994).
2. Robert Bretall, ed., *A Kierkegaard Anthology* (Princeton, N. J.: Princeton University Press, 1946), 5 (emphasis in original).
3. *Ibid.*
4. Søren Kierkegaard, *Fear and Trembling*, Howard V. Hong and Edna H. Hong, trans. (Princeton, N. J.: Princeton University Press, 1983), 55.
5. *Ibid.*
6. *Ibid.*, 57.
7. Karl Barth, *The Epistle to the Romans*, Edwyn C. Hoskyns, trans. (London: Oxford University Press, 1933). Barth cites Kierkegaard repeatedly in this, one of his earliest works.
8. Francis Schaeffer, *The God Who Is There*, in *The Complete Works of Francis A. Schaeffer*, Volume 1 (Wheaton, Ill.: Crossway Books, 1982).
9. *Ibid.*, 53.
10. *Ibid.*, 55.
11. *Ibid.*, 58.
12. Arthur L. Johnson, *Faith Misguided: Exposing the Dangers of Mysticism* (Chicago: Moody Press, 1988), 31-32.
13. Schaeffer, 64-65, emphasis added.
14. *Purgatory*: Luke 23:42-43 and 2 Cor. 5:8 indicate that believers go immediately to be with Christ at death. *Perpetual virginity of Mary*: Matt. 1:25 states that Joseph kept Mary a virgin only until Jesus' birth, and John 2:12 and Acts 1:14 reveal that Jesus had brothers. *Transubstantiation*: Heb. 7:27 and 10:12 teach that Christ made one sacrifice for sins forever; there is no need for the daily sacrifice of the Mass. *Prayers to Mary and the saints*: prayers, adoration, and

spiritual veneration offered to anyone but God is expressly forbidden by the first commandment and elsewhere throughout Scripture (Ex. 20:3; Matt. 4:10; Acts 10:25-26; Rev. 19:10; Rev. 22:8-9).

CHAPTER TWO: The Rise of Reckless Faith

1. Cited in Iain Murray, *D. Martyn Lloyd-Jones: The Fight of Faith, 1939-1981* (Edinburgh: Banner of Truth, 1990), 667.
2. Gordon H. Clark, *A Christian Philosophy of Education* (Jefferson, Md.: Trinity Foundation, 1988), 158.
3. D. Martyn Lloyd-Jones, *Romans: An Exposition of Chapters 3.20—4.25: Atonement and Justification* (Grand Rapids, Mich.: Zondervan Publishing House, 1970), 113.
4. *Ibid.*
5. *Ibid.*, 113-14.
6. *Ibid.*, 114.
7. Jay E. Adams, *A Call to Discernment* (Eugene, Ore.: Harvest House, 1987), 31.
8. *Ibid.*
9. *Ibid.*, 29.
10. *Ibid.*, 32.
11. *Ashamed of the Gospel: When the Church Becomes Like the World* (Wheaton, Ill.: Crossway Books, 1993).
12. Charles H. Spurgeon, *Autobiography, Volume 1: The Early Years* (Edinburgh: Banner of Truth, 1962 edition), v (emphasis added).
13. Bernard Ramm, *Protestant Biblical Interpretation* (Grand Rapids, Mich.: Baker Book House, 1970), pp. 17-18.
14. Adams, 28.
15. *Ibid.*, 27.
16. "What Happens When Christians Use Bad Language" (21 February 1994 news release from the Barna Research Group, Ltd.)

CHAPTER THREE: The Biblical Formula for Discernment

1. Jay E. Adams, *A Call to Discernment* (Eugene, Ore.: Harvest House, 1987), 46.
2. *Ibid.*, 75.

CHAPTER FOUR: What Are the Fundamentals of Christianity?

1. Recently republished in four volumes by Baker Book House.
2. A detailed account of how this process occurred in one institution is George Marsden's *Reforming Fundamentalism: Fuller Seminary and the New Evangelicalism* (Grand Rapids, Mich.: Wm. B. Eerdmans, 1987).
3. Foreword to James R. Spencer, *Heresy Hunters: Character Assassination in the Church* (Lafayette, La.: Huntington House, 1993), vii.
4. *Ibid.*
5. Philip Schaff, *The Creeds of Christendom*, 3 vols. (Grand Rapids, Mich.: Baker Book House, 1983 reprint), 1:531.
6. Charles Colson, *The Body* (Dallas: Word Publishing, 1992).
7. *Ibid.*, 185.

8. *Ibid.*, 104.
9. *Ibid.*
10. *Ibid.*, 170.
11. *Ibid.*, 171.
12. *Ibid.*, 186.
13. *Ibid.*, 185.
14. *Ibid.*, 186.
15. *Ibid.*, 198-99.
16. *Ibid.*, 104. Note that here Colson formulates his list in a slightly different way, separating the resurrection from the Second Coming. This makes six points of doctrine, one more than the five in Colson's numbered list on page 186. On pages 108-9 Colson gives an expanded five-point list borrowed from another source, then adds a sixth point—the authority of the inerrant Word. But in each case the core doctrines he lists are essentially the same.

    Of course, there is a world of meaning wrapped up in terms like *atonement* and *the authority of Scripture*. If Colson were appealing for faith in Scripture as the Christian's *sole* authority (excluding papal dictums and magisterial traditions), I would be more comfortable with his formula. But throughout his book he makes repeated, explicit appeals for evangelical Christians to open their arms to Catholicism and Eastern Orthodoxy.

    Therefore whatever he means by "the authority of Scripture" cannot be what the Reformers meant when they spoke of *sola Scriptura*, Scripture as our supreme and sufficient authority.
17. *The Fundamentals* included articles defending the doctrine of justification by faith alone, as well as articles titled, "Is Romanism Christianity?" and "Rome, the Antagonist of the Nation."
18. *Ibid.*, 186.
19. Schaff, 1:14-23. See also Herman Witsius, *Sacred Dissertations on the Apostles' Creed*, 2 vols. (Phillipsburg, N.J.: Presbyterian & Reformed, 1993 reprint), 1:1-15; and William Cunningham, *Historical Theology*, 2 vols. (Edmonton, Alta.: Still Waters, 1991 reprint), 1:79-93.
20. Schaff, 1:19.
21. *Ibid.*, 1:21.
22. Cunningham, 1:89.
23. Witsius, 1:30-31 (emphasis added).
24. Cunningham, 1:89.
25. Francis Turretin, *Institutes of Elenctic Theology*, vol. 1, George Musgrave Giger, trans. (Phillipsburg, N.J.: Presbyterian & Reformed, 1992), 53.
26. Owing to a misunderstanding of this article, one of the great Protestant hymns includes a line about the church's "mystic sweet communion with those whose rest is won." But far from teaching that people on earth can commune with the dead, Scripture condemns in the strongest terms any activity aimed at establishing that sort of communication (Deut. 18:10-12).
27. Cunningham, 1:89.
28. *Ibid.*, 1:90.
29. Colson, 171.
30. *Ibid.*, 112.
31. For the section that follows I am largely indebted to Witsius (*op cit.*), who includes a marvelous treatment of this very subject in volume 1, pages 16-33.

It is noteworthy that Witsius spoke of "fundamental articles" at least 250 years before the fundamentalist movement was named.

32. Turretin, 48.
33. Witsius, 1:20.
34. *Ibid.*, 1:21.
35. *Ibid.*, 1:27-29.
36. Turretin, 54.
37. *Ibid.*, 29.
38. *Ibid.*, 31.
39. *Ibid.*, 33.

CHAPTER FIVE: *Evangelicals and Catholics Together*

1. "Evangelicals and Catholics Together: Comments from Chuck Colson and Prison Fellowship Ministries," news release from Prison Fellowship dated 15 June 1994.

2. *Ibid.*

3. Timothy George, "Catholics and Evangelicals in the Trenches," *Christianity Today* (16 May 1994), 16.

4. "Evangelicals and Catholics Together: The Christian Mission in the Third Millennium," (29 March 1994), 1. All page numbers refer to the 25-page version of the document as originally distributed by Prison Fellowship. Hereafter, quotations from this document are cited in parentheses with a page number only.

5. This is by no means meant to imply that none who identify with these groups are truly Christian. There are undoubtedly people within Roman Catholicism and Eastern Orthodoxy who really do trust Jesus Christ alone for salvation, without realizing that their evangelical faith is a wholesale departure from official Catholic and Orthodox Church doctrine. It must be pointed out, however, that the Catholic Church's anathemas against anyone who affirms justification *sola fide* amounts to an automatic excommunication of all who sincerely trust in Christ alone for salvation. Such people—though they may call themselves Catholic—are officially consigned by Rome to eternal damnation. Hence the expression "evangelical Catholic" is something of a contradiction in terms.

6. Most of these quotations from the document's signatories are taken from personal letters. I am quoting their comments anonymously unless I quote from published sources.

7. George, "Catholics and Evangelicals," 16.

8. Timothy George, *Theology of the Reformers* (Nashville: Broadman, 1988), 82. Ironically, Dr. George is also the author of the *Christianity Today* editorial. In an earlier edition of this book I mistakenly identified him as a signer of the accord.

9. *Ibid.*, 82-83.

10. *Ibid.*, 80-81.

11. *Dei verbum*, 9 (emphasis added). All citations from the Vatican II documents are quoted from Walter M. Abbot, S. J., ed., *The Documents of Vatican II* (New York: America Press, 1966).

12. *Ibid.*

13. Philip Schaff, *History of the Christian Church*, 8 vols. (New York: Charles Scribner's, 1910), 7:160.

14. Philip Schaff, *The Creeds of Christendom*, 3 vols. (Grand Rapids, Mich.: Baker Book House, 1983 reprint), 1:94.
15. Quotations from the Canons and Decrees of the Council of Trent are cited in parentheses as *Trent*.
16. "New Law" refers to the Council of Trent's canons and decrees on the sacraments. The seventh session established seven sacraments: baptism, confirmation, the eucharist, penance, extreme unction, order, and matrimony—then pronounced the usual anathema on anyone who says that there are more or less than these seven sacraments (*Trent*, sess. 7, canon 1).
17. *The Gospel According to Jesus*, rev. ed. (Grand Rapids, Mich.: Zondervan Publishing House, 1994); *Faith Works: The Gospel According to the Apostles* (Dallas: Word Publishing, 1992), esp. 90-121, 242-3.
18. *Sacrosanctum Concilium* (Vatican II), 47.
19. *Lumen Gentium* (Vatican II), 59.
20. *Ibid.*, 62.
21. *Ibid.*, 67.
22. *Unitatis Reditegratio*, 21.
23. *Lumen Gentium*, 60.
24. Abbot, ed., *The Documents of Vatican II*, 91. Catholic apologist Karl Keating says any contradiction between 1 Timothy 2:5 and Mary's "saving role" as "Mediatrix of all graces" is "illusory" [Karl Keating, *Catholicism and Fundamentalism: The Attack on "Romanism" by "Bible Christians"* (San Francisco: Ignatius Press, 1988), 278]. The inescapable fact that Catholic apologists must deal with, however, is that multitudes of Catholics "venerate" Mary with a devotion that far outdoes their "worship" of Christ.
25. *Lumen Gentium*, 25.

CHAPTER SIX: Laughing Till It Hurts

1. Arthur L. Johnson, *Faith Misguided* (Chicago: Moody Press, 1988), 23.
2. Richard N. Ostling, "Laughing for the Lord," *Time* (15 August 1994), 38.
3. Daina Doucet, "Renewal Excites Canadian Churches," *Charisma* (June 1994), 52.
4. *Ibid.*, 53.
5. *Ibid.*, 52-53.
6. See, for example, Hank Hanegraaff, *Christianity in Crisis* (Eugene, Ore: Harvest House, 1993); D. R. McConnell, *A Different Gospel* (Peabody, Mass: Hendrickson, 1988); Bruce Barron, *The Health and Wealth Gospel* (Downers Grove, Ill.: InterVarsity Press, 1987); and Gordon Fee, "The Disease of the Health and Wealth Gospels" (Costa Mesa, Calif.: Word for Today, 1979). Those authors all write from a charismatic point of view, yet they are convinced that the prosperity Gospel taught by men such as Kenneth Hagin is a fatal corruption of the true Gospel.

    I have included a critique of the Word Faith movement in *Charismatic Chaos* (Grand Rapids, Mich.: Zondervan Publishing House, 1992), chapter 12.
7. "Letters," *The Challenge Weekly* (26 August 1994), 2.
8. William DeArteaga, *Quenching the Spirit* (Lake Mary, Fla.: Creation House, 1992). This book is neither scholarly nor accurate but must be addressed since

it is being used by many in an effort to give historical legitimacy to charismatic mysticism.

9. *Ibid.*, 24-25.

10. *Ibid.*, 18.

11. Other recent books that promote charismatic phenomena by appealing to the Great Awakening include Jack Deere, *Surprised by the Power of the Spirit* (Grand Rapids, Mich.: Zondervan Publishing House, 1993), 88-96; John White, "Revival and the Spirit's Power" in Gary S. Greig and Kevin Springer, eds., *The Kingdom and the Power* (Ventura, Calif.: Regal Books, 1993), 289-319; and David Pytches, *Prophecy in the Local Church* (London: Hodder and Stoughton, 1993), 253-8.

12. This is still available today in Jonathan Edwards, *Jonathan Edwards on Revival* (Edinburgh: Banner of Truth, 1984), 1-74.

13. Gerald Coates, "An Open Letter to the Editor," *Evangelism Today* (August 1994).

14. DeArteaga, 115, 249.

15. *Ibid.*, 32.

16. *Ibid.*, 52.

17. Strangely enough, DeArteaga is aware of these facts and mentions them in passing (45, 53) but never addresses the difficulty they pose for his thesis.

18. Iain Murray, *Jonathan Edwards* (Edinburgh: Banner of Truth, 1987), 211-6.

19. Edwards, 38.

20. Almost every time DeArteaga mentions Calvinism it is in a negative context. By contrast, he is extremely friendly to Catholicism. Yet Catholicism certainly has far more in common with real Pharisaism than Calvinism does.

21. *Ibid.*, 241.

22. *Ibid.*, 89.

23. *Ibid.*, 52.

24. Murray, 216.

25. Edwards, 128-29.

26. *Ibid.*

27. Murray, 217.

28. *Ibid.*, 218.

29. W. B. Sprague, cited in Murray, p. 227.

30. *Ibid.*, 227-28 (emphasis added).

31. Jonathan Edwards, *The Life of David Brainerd* (New Haven, Conn.: Yale Univ. Press, 1985), 154.

32. DeArteaga, 55.

33. *Ibid.*

34. *Ibid.*

35. DeArteaga's book ends with a rather harsh and factually inaccurate assessment of my ministry. He concludes that "MacArthur's theology becomes the perfect Pharisees' theology" (261).

36. Cited in Murray, 169. Spelling and punctuation have been modernized here.

37. Geoffrey Levey, "This man has just been given the Toronto Blessing. What in God's name is going on?" *Daily Mail* (2 September 1994), 18.

38. "Is This Revival?" *Evangelism Today* (July 1994), 1.

39. Jackie Alnor, "Holy Laughter—Is It Biblical?" *Christian Sentinel* (September 1994), 6.

40. My friend recorded these verbatim quotations in his notes.
41. Jonathan Edwards, *A Treatise Concerning Religious Affections* (New Haven, Conn.: Yale Univ. Press, 1959), 98.
42. *Ibid.*, 94.
43. *Ibid.*, 95 (emphasis added).

CHAPTER SEVEN: Looking for Truth in All the Wrong Places

1. James Ryle, *Hippo in the Garden* (Lake Mary, Fla.: Creation House, 1993), 259.
2. *Ibid.*, 261.
3. *Ibid.*, 262.
4. James Ryle, "Sons of Thunder," (Longmont, Colo.: Boulder Valley Vineyard tape ministry), preached 1 July 1990.
5. Ryle, *Hippo in the Garden*, 128.
6. *Ibid.*, 36.
7. *Ibid.*, 38.
8. *Ibid.*, 190.
9. *Ibid.*, 39.
10. *Ibid.*
11. *Ibid.*, 149-50.
12. *Ibid.*, 199.
13. *Ibid.*, 77.
14. *Ibid.*, 74.
15. Wayne Grudem, *The Gift of Prophecy in the New Testament and Today* (Wheaton, Ill.: Crossway Books, 1988), 42, 115.
16. *Ibid.*, 299.
17. *Ibid.*, 300.
18. *Ibid.*, 15.
19. *Ibid.*, 14.
20. *Ibid.*, 262.
21. *Ibid.*, 133.
22. Ryle, *Hippo in the Garden*, 30-31.
23. *Ibid.*, 32, 39, 62 (emphasis added).
24. *Ibid.*, 13-14, 15, 18, 20, 25-29, 83, 91, 113, 115-16, 142.
25. *Ibid.*, 99.
26. *Ibid.*, 292 (emphasis added).
27. In one place, Ryle says, "We must stop putting our own words in the Lord's mouth. . . . Scripture alone is our sure foundation" (*Ibid.*, 54-55). To *that* I add a hearty amen.
28. John MacArthur, *Charismatic Chaos* (Grand Rapids, Mich.: Zondervan Publishing House, 1992), chaps. 2-3.
29. Edwards's cessationist views are spelled out in his book *Charity and Its Fruits* (Edinburgh: Banner of Truth, 1969 reprint), 38, 44-47; and in even greater detail in his "Distinguishing Marks," in *Jonathan Edwards on Revival* (Edinburgh: Banner of Truth, 1984), 137ff.
30. "An Expostulatory Letter from the Late Mr. Edwards of Northampton to the Rev. Mr. Clap," cited in Iain Murray, *Jonathan Edwards* (Edinburgh: Banner of Truth, 1987), 240 (emphasis added).
31. *Ibid.*, 240.

32. *Ibid.*, 241.
33. Jonathan Edwards, *Some Thoughts Concerning the Present Revival of Religion in New England* in *The Works of Jonathan Edwards*, 2 vols. (Edinburgh: Banner of Truth, 1976 reprint), 1:404.
34. *Ibid.*
35. Edwards, *On Revival*, 104.
36. *Ibid.*, 141.
37. Kenneth Silverman, *The Life and Times of Cotton Mather* (New York: Columbia University Press, 1984), 173-75, 185-86. Mather's proneness to trust subjective phenomena—a fallacy shared by many of his colleagues—may have also kept him from acting sooner than he did to halt the Salem witch trials.
38. Murray, 241-2 (emphasis added).
39. Garry Friesen with J. Robin Maxson, *Decision Making and the Will of God* (Portland, Ore.: Multnomah Press, 1980), 127-47.
40. *Ibid.*, 130.
41. *Ibid.*, 130-1.
42. *Ibid.*, 131.
43. Haddon Robinson, *Decision Making by the Book* (Wheaton, Ill.: Victor Books, 1991), 18.
44. William DeArteaga, *Quenching the Spirit* (Lake Mary, Fla.: Creation House, 1992), 55.
45. MacArthur, *Charismatic Chaos*, 70-72.
46. Bill Hamon, "How to Receive a Personal Prophecy," *Charisma* (April 1991), 68 (emphasis added).
47. Edwards, *Some Thoughts*, 404.
48. Edwards, *On Revival*, 141.

APPENDIX ONE: Is Roman Catholicism Changing?

1. "The number of Protestants who were executed in a single province and a single reign far exceeded that of the primitive martyrs in the space of three centuries and of the Roman Empire." [Edward Gibbon, *Decline and Fall of the Roman Empire*, 7 vols. (London: Methuen, 1986), 2:139.]
2. The most conservative estimates of the death toll set the total slaughtered at 5,000; other sources say at least 30,000 were killed [Will and Ariel Durant, *The Age of Reason Begins* (New York: Simon & Schuster, 1961), 353]. Because accurate statistics were not kept, it is impossible to know the casualty figures with any accuracy, but contemporary sources said 10,000 were killed in Paris alone on the first night of the massacre.
3. John Foxe, et al., *Foxe's Christian Martyrs of the World* (Chicago: Moody Press, n.d.), 298.
4. Roland Bainton, *The Reformation of the Sixteenth Century* (Boston: Beacon Press, 1952), 171; Durant, 353-4.
5. Durant, 354. Coligny was the Huguenot leader.
6. *Ibid.*, 213-14.
7. Karl Keating, *Catholicism and Fundamentalism: The Attack on "Romanism" by "Bible Christians"* (San Francisco: Ignatius Press, 1988), 290.
8. *Ibid.*, 292. Will and Ariel Durant cite Juan Antonio Llorente, a Spanish priest who served as general secretary of the Spanish Inquisition at the end

of the eighteenth century. Llorente estimated 31,912 people were burned at the stake in Spain alone, and another 291,450 were forced to admit to heresy. "Zurita, a secretary of the Inquisition, boasted that it had burned 4,000 in Seville alone" [Durant, 215-6.] According to the Durants, Protestant historians now generally reject such estimates as exaggerations, but it must be noted that those are the figures that were recorded by the inquisitors themselves.

9. *Ibid.*, 292. Keating's assertion that the burning of witches was "almost unknown in Catholic countries" is simply inaccurate. It is true that in *some* Catholic countries, such as Portugal and Spain, witch trials were rare. But the witch mania in the heart of Europe began in the early fourteenth century, two hundred years before the Reformation—when the *only* religious authorities in Europe with the power to kill witches were Roman Catholic inquisitors.

    In 1320, Pope John XXII issued a bull *Super Illius Specula*, which authorized inquisitors to treat all sorcerers and witches as heretics. The infamous *Malleus Maleficarum* ("The Hammer Against Witches") was a Catholic document, written in 1486 by two Dominican scholars, used as a guidebook for detecting and punishing witchcraft. Its preface was a papal bull—*Summis Desiderantes Affectibus*, by Pope Innocent VIII—"confirming full papal support for the work of the inquisition against witches." [Jeffrey B. Russell, *A History of Witchcraft* (New York: Thames and Hudson, 1980), 76, 79.]

    The truth is, the Roman Catholic Church *began* the European witch craze. It was an inevitable result of the Inquisition.

10. Keating, 294-5.

11. *Ibid.*, 295.

12. *Ibid.*, 297-8.

13. The Catholic doctrine of papal infallibility did not become canon law until the First Vatican Council in 1870. The doctrine does not claim general infallibility for every word and action of the pope. It merely says that when he speaks *ex cathedra* (from the papal throne), defining a doctrine regarding faith and morals, his judgment is to be held as infallible by every Roman Catholic.

    Catholic apologists will reply that papal bulls ordering heretics and witches to be tortured and burned were not *ex cathedra* pronouncements. Indeed, all such decrees were issued several centuries before the Vatican Council even defined the concept of *ex cathedra* infallibility. Nevertheless, they were issued by men in the papal office, men who claimed supreme apostolic authority—*men who claimed to be acting infallibly in Christ's stead.*

14. Nineteen people were hanged in this tragic episode before several pastors, led by Increase Mather, insisted that the courts stop accepting testimony from "witchcraft victims"—most of them children—who claimed to be able to see into the spirit world. For a balanced account of the Puritan clergy's role in the matter, see Chadwick Hansen, *Witchcraft at Salem* (New York: Braziller, 1969).

15. Samuel Sewell, *The Diary of Samuel Sewell*, 2 vols (New York: Farrar, Straus and Giroux, 1973), 1:367.

16. G. C. Berkouwer, *The Conflict With Rome* (Philadelphia: Presbyterian and Reformed, 1957).

17. *Ibid.*, 56.

18. *Ibid.*, 58-9.

19. Martin Luther, *Table Talk*, in Helmut T. Lehman, ed., *Luther's Works*, 55 vols. (Philadelphia: Fortress Press, 1967), Theodore G. Tappert, trans., 54:185.

20. *Ibid.*, 422.

21. Berkouwer, 64.

22. Philip Schaff, *History of the Christian Church*, 8 vols. (New York: Charles Scribner's, 1910), 7:393-4.

23. Berkouwer, 60-1. Hadrian VI was a Dutchman, the last of the non-Italian popes until Pope John Paul II (of Poland) was elected in 1978.

24. Schaff, 7:394.

25. *Ibid.*

26. Berkouwer, 64.

27. *Ibid.*, 70.

28. *Ibid.*, 64.

29. Keating, 103-4.

30. Canons and Decrees of the Council of Trent, sess. 6, canons 9, 11, 30, 33. *The Catholic Encyclopedia* lists Luther, Calvin, Knox, Zwingli, and other Reformers in a table of "Heretics, Apostates, Impostors." *The Catholic Encyclopedia Dictionary* (New York: The Gilmary Society, 1941), 1063.

31. Berkouwer, 70 (emphasis in original).

32. *Ibid.*, 67 (emphasis added).

33. Pope John XXIII died in June 1963, six months after the first session concluded. His successor, Paul VI, announced at his election that he would continue the Council.

34. G. C. Berkouwer, *The Second Vatican Council and the New Catholicism* (Grand Rapids, Mich.: Wm. B. Eerdmans, 1965), 144.

35. *Ibid.*

36. Walter M. Abbot, S. J., ed., *The Documents of Vatican II* (New York: America Press, 1966), ix. All subsequent citations from the Vatican II documents are quoted from this volume.

37. *Dei Verbum*, 1; cf. *Optatum Totius*, concl.

38. *Lumen Gentium*, 52.

39. *Ibid.*

40. *Sacrosanctum Concilium*, 55.

41. *Lumen Gentium*, 25.

42. *Ibid.* (emphasis added).

43. Several of my friends who pastor churches in Quebec were arrested in the 1950s for preaching the Gospel. They actually spent time in jail at the behest of Roman Catholic authorities. Thankfully, Vatican II helped put a stop to such persecution.

44. Berkouwer, *The Second Vatican Council*, 257.

45. *Ibid.*

46. *Nostra Aetate*, 2.

47. *Ibid.*, 1.

48. *Ibid.*, 2.

49. In most ways the change is certainly a welcome one. "Dialogue and collaboration" are undoubtedly preferable to inquisitions and strife. But on the other hand, the change in tactics, without a corresponding change in doctrine, has only made the Catholic Church a more subtle adversary of the Gospel of grace.

Evangelicals need to be wary of yielding too much ground in "dialogue and collaboration" with Rome.

50. *Nostra Aetate*, 4.
51. *Ibid.*, 3.
52. *Dignitatis Humanae*, 12 (emphasis added).
53. Michael S. Horton, "Evangelicals and Catholics Together: The Christian Mission in the Third Millennium: A Critical Review," *Modern Reformation* (Jan.–Feb. 1994), 24.

SCRIPTURE INDEX

SUBJECT INDEX

Reckless Faith was typeset by the Photocomposition Department
of Crossway Books of Wheaton, Illinois.

The compositor for the project was Raymond J. Elliott;
the graphic designer was Mark Schramm.
The cover design was by The Puckett Group.
Editorial production work was done by Ted Griffin;
editing was done by Leonard G. Goss.

The text type was set in 11 point Caslon 540,
the original face for which was produced about 1725
and based on Dutch styles of the seventeenth century.

This book was printed on Cream White Lyons Falls Lite
Antique 50-pound paper by R.R. Donnelley & Sons,
Crawfordsville, Indiana.